Morphological Investigations

Editors: Jim Blevins, Petar Milin, Michael Ramscar

In this series:

Further investigations into the nature of phrasal compounding

Edited by

Carola Trips

Jaklin Kornfilt

language
science
press

Carola Trips & Jaklin Kornfilt (eds.). 2017. *Further investigations into the nature of phrasal compounding* (Morphological Investigations 1). Berlin: Language Science Press.

This title can be downloaded at:
http://langsci-press.org/catalog/book/156
© 2017, the authors
Published under the Creative Commons Attribution 4.0 Licence (CC BY 4.0):
http://creativecommons.org/licenses/by/4.0/
ISBN: 978-3-96110-012-5 (Digital)
      978-3-96110-013-2 (Hardcover)
DOI:10.5281/zenodo.885113
Source code available from www.github.com/langsci/156
Collaborative reading: paperhive.org/documents/remote?type=langsci&id=156

Cover and concept of design: Ulrike Harbort
Typesetting: Felix Kopecky, Sebastian Nordhoff, Iana Stefanova
Proofreading: Ahmet Bilal Özdemir, Andreas Hölzl, Andreea Calude, Eitan Grossman, Gerald Delahunty, Jean Nitzke, Jeroen van der Weijer, Ka Yau Lai, Ken Manson, Luigi Talamo, Martin Haspelmath, Parviz Parsafar, Steven Kaye, Steve Pepper, Valeria Quochi
Fonts: Linux Libertine, Arimo, DejaVu Sans Mono
Typesetting software: XƎLATEX

Language Science Press
Unter den Linden 6
10099 Berlin, Germany
langsci-press.org

Storage and cataloguing done by FU Berlin

Freie Universität Berlin

Contents

Chapter 1

Further insights into phrasal compounding

Carola Trips
Universität Mannheim

Jaklin Kornfilt
Syracuse University

1 Further insights into phrasal compounding from a typological and theoretical perspective

This collection of papers on phrasal compounds is part of a bigger project whose aims are twofold: First, it seeks to broaden the typological perspective by providing data for as many different languages as possible to gain a better understanding of the phenomenon itself. Second, based on these data, which clearly show interaction between syntax and morphology, it aims to discuss theoretical models which deal with this kind of interaction in different ways. For example, models like Generative Grammar assume components of grammar and a clear-cut distinction between the lexicon (often including morphology) and grammar which mostly stands for the computational system (syntax). Other models, like construction grammar do not assume such components and are rather based on a lexicon including constructs. A comparison of these models makes it then possible to assess their explanatory power.

The field of morphology and syntax started to acknowledge the existence of phrasal compounds predominantly in the context of Lexicalist theories because a number of authors realised that they are not easy to handle in models of linguistic theory which demarcate the lexicon (morphology) from syntax. Commenting on

Carola Trips & Jaklin Kornfilt. Further insights into phrasal compounding. In Carola Trips & Jaklin Kornfilt (eds.), *Further investigations into the nature of phrasal compounding*, 1–11. Berlin: Language Science Press.
DOI:10.5281/zenodo.885107

the difference between base and derived forms Chomsky said in his "Remarks on Nominalization":

> "However, when the lexicon is separated from the categorial component of the base and its entries are analyzed in terms of contextual features, this difficulty disappears."
> (Chomsky (1970: 190))

This assumption was dubbed The Lexicalist Hypothesis and in the course of time a number of different versions surfaced. For example, Lapointe (1980: 8) put forward the Generalized Lexicalist Hypothesis which stated that "No syntactic rule can refer to elements of morphological structure." Botha (1981: 18) took the perspective from morphology and established The No Phrase Constraint which postulated that "Syntactic phrases cannot occur inside of root compounds." In 1987, Di Sciullo & Williams summarised these hypotheses and constraints in their Atomicity Thesis:

> "Words are "atomic" at the level of phrasal syntax and phrasal semantics. The words have "features" or properties, but these features have no structure, and the relation of these features to the internal composition of the word cannot be relevant in syntax – this is the thesis of the atomicity of words, or the lexical integrity hypothesis, or the strong lexicalist hypothesis (as in Lapointe 1980), or a version of the lexicalist hypothesis of Chomsky (1970), Williams (1978; 1978a), and numerous others."
> (Di Sciullo & Williams 1987:49)

Some of these authors commented on instances of phrasal compounding like Botha (2015) (who coined the term "phrasal compounds") and Savini (1984) and came to the conclusion that they constitute negative evidence for these constraints because they clearly showed interaction between syntax and morphology (see the following examples from Dutch):

(1)   a. uit-die-bottel-drink   alkoholis
              from-the-bottle-drink alcoholic
              'alcoholic who drinks straight from the bottle'
              (Botha 1980:143)

        b. laat-in-die-aand   drankie
              late-in-the-evening drink
              'drink taken late in the evening'
              (Savini 1984: 39)

In the same vein, Lieber (1988; 1992) put forward examples for English and came to the conclusion that they violate these constraints, or in more general terms, the Lexical Integrity Hypothesis:

(2) a. slept all day look
     b. a who's the boss wink
         (Lieber 1992:11)

But despite these rather sporadic discussions of the phenomenon no comprehensive study of phrasal compounds in individual languages or cross-linguistically existed.

Fortunately, with a growing interest in compounding as an interface phenomenon the situation has changed in the last five years. This can be seen by the publication of a number of volumes dedicating themselves explicitly to this type of word formation by providing detailed accounts of types of compounds across languages (see e.g. Scalise & Vogel (2010); Štekauer & Lieber (2009)), and this development brings phrasal compounds now to the fore as well.

To gain a better understanding of phrasal compounds, in 2013 a workshop with the topic "Phrasal compounds from a typological and theoretical perspective" brought together scholars who had been working on (phrasal) compounding in different languages and from different theoretical perspectives. The outcome of this fruitful workshop was a collection on the topic which was published in 2015 as a special edition of STUF (Trips & Kornfilt 2015). The languages under investigation were German, English, Italian, Turkish, some additional Turkic languages and Greek. Concerning the approaches chosen for an analysis of the phenomenon, some authors (Pafel, Göksel) analysed the phrasal non-head of phrasal compounds in terms of quotes, quotations, citations whereas authors like Meibauer and Trips favoured a semantic analysis which attributes an important role to pragmatics (Trips to some degree in the form of coercion, Meibauer even more so in terms of pragmatic enrichment). Some of the authors (Bisetto, Bağrıaçık & Angela Ralli) made a distinction between phrasal compounds that are lexical/morphological and syntactic (either within one and the same language or comparing languages) and some authors (Trips & Kornfilt) found similar semantic restrictions in diverse languages (Germanic, Turkish) but also clear structural differences.

Despite this valuable contribution to a phenomenon underrepresented in current research, it became evident quickly that to come closer to fulfilling the aims defined above it would be necessary to add further languages, on the one hand, and to deepen the theoretical discussion, on the other hand.

Concerning the typological aspect of (phrasal) compounding we wanted to include further languages which had not been investigated so far; especially interesting are, for example, Slavic languages, because they seem to exhibit compounds, but they occur less frequently than for example in the Germanic languages. Another aspect worth investigating is whether all Germanic languages behave in the same way. One very interesting example is Icelandic which has much more inflectional morphology than the other contemporary Germanic languages. Can we then expect that Icelandic behaves differently because of different morphology? Another, more general question is if languages which are of the same syntactic type (e.g. SOV) behave in the same way when it comes to PCs. Would we, for example, expect to find the same patterns we identified for German as an SOV language in another SOV language like Japanese? And what about languages in contact? Would we expect to find the borrowing of phrasal compounding from a source language to a recipient language since, after all, they are complex (under the assumption that contact generally leads to simplification)?

Concerning questions relevant for linguistic theory it would be worthwhile investigating if there is a correlation between the morphological and syntactic typology of a language. So for example is the rightheadedness in morphology (always) related to SOV? Or is a rich inflectional system a prerequisite for rightheadedness in morphology? Another interesting question is whether the distinction between PCs containing a predicate and PCs not containing a predicate made by Trips related to the property of the nominal head requiring an argument (or not) as the non-head? Focussing on the semantic relation between the non-head and the head in languages like English and German we find a tight semantic relation. The same is true for Turkish, but in addition we have selectional restrictions. In contrast, languages like Sakha (Turkic) show looser semantic relations between the non-head and head. So would we find these similarities/differences in other language pairs? And, from a more general point of view, are there theories which model the general properties of phrasal compounds more adequately than others? And if so, which properties would such a theory have?

Our interest in these questions made us open up our workshop in 2015 as well as this special issue to papers conceived in different frameworks. While we cannot answer these evaluative questions yet, we hope that this collection of case studies conducted in a variety of models will bring us closer to such answers.

Turning back to structural and semantic properties of phrasal compounds, questions about the relationship of the head and the non-head of phrasal compounds were addressed by the presentations at the workshop and continue to be a focus in the contributions to this special issue. In many simple as well as phrasal compounds, the semantics appear to be similar to that of a predicate – argument relationship, as in Turkish and German:

(3) Turkish
    dilbilim   öğrenci-si
    linguistics student-CM
    'linguistics student'

(4) German
    Linguistikstudent
    linguistics-student
    'linguistics student'

However, especially with respect to quotative phrasal compounds, it is clear that much more general semantic relationships must be allowed to hold. This is shown quite clearly in the examples above, especially by those in (2).

Another issue that contributions have focused on is the overt (syntactic and/or morphological) expression of the head – non-head relationship in compounds, and in phrasal compounds in particular. As illustrated in (3), Turkish (nominal) compounds have a compound marker (CM) on their head; similar compounds in German and English don't have such a marker; Greek does, as well as Pharasiot, a variety of Asia Minor Greek influenced by Turkish. However, the compound markers of these Greek varieties differ with respect to their sources and their shapes – one of the issues discussed in one of the contributions in this volume. Does the presence versus absence of a compound marker determine other properties of a compound, whether phrasal or otherwise? This is a fascinating question whose answer has been attempted in the contribution on Pharasiot, but one which can only be answered more definitively after a good deal of further cross-linguistic research.

One property which appears to hold cross-linguistically is adjacency between the head and the non-head in compounds, setting them apart from phrases:

(5) a. (çalışkan) dilbilim   (*çalışkan) öğrenci-si (Turkish)
       (diligent) linguistics diligent   student-CM
       'diligent linguistics (*diligent) student'
    b. der (fleißige) Linguistik(*fleißige)student (German)
       the diligent   linguistics-diligent-student
       'the diligent linguistics (*diligent) student'
    c. the (diligent) linguistics (*diligent) student (English)

Thus, adjacency turns out to be a reliable diagnostic device for distinguishing compounds from phrases. This becomes particularly important when distinguishing phrasal compounds from phrases, given that in both, the non-head constituent is phrasal, making the relevant distinction less clear at first glance.

The non-head in phrasal compounds can be expressed in a variety of different ways cross-linguistically. Limiting attention to clausal non-heads in phrasal compounds, we see that in some languages, that constituent can be either identical to a root clause (and thus a "quotative"), or it can show up in the typical shape of an embedded clause in the language in question. Thus, in Turkic languages, embedded clauses typically show up as gerund-like nominalizations, and this is a pattern that shows up in Turkish phrasal (non-quotative) compounds:

(6) [en çabuk nasıl zengin ol   -un -duğ   -u] (*ilginç)
     most fast how rich   become -PASS -FACT-NOM -3.SG (interesting)
     soru   -su
     question -CM
     'The (interesting) question (of) how one gets rich fastest'

In German, on the other hand, embedded clauses typically show up as fully finite, verb-final clauses, in contrast to root clauses which are verb-second; not surprisingly, this is a pattern that shows up in German phrasal (non-quotative) compounds:

(7) die (interessante) [wie man am schnellsten reich wird] (*interessante)
     the interesting   how one the fastest   rich gets interesting
     Frage
     question
     'The (interesting) question (of) how one gets rich fastest'

In quotative phrasal compounds, we find the non-head exhibiting the morphosyntactic properties of the root clause; this appears to be similar cross-linguistically, as illustrated in (8a) for Turkish, German, and English:

(8) a. Turkish
         [en çabuk nasıl zengin ol   -un -ur]   (*ilginç)
         most fast   how rich   become -PASS -AORIST interesting
         soru-su
         question-CM
         'The "how does one get rich fastest" (*interesting) question'

b. German
die [wie wird   man am schnellsten reich] (*interessante) Frage
the how become one the fastest   rich interesting   question

'The "how does one get rich fastest" (*interesting) question'

Similar semantics can be expressed by phrases rather than compounds in many
instances. Often, a preposition or a postposition is involved in the equivalent
phrase, heading the clause; this is illustrated in (9) for Turkish and German, respectively:

(9) a. [en çabuk nasıl zengin ol   -un -duğ   -u] hakkında
most fast   how rich   become -PASS -FACT-NOM -3.SG about
(ilginç)   soru-lar
(interesting) question-pl

'(interesting) questions about how one gets rich fastest'

b. (interessante) Fragen   darüber, [wie man am schnellsten reich
interesting   questions about how one the fastest   rich
wird]
becomes

'(interesting) questions about how one becomes rich fastest'

The possibility of non-adjacency between the phrasal (here, clausal) non-head
and the head shows, for both Turkish and German, that these constructions are
not compounds, but rather phrases. In addition, the fact that in the Turkish example there is no compound marker strengthens this observational claim.

We thus see that phrasal compounds exhibit similarities as well as differences
cross-linguistically. Among the latter, we saw that in Turkish, clausal non-heads
in phrasal compounds can be nominalized; this is not an option in German and
English phrasal compounds. Furthermore, Turkish phrasal compounds exhibit a
compound marker attached to the head; no such marker is ever found in German
or English phrasal compounds. Future research will, we hope, show explanations
for these differences, beyond those we were able to sketch in this brief overview.

To come closer to an answer to these questions, a second workshop on phrasal
compounding from a typological and theoretical perspective took place in 2015
adding further languages and theoretical models. The present volume is a collection of these contributions.

Kristín Bjarnadóttir provides a description of compounding in Icelandic in
general terms including phrasal compounding as a marked case. She shows that

compounds are extremely productive in Icelandic and are traditionally grouped into a class containing stems and a class containing inflected words (mainly genitive) as non-heads. Phrasal compounds are also found, and a more common type, well established in the vocabulary, can be distinguished from a more current, complex type. Interestingly, phrasal compounds may also contain a genitive non-head and then the question arises how they can be distinguished from the genitival non-phrasal compounds.

Bogdan Szymanek discusses compounding in Polish (and more generally, in Slavic). He shows that compounds exists in Polish but that they are much less productive than in German or English. Phrasal compounds do not seem to occur at all, as in all the other Slavic languages. The author identifies a number of reasons why this type of word formation is absent, for example the presence of 'multi-word units' that are frequently used to express complex nominal concepts.

Alexandra Bagasheva provides a study of phrasal compounds in Bulgarian. Despite the fact that this type of compound is said not to exist in Slavic languages she shows that they do, especially so in life style magazines. The author discusses her data in the constructionalist framework and proposes the process of "pattern" borrowing from English as an explanation of why phrasal compounds have started to emerge in Bulgarian.

Katrin Hein provides a comprehensive description of phrasal compounds in German and models the different types found in construction grammar. She prefers this model because "traditional" generative approaches do not allow for syntax in morphology and because such an approach also fails to explain why a speaker chooses to use a phrasal compound instead of a nominal compound. Based on a corpus study she shows that the types of phrasal compounds she found can all be captured as form-meaning pairings in this model and that their frequency and productivity justify defining them as constructions. In addition, she notes that the model serves well to explain why the second constituent with its semantic properties has to be seen as the main element and not the first constituent with its abstract syntactic properties.

Kunio Nishiyama describes and categorizes various types of compounds in Japanese whose non-heads are phrasal. Nishiyama proposes that the main criterion of categorization is whether noun incorporation is involved or not in the formation of a given phrasal compound in Japanese. The author is careful not to take a stand on whether an explicit Baker-type incorporation is involved or not, but the derivation he assumes is based on a head-movement approach, similar to a Baker-type noun incorporation, given that the evidence for noun incorporation having taken place is the appearance of "modifier stranding" effects, i.e. that a "modifier" can be separated from its head only when it is stranded (as a result of incorporation). If noun incorporation has applied in the derivation of a phrasal compound, a further division is made according to whether the "predicate", i.e. the verbal noun which is the host of the incorporated noun, is of Sino-Japanese or of native origin. Nishiyama proposes that there are two licensing conditions for modifier stranding: the complement of the verbal noun, i.e. the left-hand element of the compound, should be a relational noun or a part of a cliché.

If no noun incorporation is involved, there are four subclasses, depending on the phrasal non-head: a modifying non-head, a coordinate structure as a non-head, phrasal non-heads to which prefixes (which the author is inclined to analyze as proclitics) are attached, and non-heads to which suffixes (which, again, the author suggests are enclitics in contemporary Japanese) are attached. Nishiyama further proposes that in phrasal compounds whose non-heads are modifying structures and coordinate structures, the licensing condition is again cliché.

Metin Bağrıaçık, Aslı Göksel & Angela Ralli The paper argues that compounding in Pharasiot Greek (PhG), an endangered Asia Minor Greek variety, is selectively copied from Turkish, based on differences between PhG compounds and Hellenic compounds on the one hand, and similar properties between PhG compounds and Turkish compounds, on the other: As opposed to various other Hellenic varieties, compounds in PhG are exclusively composed of two fully inflected nouns, where the non-head, the left-hand constituent, is marked with one of the two compound markers, -u and -s, whose shape is conditioned morphologically. According to the authors, these compound markers have been exapted from the genitive markers in PhG. Hellenic compounds have a compound marker, as well, located similarly between the head and the non-head, but it is quite a different marker, with a different history; it has been exapted from an Ancient Greek thematic vowel. Furthermore, in Hellenic compounds, there has to be at least one (uninflected) stem. Similarities between PhG and Turkish compounds include, in addition to certain structural common features, the provenance of the respective compound markers: in Turkish, the compound marker is identical to the third person singular possessive (agreement) marker and is placed, just like that agreement marker in possessive constructions, on the head, i.e. the rightmost nominal element. In PhG, the compound marker has the shape of a genitive marker and is placed, just like the genitive, on the non-head. A parallel is drawn by the authors between the respective sources of the compound markers in Turkish and PhG (i.e. the possessive agreement marker in Turkish, and the genitive marker in PhG), basing their view on a possible identification of the genitive in

PhG with the Turkish possessive agreement marker (rather than with the genitive in Turkish, which is placed on the non-head in Turkish possessives). The paper discusses, in addition to the similarities between PhG and Turkish compounds, also differences between them: Turkish compounds can have phrasal (and even clausal) non-heads, while PhG compounds cannot. This difference is attributed mainly to the location of the compound marker within the compound: the PhG compound marker, being a purely morphological affix, attaches to stems, similar to all affixes in the language (as well as in all Hellenic varieties). Therefore, no phrasal constituent can be hosted in the position to which the compound marker attaches. In Turkish, on the other hand, since the compound marker attaches to the head, the non-head can host phrasal constituents. This correlation is claimed to also hold in Khalkha Mongolian, an Altaic language like Turkish, in which, however, the compound marker attaches to the non-head. The authors claim that similar to PhG, but unlike Turkish, phrasal constituents cannot be hosted in the non-head position in Mongolian, thus supporting the correlation they propose between the locus of the compound marker and the availability of phrasal non-heads. Apparent counterexamples in Khalkha, they argue, involve a covert preposition which assigns genitive Case, thus imposing a phrasal, rather than a compound, structure on these counterexamples.

Jürgen Pafel takes a theoretical stance and discusses the morphology-syntax relation in modular approaches. He analyses phrasal compounds in the conversion approach in a number of languages and shows, contra the Lexical Integrity Hypothesis, that morphology and syntax are separate levels of grammar with separate structures and distinct properties. Further, the properties of phrasal compounding speak in favour of a parallel architecture framework, where general interface relations constrain their properties.

Acknowledgements

We would like to thank the participants of the workshop for interesting talks and fruitful discussions.

References

Botha, Rudolf P. 1981. A base rule theory of Afrikaans synthetic compounds. In Michael Moortgat, Harry van der Hulst & Teun Hoekstra (eds.), *The scope of lexical rules*, 1–77. Dordrecht: Foris.

Botha, Rudolf P. 2015. Do Romance languages have phrasal compounds? A look at Italian. *STUF–Language Typology and Universals* 68. 395–419.

Chomsky, Noam. 1970. Remarks on nominalization. In R. Jacobs & P. Rosenbaum (eds.), *Readings in english transformational grammar*. Waltham, Mass.: Ginn & Co.

DiSciullo, Anna-Maria & Edwin Williams. 1987. *On the definition of word*. 2nd edn. Cambridge, Mass.: The MIT Press.

Lapointe, S. G. 1980. *A theory of grammatical agreement*. Amherst: University of Massachusetts dissertation.

Lieber, Rochelle. 1988. Phrasal compounds and the morphology-syntax interface. *Chicago Linguistic Society* II Parasession on agreement in grammatical theory(24). 202–222.

Lieber, Rochelle. 1992. *Deconstructing morphology. Word formation in syntactic theory*. Chicago: University of Chicago Press.

Savini, Marina. 1984. Phrasal compounds in Afrikaans: A generative analysis. *Stellenbosch Papers in Linguistics* 12. 34–114.

Scalise, Sergio & Irene Vogel (eds.). 2010. *Cross-Disciplinary issues in compounding*. Amsterdam/Philadelphia: Benjamins.

Štekauer, Pavol & Rochelle Lieber (eds.). 2009. *The Oxford handbook of compounding*. Oxford: Oxford University Press.

Trips, Carola & Jaklin Kornfilt (eds.). 2015. *Phrasal compounds from a typological and theoretical perspective*. Vol. 68. Berlin: De Gruyter. Special edition of STUF.

Chapter 2

Phrasal compounds in Modern Icelandic with reference to Icelandic word formation in general

Kristín Bjarnadóttir

The Árni Magnússon Institute for Icelandic Studies, University of Iceland

In Icelandic, as in many other languages, phrasal compounds are an interface phenomenon of the different components of grammar. The rules of syntax seem to be preserved in the phrasal component of Icelandic compounds, as they show full internal case assignment and agreement. Phrasal compounds in Icelandic can be divided into two distinct groups. The first group contains common words which are part of the core vocabulary irrespective of genre, and these are not stylistically marked in any way. Examples of these structures can be found in texts from the 13th century onwards. The second group contains more complex compounds, mainly found in informal writing, as in blogs, and in speech. These seem to be 20th century phenomena. Phrasal compounds of both types are relatively rare in Icelandic, but other types of compounding are extremely productive. Traditionally, Icelandic compounds are divided into two groups, i.e., compounds containing stems and compounds containing inflected word forms, mostly genitives, as non-heads. Phrasal compounds in Icelandic also have genitive non-heads, raising questions on the difference between the processes in non-phrasal and phrasal compounding in Icelandic.

1 Introduction

Compounding is extremely productive in Icelandic, and an indication of this can be seen in the proportions of non-compounds (base words) vs. compounds in The Database of Modern Icelandic Inflection (DMII, Bjarnadóttir 2012), a full-form database of inflectional forms produced at The Árni Magnússon Institute

Kristín Bjarnadóttir. Phrasal compounds in Modern Icelandic with reference to Icelandic word formation in general. In Carola Trips & Jaklin Kornfilt (eds.), *Further investigations into the nature of phrasal compounding*, 13–48. Berlin: Language Science Press. DOI:10.5281/zenodo.885105

for Icelandic Studies and its forerunner, The Institute of Lexicography.[1] The DMII contains the core vocabulary of Modern Icelandic, with approximately 280,000 paradigms. The vocabulary is not selected by morphological criteria, apart from the self-explanatory fact that only inflected words are included. The sources of the DMII are lexicographic data, both from traditional dictionary archives and corpora. Out of 278,764 paradigms in the DMII on Dec. 15th 2015, 32,118 entries were non-compounds, and the remaining 246,646 entries were compounds. The DMII contains both lexicalized compounds and purely productive ones, but the same rules of word formation pertain to both, i.e., they are morphologically identical.

The DMII only contains compounds written as continuous strings, in accordance with current Icelandic spelling conventions. These spelling conventions are a feature of Modern Icelandic and they do not hold in older forms of the language. To give a very simple and common example, patronyms are written as a continuous string in Modern Icelandic, e.g. *Bjarnadóttir* 'daughter of Bjarni', not *Bjarna dóttir* as evidenced in older texts. Residues of the older spelling are still found in some instances in Modern Icelandic, as when the names of the sagas are written discontinuously: *Njáls saga* 'The Story of Burnt Njáll'. This is traditional in the names of the sagas and recommended in the current spelling rules for Icelandic, but otherwise the continuous string is the norm. Spelling mistakes in present-day Icelandic do, however, very often involve the splitting of compounds, and these are most commonly found in informal texts where phrasal compounds (PCs) are very often found. These problems with spelling make PCs elusive both in traditional lexicographic archives and in automatic word extraction. PCs are here taken to be compounds where the non-head contains any kind of syntactic phrase, from noun phrases and prepositional phrases up to full finite sentences.

Discussion of PCs is largely absent from the linguistic literature on Icelandic, and probably first mentioned in Bjarnadóttir 1996[2005], citing examples not adhering to Botha's (1981) No Phrase Constraint. The Icelandic examples cited in Bjarnadóttir 1996[2005] are now a part of a private collection of over 200,000 Icelandic compounds, with full analysis of structure and constituent parts. The sources for this collection are to a large extent the same as for the DMII. The following analysis of PCs is based on this collection, with approx. 200 additional

---

[1] The DMII was initially conceived as a language resource for natural language processing, but was also intended for use in lexicography and linguistic research. The paradigms are accessible online as a reference tool and are used as such by the general public. Downloadable data and website: http://bin.arnastofnun.is.

PCs from other sources, such as *Íslenskur orðasjóður* (Wortschatz, University of Leipzig, see Hallsteinsdóttir et al. 2007), a corpus of texts from Icelandic websites, which is a good source of informal language. The total number of PCs used in this study is approx. 900. The problems involved in finding the more informal PCs are described in §3, cf. (16). At the present stage of technology, the data is sparse, and the full picture of PCs in Icelandic therefore awaits a better analysis of multiword lexical items.

In this study, PCs in Modern Icelandic are divided into two groups, based on structure, and usage or genre. The first group (Phrasal Compounds I, PCIs) contains structures which are attested by examples from the 13th century onwards, as in the Dictionary of Old Norse Prose (ONP). These PCIs are very much a feature of Modern Icelandic, they are not marked in any way stylistically, and they may appear in any genre. The most common structures of phrasal non-heads in this group are prepositional phrases (1a), and genitive noun phrases (1b), both showing full inflection or agreement:[2]

(1) a. milli   ríkja   samningur
     between.PREP state.N.NEUT.GEN.PL contract.N.MASC
     'international agreement'

    b. tveggja   manna   far
     two.NUM.GEN.PL man.N.MASC.GEN.PL vehicle
     'a boat for two'

The second group (Phrasal Compounds II, PCIIs) contains PCs that are found in certain informal genres, i.e., in blogs, social media, and speech, etc. All the examples are recent, they are often considered a little strange, and the question "Is this really a word?" is sometimes heard in connection with them. The structure of the non-head in PCIIs ranges from nominative noun phrases (2a) to fully-fledged sentences (2b):

(2) a. maður   -á   -mann   aðferð
     man.NOM to.PREP man.ACC method
     ' "man to man" method'

    b. ég- er- bara- einn- af- ykkur- strákunum   -brosið
     I   am just   one   of you   boy.DAT.DEF.PL smile.NOM.DEF
     'the "I am just one of you boys" smile'

---

[2] The compounds are aligned to the glosses, but Icelandic spelling conventions stipulate that they are written continuously. Hyphens are shown when part of the spelling.

This study presents a classification of PCs in Icelandic based on their morphological structure. Section 2 contains an introduction to the relevant features of Icelandic compounding in general, demonstrating both stems and inflected forms of nouns and adjectives as non-heads of compounds. Section 3 contains a classification of the PCs, divided into the traditional, not marked in any way by style or genre (PCI), and the more informal (PCII). The PCII constructions do, for the most part, have counterparts in Carola Trips' analysis of English PCs (Trips 2016). Section 4 contains the conclusion, along with a few words on future work.

2 Compounding in Icelandic

A comprehensive description of Icelandic compounding drawing on empirical data has not yet been written, and apart from short chapters in textbooks, the grammatical literature on Icelandic compounds is fragmentary and mostly written in Icelandic. A description of relevant aspects of Icelandic compounding is therefore in order here.

2.1 Binary branching and stress pattern

Following Eiríkur Rögnvaldsson's textbook on Icelandic morphology (Rögnvaldsson 1986), linguists have assumed binary branching for Icelandic compounds. Recent experiments with automatic compound splitting have confirmed this observation (Daðason & Bjarnadóttir 2014). Morphologically, Icelandic compounds are right-headed, and inflectional endings of compounds attach to the word-final element. All word classes can appear both as head and non-head, but noun-noun compounds are by far the most productive (Bjarnadóttir 1996[2005]). As almost all the PCs discussed here are nouns, with a marginal number of adjectives, the topic of this section is limited to compounds with nouns or adjectives as heads.

The word formation rules for lexicalized and productive compounds in Icelandic are morphologically identical, as the data in the DMII shows. That resource is intended for use in language technology and the vocabulary is therefore chosen to be as inclusive as possible, including data both from lexicographic sources and corpora.

As stated above, compounds are expected to be written as continuous strings in Modern Icelandic. As the spelling can fluctuate, this is sometimes not a very definitive criterion, and it would be of great interest to define compounds either with reference to syntactic analysis or by using phonological aspects, such as intonation and stress (Árnason 2011, and references cited there). Empirical data of this kind, however, does not exist as yet.

In spite of this, the basic stress pattern of Icelandic words can be a guideline in determining whether an item is a compound or phrase. This pattern is fairly simple, with word initial stress, and secondary stress, etc., on constituents according to morphological binary trees, as in *¹kransæðar³hjáveitu²græðlingur* 'coronary bypass transplant' in Figure 1. The prosodic pattern is therefore determined by the morphological structure, with the numbers 1, 2, 3, in the binary tree in Figure 1 signifying primary, secondary and tertiary stress.

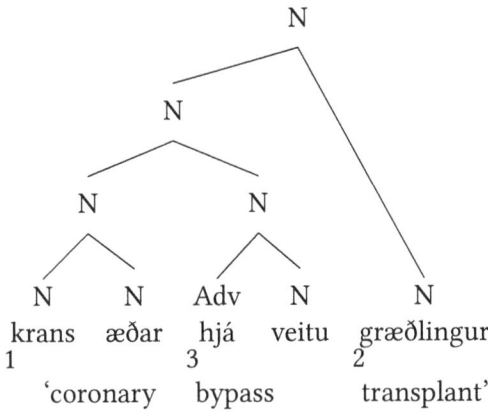

Figure 1: The stress pattern of an Icelandic compound

The compounds discussed in §2 are assumed to conform to this basic stress pattern, as do most of the PCIs in §3.1, but there is still insufficient research on the topic for an exact description of the exceptions. The complex structures in the PCIIs in §3.2 below are more of a problem where stress is concerned, as the relatively simple rules of word stress do not apply to syntactic phrases as non-heads. Informally, the observation that the head of the PCIIs is stressed has been confirmed by native speakers, but proper experiments have not been carried out. The question whether these are indeed compounds phonologically therefore remains open, but comparative data from other languages shows that similar structures are analysed as PCs in those, as is the case in Trips (2016) for English. As most of the examples of PCIIs here are from written texts or transcriptions where the original sound files are unavailable, the question of phonology may be a moot point.

2.2 Recursion

Noun-noun compounds are by far the most common type of compounds in Icelandic, and also the most structurally complex. As stated above, Icelandic compounds are right-headed, but the constituent structure in recursive compounds can be either left- or right-branching, cf. examples in (9–13). Theoretically there is no limit to the length of compounds, and the classic example of this is the frequently quoted word in (3) *Vaðlaheiðarvegavinnuverkfærageymsluskúrsútidyralyklakippuhringur*, where *Vaðlaheiði* is a compound place name.

(3) Vaðlaheiðar vega vinnu verk færa geymslu skúrs úti dyra lykla kippu
     V.   road works work tools storage shed out door key bunch
     hringur
     ring
     'key ring of the key chain of the outer door to the storage tool shed of the road works on the Vaðlaheiði plateau'

Overlong compounds are apt to be split up in Icelandic, using prepositional phrases at need, and in reality more than seven constituents are rare (Snædal 1992; Daðason & Bjarnadóttir 2014). The compound in (3) could be rephrased as

(4) lyklakippuhringur fyrir útidyrnar á verkfærageymsluskúr vegavinnunnar
     á V
     'a key chain ring for the outside door of the tool storage shed of the roadworks on V.'

In spite of the trend towards splitting, overlong compounds do sometimes occur, such as *Norðausturatlantshafsfiskveiðinefndin* 'The North East Atlantic Ocean Fisheries (lit. Fish-Catching) Committee'. Long PCs should therefore not cause a problem for Icelanders just because of their length, even if they are not common.

2.3 Inflection or compound markers?

Nouns and adjectives as non-heads in Icelandic compounds appear in different forms, i.e., as stems or inflectional forms, mostly genitive. Dative non-heads are also found in compounds, as in *gyðjumlíkur* 'goddess.N.FEM.DAT.PL like.ADJ' (Bjarnadóttir 2002). A very limited number of non-head combining forms are also found, e.g., *kven-* of the feminine noun *kona* 'woman' where the regular non-head would be *konu* (GEN.SG) or *kvenna* (GEN.PL). Linking phonemes also occur, but these are rare, with the proportion 0.005% in 38,000 non-heads in compounds in Bjarnadóttir 1996[2005]. The discussion here will be limited to stems and genitive forms as non-heads, as these are very frequent, whereas the other types are very rare.

The analysis of genitives as such in Icelandic compounds is traditional in the Icelandic grammatical literature, dating back to Rasmus Christian Rask's seminal work on Icelandic grammar Rask (1811). According to this analysis, nouns as non-heads appear as stems or genitive forms, singular or plural. Corresponding structures in Faroese and some West Norwegian dialects are analysed in the same manner in Indriðason (2014) and Thráinsson et al. (2004)

The nature of these genitives in Icelandic compounds and the question whether these are true inflectional forms or linking phonemes are matters of debate, especially in theories that specify a strict ordering of derivation, compounding and inflection. The argumentation that these genitives are not a part of morphological structures, but attributes within noun phrases, is difficult to maintain for the following reasons: The stress pattern described in §2.1. can be used to determine whether a structure is a compound or phrase, but additionally, basic Icelandic word order provides clues, as genitive attributes are usually placed after the nominal head in a sentence: *bók Kristínar* 'Kristín's book'. The reverse order, *Kristínar bók*, is usually found with contrastive stress (cf. Thráinsson 2007: 92–96). Furthermore, this analysis would leave almost half of the vocabulary, i.e. the so-called weak inflection, unavailable for compound formation as these can never appear as stems in non-heads, cf. §2.5.[3]

The case against analysing the genitive non-heads in Icelandic compounds as compound markers or linking phonemes for Icelandic also rests on the fact that the non-heads appear as the correct genitive forms, in spite of the complexity of the inflectional patterns. Inflectional variants are very common, and the paradigms in the DMII reflect this, with 594 inflectional patterns listed for the major word classes, i.e., nouns, adjectives, verbs, and adverbs (Bjarnadóttir 2012). The reason for the high number of inflectional patterns in the DMII is that each paradigm contains all inflectional variants, i.e., a word is not assumed to belong to more than one inflectional class, as in the traditional classification in Icelandic textbooks. The rampant variation found among genitive singular inflectional forms is fully reflected in the form of the non-heads.

---

[3] Further argumentation against level ordering or split morphology can be found in Icelandic derivation, as some suffixes can attach to genitive non-heads: *mannlegur* man.N.MASC.STEM -ly.SUFF.ADJ 'human', *mannslegur* man.N.MASC.GEN.SG -ly.SUFF.ADJ 'manly', *mannalegur* man.N.MASC.GEN.PL -ly.SUFF.ADJ 'pompous, conceited' (Bjarnadóttir 1996[2005]; Indriðason 1994).

The non-heads appear as correct genitive forms, as shown in all the examples in §2.4.[4] To give an example, the base word *vegur* 'way, road' has the genitive singular forms *vegar* and *vegs*, the first of which is much more frequent. Both *-ar* and *-s* appear in the non-heads of compounds, i.e., *vegarendi* 'end of road', *vegsauki* 'increase of way', i.e., 'promotion'. (The genitive plural *vega* is also used in compounds: *vegamót* 'joint of roads, i.e., crossroads'). Compounds with the head *vegur* can exhibit variants in the same way as the base word, but the crux of the matter is that these variants can be reflected in the non-heads of compounds as well, as in (5b–c). However, some compounds with the head *vegur* only have *-s* as a genitive ending, thus exhibiting a different inflectional pattern from the base words, which is interesting in light of Lieber's theories of percolation (1989). This genitive is always reflected in the non-heads of recursive compounds, as in *útvegur* 'out-way', i.e., 'fishing, fisheries', and *farvegur* 'passage way', i.e., 'channel, course' (5d–e). Underscoring marks the genitive endings:

(5)   Lemma   Gen.sg.

   a. *vegur* 'way, road'   *veg<u>ar</u>, veg<u>s</u>*
      Compounds:
      veg<u>ar</u>endi 'end of road'
      veg<u>s</u>auki 'increase of way', i.e., 'promotion'

   b. *reiðvegur* '(horse) riding road'   *reiðveg<u>ar</u>, reiðveg<u>s</u>*
      Compounds:
      reiðveg<u>ar</u>spotti 'stretch of riding road'
      reiðveg<u>s</u>framkvæmd 'riding road construction'

   c. *Laugavegur* 'pool way' (street name) *Laugaveg<u>ar</u>, Laugaveg<u>s</u>*
      Compounds:
      Laugaveg<u>s</u>apótek 'Pool Street Drug Store'
      Laugarveg<u>ar</u>ganga 'a walk along Pool Street'

   d. *útvegur* 'out-way' ('fisheries, fishing') *útveg<u>s</u>*
      Compound:
      útveg<u>s</u>þorp/ *útveg<u>ar</u>þorp 'fisheries village'

   e. *farvegur* 'passage way'   *farveg<u>s</u>*
      Compound:
      farveg<u>s</u>breyting/*farveg<u>ar</u>breyting 'change of course'

The conclusion is that *-s* and *-ar* are inflectional endings in Icelandic compounds and not linking phonemes. This is directly opposite to the case of German, where paradigmatically incorrect forms such as *liebesbrief* 'love letter' are

---

[4] The exceptions are few, and can for the most part be explained by historical changes. These obsolete inflectional forms are only a feature of lexicalized compounds.

analysed as containing a prosodic marker, here -*s*-. With the correct feminine genitive, the compound would be *liebebrief* (Trips, personal communication).

The function of the genitive in compounding is considered in Indriðason (1999; 2014) in the light of the split morphology hypothesis (Perlmutter 1988) and the split inflection theory (Booij 1994), and his conclusion is that "the genitive in Icelandic compounds can formally be categorized as contextual inflection but functionally as inherent inflection. This dual role of the genitive is unique and creates problems for the theories previously mentioned" (Indriðason 2014: 30). The aim here is to present these so-called genitive forms, to be able to compare them with the genitives in the PCs in §3, as these undoubtedly contain inflectional forms. The question is, then, whether the "ordinary" (i.e., non-phrasal) compounds contain true genitives.

2.4 Non-head in compounds: Nouns

Examples of the different forms found in the non-heads of noun-noun compounds are shown in (6) (see Bjarnadóttir 2002). These nouns are all written as continuous strings without hyphens. The lemma forms are shown in parentheses, as in *naglrót* (*nögl+rót*). Underscoring is used for genitive endings and for emphasis, as in *nögl*, to mark the umlaut.

(6) Form of non-head in noun-noun compounds

   A. Stem

      1. Lemma form[5]

        a. orð   myndun   (orð+myndun)
           word.N.NEUT formation.N.FEM
           'word formation'

      2. Without umlaut

        b. nagl   rót   (nögl+rót)
           nail.N.FEM root.N.FEM
           'base of finger/toe-nail'

      3. With umlaut (rare)

        c. lög   brot   (lög+brot)
           law.N.NEUT.PL breaking.N.NEUT
           'infraction of law'

---

[5] Lemma form without nominative ending where applicable, as in *hest* for the masculine *hestur*, subtracting the masculine nominative ending -*ur*.

4. Irregular (rare change in stem)

   d. mann   tal   (maður+tal)
      man.N.MASC count.N.NEUT
      'census'

B. Inflectional forms

  1. Genitive singular

    e. bor<u>ðs</u>   horn   (borð+horn)
       table.N.NEUT.GEN.SG corner.N.NEUT
       'corner of a table'

    f. hund<u>s</u>   haus   (hundur+haus)
       dog.N.MASC.GEN.SG head.N.MASC
       'head of a dog'

    g. katt<u>ar</u>   haus   (k<u>ö</u>ttur+ha<u>u</u>s)
       cat.N.MASC.GEN.SG head.N.MASC
       'head of a cat'

    h. penn<u>a</u>   strik   (penni+strik)[6]
       pen.N.MASC.GEN.SG stroke.N.NEUT
       'stroke of a pen'

    i. per<u>u</u>   tré   (pera+tré)
       pear.N.FEM.GEN.SG tree.N.NEUT
       'pear tree'

    j. bók<u>ar</u>   kápa   (bók+kápa)
       book.N.FEM.GEN.SG coat.N.FEM
       'dust jacket'

  2. Genitive plural[7]

    k. orð<u>a</u>   bók   (orð+bók)
       word.N.NEUT.GEN.PL book.N.FEM
       'dictionary'

    l. bíl<u>a</u>   stæði   (bíll+stæði)
       car.N.MASC.GEN.PL place.N.NEUT
       'car place, parking lot'

---

[6]The use of stems is limited in some inflectional classes, cf. §2.5.

[7] The genitive plural of all nouns ends in -*a* (or -*na* for some feminine and neuter nouns).

    m. bók<u>a</u>   búð   (bók+búð)
        book.N.FEM.GEN.PL store.N.FEM
        'book shop'

    n. dúf<u>na</u>   kofi   (dúfa+kofi)[8]
        pigeon.N.FEM.GEN.PL hut.N.MASC
        'pigeon hut'

The genitive forms of the non-head in compounds are in accordance with the correct genitives, as they occur in the paradigms in the DMII. To give examples, the genitives of the masculine nouns *hundur* 'dog' and *köttur* 'cat' are *hunds/*hundar* and *kattar/*kötts*, and always appear as such when the genitive is used in the non-heads of the compounds of these words (cf. B.1.f and g in (6)). A choice of identical linking phonemes to the correct genitive endings is less than convincing, especially as the choice of endings on individual words is for the most part idiosyncratic. PCs with genitive phrases as non-heads also invariably contain the correct genitive forms.

The choice of stem or inflected form seems to be arbitrary for compounds where the non-head is a base noun, i.e., not a compound (Bjarnadóttir 1995), with the exceptions discussed below (this section). The compounds *bóksala* and *bókabúð* shown in (7) thus contain the stem and the genitive plural of the word *bók* 'book' as non-heads without any discernible reason for the difference, as the compounds are semantically identical with synonyms as heads. The distribution is not phonetically conditioned either, as seen in *blekborði (k+b)* 'ink strip' (cf. *bókabúð*), and *bókasafn* (ka+s) 'book museum', i.e., 'library' (cf. *bóksala*) occurring freely on morpheme boundaries:

(7)   a. bók.N.FEM.STEM sala.N.FEM 'book shop'

        b. bóka.N.FEM.GEN.PL búð.N.FEM 'book shop'

The choice of stem or genitive construction may be arbitrary in non-recursive compounds, as in (7), but it turns out that it is not free, i.e., the form itself can be lexicalized, so to speak, as users will only accept the expected variant, thus *bóksala, bókabúð* vs. **bókasala, *bókbúð*. The same can apply to the choice between genitive singular and plural, which is often not semantically significant, as in (8a–b) where *barns/barna* can refer to one or more children.[8]

---

[8] The difference between genitive singular and plural can be significant, as in *bróður-sonur* 'brother's.N.MASC.GEN.SG son.N.MASC.SG' ('the son of (your) brother'), *bróðursynir* 'brother's.N.MASC.GEN.SG sons.N.MASC.PL' ('the sons of (your) brother'), and *bræðrasynir* 'broth-

(8) a. barns   meðlag
         child.N.NEUT.GEN.SG support.N.NEUT
         'child support' (paid by parent)

     b. barna   lífeyrir
         child.N.NEUT.GEN.PL support.N.MASC.PL
         'child support' (paid by state, etc.)

     c. barns   vagga
         child.N.NEUT.GEN.SG crib.N.FEM
         'baby's crib'

     d. barna   rúm
         child.N.NEUT.GEN.PL bed.N.NEUT
         'baby's cot'

The choice between stem and genitive appears to be less free in recursive compounding, with left-branching compounds ([[N N] N]) tending to result in genitive constructions (Jónsson 1984), when the corresponding non-recursive compound does not, as in the pairs *skrifborðsfótur* (9a) and *borðfótur* (9b), and *olíuverðshækkun* (9c) and *verðhækkun* (9d):

(9) a. [skrif   borðs]   fótur
         write.N.NEUT.STEM desk.N.NEUT.GEN.SG leg.N.MASC
         'writing desk leg'

     b. borð   fótur
         desk.N.NEUT.STEM leg.N.MASC
         'desk leg'

     c. [olíu   verðs]   hækkun
         oil.N.FEM.GEN.SG price.N.NEUT.GEN.SG rise.N.FEM
         'rise in oil price'

     d. verð   hækkun
         price.N.NEUT.STEM rise.N.FEM
         'price rise'

---

ers'.N.MASC.GEN.PL sons'.N.MASC.PL ('the sons of (your) brothers'). The compound *bræðrasonur* 'brothers'.N.MASC.GEN.PL son'.N.MASC.SG ('the son of (your) brothers') is not found. Some nouns exhibit agreement of number between non-head and head, as in the singular *mannsnafn* 'persons'.N.MASC.GEN.SG name' .N.NEUT.SG (i.e., 'Christian name') vs. the plural *mannanöfn* 'persons' .N.MASC.GEN.PL names.N.NEUT.PL (i.e., 'Christian names'). It is unclear how extensive number agreement of this type is in compounds and the topic awaits further research.

Left-branching recursive compounds with stems of compounds as non-heads do also occur, although they are much rarer than the corresponding genitive constructions. These are of two kinds, i.e., with a stem compound as first part of the non-head [[N.STEM N]STEM N] (cf. *saltfiskútflutningur*, 10b), and with a genitive compound as first part of the non-head [[N.GEN N]STEM N] (cf. *fjárhúsdyr*, 10c):

(10) a. [kú   fisk]   plógur
        COW.N.FEM.STEM fish.N.MASC.STEM plough.N.MASC

        'ocean quahog plough'

    b. [salt   fisk]   útflutningur
        salt.N.NEUT.STEM fish.N.MASC.STEM export.N.MASC

        'salt fish export'

    c. [fjár   hús]   dyr
        sheep.N.NEUT.GEN.SG house.N.NEUT.STEM door.N.FEM.PL

        'sheep house door'

    d. [betrunar   hús]   vist
        betterment.N.FEM.GEN.SG house.N.NEUT.STEM stay.N.FEM.SG

        'stay in jail'

    e. [rentu   kammer]   bréf
        rent.N.FEM.GEN.SG chamber.N.NEUT.STEM letter.N.NEUT.SG

        'letter from the (Danish) ministry of finance' (*renta*: 'rent, interest')

The observation in Jónsson 1984 of the strong tendency towards genitive in compound non-heads holds for the most part, but stem compounds as in (10a–b) do also exist in compound non-heads, sometimes even as variant forms, as in (10b) *saltfiskútflutningur* [[N.STEM N].STEM N] where the corresponding *saltfisksútflutningur* [[N.STEM N]GEN N] is also found.[9] The compounds in (10c–d) are more problematic, as these contain a stem ending in -*s* where the genitive ending would also be an -*s*. The syllables containing the genitive are unstressed, moreover, as can be inferred from Figure 1 above, and the difference in vowel length normally occurring in such genitives (i.e., *hús* vs. *húss*) may thus not be discernible (Árnason 2011). This could therefore be a matter of spelling, although the genitive -*s* is usually preserved in such cases. The compound in (10e), *rentukammerbréf*, contains an undisputed genitive construction in *rentu*.N.GEN.SG.*kammer*, but the first part is in fact a weak feminine noun which can never appear as a

---

[9] In this case the stem compound *saltfiskútflutningur* seems to be much more common than the genitive compound *saltfisksútflutningur*. The frequency on timarit.is (The National Library's corpus of newspapers and journals) is 372/104.

stem, as is the case in the word *olía* in (9c) (cf. §2.5). The evidence for the construction [[N.GEN N]STEM N] therefore does not seem to be very strong.

Right-branching recursive compounds do not exhibit similar restrictions as the left-branching ones do, as stem constructions and genitive constructions mix freely:

(11) I. [N.STEM [N.STEM N]]

   a. [stál   [borð   búnaður]]
       steel.N.NEUT.STEM table.N.NEUT.STEM equipment.N.MASC.SG
       'steel cutlery'

   b. [stíl   [hug   sjón]]
       style.N.MASC.STEM mind.N.MASC.STEM vision.N.FEM.SG
       'ideal of style'

   c. [her   [flug   maður]]
       army.N.MASC.STEM flight.N.NEUT.STEM man.N.MASC.SG
       'military pilot'

  II. [N.GEN. [N.STEM N]]

   d. [togara   [sjó   maður]]
       trawler.N.MASC.GEN.SG sea.N.MASC.STEM man.N.MASC.SG
       'trawler fisherman'

   e. [bómullar   [hand   klæði]]
       cotton.N.FEM.GEN.SG hand.N.FEM.STEM cloth.N.NEUT
       'cotton towel'

   f. [atvinnu   [flug   maður]]
       profession.N.FEM.GEN.SG flight.N.NEUT.STEM man.N.MASC.SG
       'professional pilot'

 III. [N.STEM [N.GEN. N]]

   g. [plast   [hnífa   par]]
       plastic.N.NEUT.STEM knife.N.MASC.GEN.PL pair.N.NEUT.SG
       'plastic cutlery' (usually set of knife, fork & spoon)[10]

   h. [hör   [vasa   klútur]]
       linen.N.MASC.STEM pocket.N.MASC.GEN.SG cloth.N.MASC
       'linen handkerchief'

---

[10] The spoon may be optional, but this is emphatically not a pair of two plastic knives, i.e., not [[*plast hnífa*] *par*].

i. [grunn [fjár festing]]
    base.N.MASC.STEM capital.N.NEUT.GEN.SG fastening.N.FEM

    'basic investment'

IV. [N.GEN.[N.GEN. N]]

j. [biskups [skjala safn]]
    bishop.N.MASC.GEN.SG document.N.NEUT.GEN.PL collection.N.NEUT

    'archives of the bishop'

k. [blúndu [vasa klútur]]
    lace.N.FEM.GEN.SG pocket.N.MASC.GEN.SG cloth.N.NEUT

    'lace handkerchief'

l. [hernaðar [leyndar mál]]
    warfare.MASC.GEN.SG secret.N.FEM.GEN.SG matter.N.NEUT

    'military secret'

The examples in (11g–i) are critical in respect to theories with any kind of ordering of stem and genitive compounds. Imposing a left-branching structure on (11g) would change the meaning of *plasthnífapar* from 'a set of knife and fork made from plastic' to 'a pair of knives …'. Posing different structures for (11h) *hörvasaklútur* 'linen handkerchief' and (11k) *blúnduvasaklútur* 'lace handkerchief' and the corresponding set of towels in (12a–b) seems semantically counterintuitive:

(12) a. [hör [hand klæði]]
      linen.N.MASC.STEM hand.N.NEUT.STEM cloth.N.MASC

      'linen towel'

   b. [bómullar [hand klæði]]
      cotton.N.FEM.GEN.SG hand.N.NEUT.STEM cloth.N.MASC

      'cotton towel'

   c. [hör [vasa klútur]]
      linen.N.MASC.STEM pocket.N.MASC.GEN cloth.N.MASC

      'linen handkerchief'

   d. [blúndu [vasa klútur]]
      lace.N.FEM.GEN.SG pocket.N.MASC.GEN cloth.N.MASC

      'lace handkerchief'

An explanation based on the fact that *handklæði* and *vasaklútur* are lexicalized compounds will not suffice either, as fully productive compounds with these structures are easily made:[11]

---

[11] These compounds are nonce formations. All nonce formations in this text are clearly marked as such.

(13) a. [plast   [penna   dallur]]
           plastic.N.NEUT.STEM pen.N.MASC.GEN tub.N.MASC

           'plastic pen container'

     b. [postulíns   [penna   dallur]
           porcelain.N.NEUT.GEN.SG pen.N.MASC.GEN tub.N.MASC

           'porcelain pen container'

The modifiers *plast* and *postulín* refer to the material of the container, not the pens stored in it.

2.5 Restriction of the use of stems as non-heads

Words from some inflectional classes can never appear as stems in compounds and there the genitive forms are always used. This applies to the so-called weak inflection of feminine and masculine nouns, e.g., feminine nouns ending in *-a* in the nominative singular, as in *olía* in *olíuverðshækkun* 'a rise in the price of oil' in (9c), and masculine nouns ending in *-i* in the nominative singular, as in *vasi* in *vasaklútur* '(pocket) handkerchief' in (12). Words of this type are very numerous, as seen in the DMII which contains 27,381 non-compounds. Out of a total of 13,116 masculine and feminine nouns, 6,540 belong to the weak inflection, or just under 50%.

This fact should not be forgotten when the proportions of stem compounds and genitive compounds are considered, as the result is that a large proportion of the vocabulary is unavailable for stem compounds.[12] The consequences of this for any kind of ordering based on the difference of stems and inflected non-heads in compounds are unclear, but the option of specifying that half of the vocabulary is unavailable at any given level seems counter-intuitive.

2.6 Non-heads in compounds: Adjectives

Adjectives as non-heads of compounds exhibit similar variants as nouns do, i.e., stems (*lítil* 'small' in *lítilmenni* 'insignificant character' (A.b in 14) and genitives (*lítils* in *lítilsverður* 'insignificant' (B.c in 14)). Internal inflection is also found in adjectives as non-heads in compounds with nominal heads, where agreement of gender, case, and number is exactly the same within the compounds as in

---

[12] There are a few exceptions where the combining forms of weak masculine nouns are stems, e.g., *sím-* for *sími* 'telephone', e.g., *símhringing* 'telephone call', where *síma-* would be expected. These cases are extremely rare and most compounds with *sími* have the genitive non-head *síma*, e.g., *símasamband* 'telephone connection'.

syntax, as in the nominative *litlifingur* 'little finger, pinkie', where the ending *-i-* in the non-head is a portmanteau adjectival ending for masculine, singular, nominative, definite, and the accusative *litlafingur*, where the ending *-a-* is a portmanteau adjectival ending for masculine, singular, accusative, definite, cf. (14C.). A comparison of agreement within a compound and in syntax is shown in Table 1.

(14) *Form of adjectives as non-heads of compounds*

A. Stem

   a. blá   ber   (blár+ber)
      blue.ADJ.STEM berry.N.NEUT
      'blueberry'

   b. lítil   menni   (lítill+-menni (*menni*=bound form))
      small.ADJ.STEM man.N.MASC
      'insignificant character'

B. Inflection, genitive (indefinite)

   c. lítils   verður   (lítill+verður)
      small.ADJ.GEN.SG.INDEF worthy.ADJ
      'insignificant'

   d. sjúkra   hús   (sjúkur+hús)
      sick.ADJ.GEN.PL.INDEF house.N.NEUT
      'hospital'

C. Inflection, internal[13]

   1. Positive degree

      e. litli   fingur
         little.ADJ.MASC.DEF finger.N.MASC.INDEF
         (*lítill+fingur*; Acc. *litlafingur*)
         'pinkie, little finger'

      f. Bratta   brekka
         steep.ADJ.FEM.DEF hill.N.FEM
         (*brattur+brekka*; Acc. *Bröttubrekku*)
         'Steep Hill' (placename)

---

[13] Degree, as shown in the superlative *hæstiréttur* 'supreme court' in (14) (C)g, is not an instance of internal inflection but a contextual feature (Indriðason 2014: 21). Internal inflection in the comparative only appears in place names in Modern Icelandic and is not shown here.

2. Superlative

    g. hæsti   réttur
        highest.ADJ.MASC.SUP.DEF court.N.MASC.INDEF
        (*hár+réttur*; Acc. *hæstarétt*)
        'supreme court'

Definiteness is an inflectional feature of Icelandic adjectives (cf. Table 1). The genitives in B in (14) are indefinite forms, but adjectival non-heads in C in (14) are always definite, irrespective of the definiteness of the compound as a whole. For explanation, Table 1 contains the paradigms for the noun phrase *lítill fingur* 'little finger' in column 1 and 2, and the internal inflection for the compound *litlifingur* 'pinkie' in the compound in column 3.

Table 1: Paradigms for noun phrases and internal adjectival inflection

singular	indefinite	definite	compound
NOM.	lítill fingur	litli fingurinn	litlifingur
ACC.	lítinn fingur	litla fingurinn	litlafingur
DAT.	litlum fingri	litla fingrinum	litlafingri
GEN.	lítils fingurs	litla fingursins	litlafingurs
plural			
NOM.	litlir fingur	litlu fingurnir	litlufingur
ACC.	litla fingur	litlu fingurna	litlufingur
DAT.	litlum fingrum	litlu fingrunum	litlufingrum
GEN.	lítilla fingra	litlu fingranna	litlufingra

Note that the internal inflection in the compound in column 3 in Table 1 is identical to the definite inflectional form in column 2. This is in fact the case in all compounds of this type in the DMII, but the construction is not very common, except in place names. The form of the compound is indefinite, however, and the cliticized definite article can be attached, in the same manner as in other nouns, as seen in the examples in (15):

(15)   a. Hann braut litlafingur,   held ég.
           he   broke littlefinger.N.MASC.ACC.SG.INDEF, think I
           'He broke a pinkie, I think.'

b. Hann braut á sér litlafingurinn
  he broke on himself (the) littlefinger.N.MASC.ACC.SG.DEF

  'He broke his pinkie.'

c. Litlifingurinn brotnaði.
  the-littlefinger.N.MASC.NOM.SG.DEF broke

  'The pinkie broke/was broken.'

The genitive constructions with adjectival non-heads have direct counterparts in PCs, in the same manner as nouns. They are, however, quite rare, cf. §3.1.2.

2.7 The relevant features of non-phrasal compounding for PCs

The salient points in this section in connection with the PCs discussed in the next section are these:

- Genitive non-heads are one of two basic options in forming Icelandic non-phrasal compounds. The other main option is to have non-head stems. Genitive non-heads are also found in PCs, as will be discussed in §3.

- The distribution of genitives and stems as non-heads in compounds is partly dependent on the inflectional class of the non-head, as masculine and feminine words from the so-called weak inflection cannot appear as stems in compounds, with exceptions mentioned in Footnote 13. Right-branching compounds with genitive non-heads in a lower node than stem non-heads are quite common. Therefore, it is difficult to maintain strict ordering of stems and genitives as non-heads of compounds for Icelandic.

- The inflected non-heads are in accordance with the "correct" inflection of the respected unbound forms. This also applies in PCs.

- The internal inflection of adjectival non-heads could perhaps be analysed as a phrase-to-word conversion. §3.1.4 contains PCs with prepositional phrases which could also be analysed as phrase to word conversion, as could some of the PCII structures in §3.2, cf. also Footnote 16. The process of phrase to word conversion (or nominalization) will not be discussed in any detail, as the necessary research is not available.

3 Phrasal compounds

Below, Icelandic PCs are divided into two groups. The first group (§3.1) contains common words which are not stylistically marked in any way, some of which are attested from medieval times to the present day. This group of PCs contains genitive noun phrases and prepositional phrases as modifiers of nouns, as in Table 2. (Examples of all constructions are given in the following sections.)

Table 2: Phrasal Compounds I, from lexicographic sources

a.	NP.GEN. + N	Phrase internal agreement
b.	AdjP.GEN. + N	Phrase internal agreement (rare)
c.	PP + N	Case assignment by preposition

The second group contains more complex PCs, mainly found in informal writing and in speech. The structures are variable, up to full main clauses. The evidence for some of the structures is weak, down to single examples. The classification in §3.2 reflects this. It should be noted that the more traditional PC types shown in Table 2 also appear in the more informal texts used as sources for PCIIs.

Table 3: Phrasal Compounds II, from the web, etc.

a.	[N.NOMINATIVE + PP]NP + N	Case assignment by preposition
b.	Miscellaneous non-predicates:	AdjP, AdvP, negation, etc.
c.	Predicates:	Imperatives, questions, finite S, etc.

As the second type of PCs is very much a feature of informal speech and text, the spelling tends to be varied. In fact, Icelandic spelling rules do not include any indication of the correct form in these cases.[14] The PCs are therefore a free-for-all in Icelandic spelling, which makes them very difficult to extract automatically from text. The examples in (16) show spelling variations with different quotation marks, hyphenation, and spaces, found in data from a corpus of Icelandic websites, *Íslenskur orðasjóður* (Hallsteinsdóttir et al. 2007):

---

[14] The only indication is the spelling of compounds containing multiword first parts of foreign origin, such as the translation of *New York City*, i.e., *New York-borg*, where the spelling rules place a hyphen before the compound head *borg* 'city'. The space in *New York* from the English original is maintained. Judging by all the mistakes made, this spelling rule seems to be hard to learn, and extending it to phrasal compounds seems to be counter-intuitive as spelling as in (16f) (*munn við munn-aðferð*) is hardly ever found.

(16) a. *„allt eða ekkert" aðferðin* ·   'the all or nothing method'

     b. *"allt eða ekkert" dæmi*   '[an] all or nothing example'

     c. *'allt eða ekkert' týpa*   '[an] all or nothing type', i.e., 'guy'

     d. *allt eða ekkert dæmi*   '[an] all or nothing example'

     e. *munn-við-munn-öndun*   '[a] mouth to mouth breathing'

     f. *munn við munn-aðferð*   '[a] mouth to mouth method'

     g. *allt-eða-ekkert hugsunarháttur*   '[an] all or nothing way of thinking'

The possible spelling varieties are not exhausted in this search, but at present, tools for an automatic search do not exist. No attempt is made here to normalize the spelling in these examples, resulting in strange quotation marks at times.

The PCs discussed here are a subset from a collection of over 200,000 compounds compiled by the author over a period of over 30 years. The sources are mostly the same as those for the DMII mentioned above (Bjarnadóttir 1996[2005]; 2012), and the analysis contains lemmatization and full analysis of the constituents of the compounds. This resource returned ca. 700 PCs, almost all of which are PCIs. In addition, ca. 200 PCs from the web, from blogs, social media, radio, and TV, were collected from *Íslenskur orðasjóður*, and from miscellaneous sources, personal communication, etc. Finding data for PCIIs turned out to be difficult, because of unstandardized spelling. The remainder of this section contains a classification of these 900 PCs.

3.1 Phrasal compounds I

3.1.1 Genitive noun phrase and nominal head

Genitive noun phrases with adjectives are common in any genre as non-heads of compounds. There is full agreement of gender, case and number within the noun phrases, as in *Góðrarvonarhöfði* 'Cape of Good Hope' (17c). where the adjective *góður* 'good' agrees in gender with the feminine noun *von* 'hope', and both agree in case (gen.), and number (sg.). The head *höfði* 'cape' is a masculine noun.

(17) a. [hálfs   mánaðar]NP   blað

        half.ADJ.MASC.GEN.SG month.N.MASC.GEN.SG paper.N.NEUT.SG

        'biweekly journal'

     b. [heils   árs]PP   dekk

        whole.ADJ.NEUT.GEN.SG year.N.NEUT.GEN.SG tyre.N.NEUT.SG

        'all year tyre'

    c. [Góðrar   vonar]NP   höfði
         good.ADJ.FEM.GEN.SG hope.N.FEM.GEN.SG cape.N.MASC.SG
         'Cape of Good Hope'

    d. [allra   sálna]NP   messa
         all.ADJ.FEM.GEN.PL soul.N.FEM.GEN.PL mass.N.NEUT.SG
         'All Souls' Day' Nov. 2nd

PCs of this type are found in Old Icelandic, as in *allramannagisting* 'all men's night lodging' and *allralandamaður* 'all countries' man' (AM 132 fol., AD c1300–1350, cf. ONP). These two PCs do not appear to be lexicalized as an entity, as the head can easily be changed as in the nonce formation *allramannalygi* 'all men's lies' (nonce formation by Jóhannes Bjarni Sigtryggsson). The PCs in (17) are lexicalized, with the possible exception of (17a), and the stress pattern of unlexicalized PCs of this type needs to be investigated as there is a tendency to split them apart in writing.

3.1.2 Genitive adjectival phrase and nominal head

PCs with adjectival phrases as heads are rare. There is agreement for case and number in the example below, but gender is indistinct in the genitive plural:

(18) [allra   heilagra]ADJP   messa
      all.ADJ.GEN.PL holie.ADJ.GEN.PL mass.N.FEM.SG
      'All Saints' Day' Nov. 1st

The construction is similar to *allrasálnamessa* (17d) above. The PC in (18) is also found in Old Icelandic (GKS 1812 4°, cf. ONP), along with variants, e.g., *allraheilagradagur* 'All Saints' Day', *allraheilagrahátíð* 'All Saints' Feast'.

3.1.3 Noun phrase with numeral and nominal head

The cardinal numbers 1–4 inflect for gender and case in Icelandic, and these appear in PCs with the same construction as the adjectives in §3.1.1 There is full agreement of numeral and noun for case and number. Gender is distinguished in the singular, but the genitive plural is the same for numerals in all genders, as in adjectives.

(19) a. [eins   manns]NP   herbergi
        one.NUM.MASC.GEN.SG man.N.MASC.GEN.SG room.N.NEUT.SG
        'single room'

b. [tveggja   manna]NP   herbergi
two.NUM.MASC.GEN.PL men.N.MASC.GEN.PL room

'double room'

c. [fimm   ára]NP   áætlun
five.NUM year.N.NEUT.GEN.PL plan.N.FEM.SG

'five year plan'

d. [sex   liða]NP   háttur
six.NUM parts'.N.MASC.GEN.PL meter.N.MASC.SG

'hexameter'

The phrases in PCs in (19) are fully transparent and not lexicalized, as can be demonstrated by the free replacement of the numerals, cf. (19b–d):

(20)   a. [níu   manna]NP   herbergi
nine.NUM men.N.MASC.GEN.PL room.N.NEUT.SG

'a room for nine'

b. [þriggja ára]NP   áætlun
three.NUM year.N.NEUT.GEN.PL plan.N.FEM.SG

'three years' plan'

c. [sjö   og hálfs   árs]NP   áætlun
seven.NUM and half.NEUT.GEN.SG year.N.NEUT.GEN.SG plan.N.FEM.SG

'seven and a half year plan'

d. [ellefu   liða]NP   háttur
eleven.NUM part.N.MASC.GEN.PL meter.N.MASC.SG

'a (hypothetical) meter with 11 parts'

A similar construction in German does not exhibit this agreement, and is in fact used as an argument against a phrasal analysis, as in Pafel (2015) on words like *Zweibettzimmer*, partly because "their parts do not agree as the parts of the corresponding phrase would do". Icelandic PCs containing NPs with numerals always show agreement, as do those with adjectives. They would therefore seem to point to a different conclusion from Pafel's and be considered true PCs and not 'pseudo-phrasal' compounds like the German construction.

The agreement of numeral and noun within PCs obeys the same rules as in syntax, as can be seen in the following examples of PCs and corresponding sentences:

(21) a. [einnar   hæðar]NP   skýjakljúfur
        one.NUM.FEM.GEN.SG storey.N.FEM.GEN.SG skyscraper.N.MASC.SG
        Ég ætla að_fá einn   [súpu   disk]
        I   FUT   have   one.NUM.MASC.SG soup.N.FEM.GEN.SG plate.N.MASC.SG
        'I'll have one plate of soup'

     b. [tveggja   hæða]NP   hús
        two.NUM.FEM.GEN.PL storey.N.FEM.GEN.PL house.N.NEUT.SG
        Ég ætla að_fá tvo   [súpu   diska]
        I   FUT   have   two.NUM.MASC.PL soup.N.FEM.GEN.SG plate.N.MASC.PL
        'I'll have two plates of soup'

     c. [tuttugu-og-einnar   hæðar]NP
        twenty-one.NUM.FEM.GEN.SG storey.N.FEM.GEN.SG
        skýjakljúfur
        skyscraper.N.MASC.SG
        Ég ætla að_fá [tuttugu_og_einn]   [súpu
        I   FUT   have   twenty-one.num.masc.sg soup.N.FEM.GEN.SG
        disk   ]
        plate.N.MASC.SG
        'I'll have twenty-one plates of soup'

The peculiarity of the agreement with the last part of the numeral is always observed, i.e., any number that ends in *einn* 'one' takes the singular, irrespective of it being 1, 21 or 1001, both in syntax and within compounds: *Ég var að lesa Þúsund og eina nótt*SG. 'I've been reading *Thousand and One Night[s]*'.

3.1.4 Prepositional phrase and nominal head

The most common type of PCs in Icelandic contains a prepositional phrase as a non-head. The prepositions occurring in these PCs govern the genitive, and case assigned by the preposition is always maintained. The stress pattern is regular, as shown in Figure 1. Most of these PCs are easily rephrased as sentences, as in *milliríkjasamningur* (cf. translation in 22a) vs. *samningur milli ríkja* 'a contract between states'.

(22) a. [milli   ríkja]PP   samningur
        between.PREP state.N.NEUT.GEN.PL contract.N.MASC.SG
        'international agreement'

b. [milli   landa]PP   flug

   between.PREP country.N.NEUT.GEN.PL flight.N.MASC.SG

   'international air transport'

c. [innan   dyra]PP   þægindi

   inside.PREP door.N.FEM.GEN.PL conveniences.N.NEUT.PL

   'indoor conveniences'

d. [innan   lands]PP   markaður

   inside.PREP country.N.NEUT.GEN.SG market.N.MASC

   'domestic market'

e. [neðan   jarðar]PP   lest

   below.PREP earth.N.FEM.GEN.SG train.N.FEM

   'subway, underground train'

Prepositional phrases also seem to be converted to adverbials or adjectives (Bjarnadóttir 1996[2005]), as in *innanhúss* 'indoors' shown successively in (23a, b, c) as an adverb, an adjective and a full prepositional phrase with the definite article. This type of word formation in Icelandic is a neglected field, but it is very common.[15]

(23) a. mótaröð   í frjálsum   innanhúss

       series.of.events in free.ADJ.DAT.PL indoors.ADV

       'a series of track and field events indoors' (frjálsar.ADJ.FEM.PL 'track and field')

   b. innanhúss   knattspyrnuskór

       indoors.ADJ soccer.shoes.N.MASC.PL.INDEF

       'indoors soccer shoes'

   c. Hópurinn starfar innan.PREP hússins.N.NEUT.GEN.DEF

       'The group works inside the house'

The compound *innanhúss* in (23a) is not lexicalized, in the lexicographer's sense of the meaning being different from the sum of the parts (see Svensén 1993: 42), as demonstrated by nonce compounds such as *innanbókarvísun* 'inside

---

[15] The analysis of phrase to word conversion seems to be obvious, and the phenomenon is supported by words like the verb *svei-mér-þá-a* 'shame.INTERJ.me.PRON.DAT.now.ADV, with infinitival ending -a, as in *Hann svei-mér-þá-aði sér duglega* 'He said "shame-on-me" with gusto"'. (Bjarnadóttir 1996[2005]). There are not many such cases; *gleym-mér-ei* 'forget me not' is probably the most common.

(a) book citation', which are easily formed.[16] They cannot be modified in the same manner as the sentence in (23c), e.g., *innanbókarinnarvísun* 'inside-the-book citation'.

This type of PC is quite common in Modern Icelandic, and the construction also exists in Old Icelandic. The word *innanfjórðungsmaður* 'inside the quarter man' (i.e., 'an inhabitant of a district (quarter)') appears in *Grágás* 'The Gray Goose Law' (GKS 1157 fol., AD 1260?). The modern term for 'vagrant' is the PC *utangarðsmaður* 'outside garden/wall man' first attested in a Norwegian diploma in AD 1300 (AM dipl norv facs I 12).[17]

3.1.5 Prepositional phrase and adjectival head

PCs with adjectival heads are held to be marginal (Meibauer 2007: 237) or not in accordance with the properties of PCs in Germanic languages, as in Trips (2016: 153).

The adjective *utanríkispólitískur* 'of foreign politics' in (24b) is a PCI with a possible adjectival head found in the DMII but not present in the data used for this study. Google returns 58 examples of this PC, from the media and the website of Alþingi, the Icelandic Parliament. (For comparison, about 1,400 instances of the adjective *flokkspólitískur* 'party political' are found on Google.) Google returns about 4,140 instances of the corresponding noun *utanríkispólitík* 'foreign politics', which has the structure in (24a) (cf. §3.1.4, 22). The parallel analysis of the adjective is shown in (24b). If the possibility of recursive compounding and derivation is considered allowable, the analysis in (24c) is the result, deriving the adjective from the PC.

(24) a. [utan   ríkis]PP   pólitík
          outside.PREP state.N.NEUT.GEN.SG politics.N.FEM
          '(the) politics of foreign affairs'

      b. [utan   ríkis]PP   pólitískur
          outside.PREP state.N.NEUT.GEN.SG political.ADJ
          'pertaining to foreign politics'
          (as in *utanríkispólitískur veruleiki* '(the) reality of foreign politics')

      c. [[utan   ríkis]PP   pólitík]   +skur
          outside.PREP state.N.NEUT.GEN.SG politics.N.FEM +al.ADJ.SUFF

---

[16] Spontaneous creation by Jóhannes Bjarni Sigtryggsson referring to citation in the present volume, Feb. 12th 2016.

[17] All examples from Old Icelandic are derived from *The Dictionary of Old Norse Prose* (ONP).

Recursive compounding and derivation have been proposed for Icelandic (Bjarnadóttir 1996[2005]) which solves issues of bracketing paradoxes that are otherwise common for Icelandic, but are of course not compatible with most current models of the language architecture. PCs with adjectival heads are certainly very rare in Icelandic, but two more PCIIs are shown in (29) in §3.2.2.

3.2 Phrasal compounds II

Informal speech and texts provide examples of constructions of PCs not found in other genres. These constructions range from types of noun phrases not described in the previous section to full predicate phrases, such as *ég-verð-að-vita-hvað-gerist-næst-bók* 'I must (to) know what happens next book'. In this section the PCs are divided into non-predicative (§3.2.1–2) and predicative PCs (§3.2.3. The classification in this section is partly based on Carola Trips' analysis of English PCs (Trips 2016).

These PCs can be humorous, as in *ég-er-bara-einn-af-ykkur-strákunum-brosið* '"I'm just one of you boys" smile', but that is certainly not always the case. The head of the Icelandic Confederation of Labour certainly did not have anything humorous in mind when he used the word *ef-og-þá-kannski-hlutir* 'if and then maybe things' of vague offers in negotiations, on the brink of a general strike.[18] The PCs are very often spontaneous ad hoc constructs, but occasionally they do catch on and become a part of everyday language, sometimes as a part of the jargon within small groups as when linguists in Iceland refer to chapters on future work as *gaman-væri-að-kaflinn* 'the "it would be fun to" chapter'.

The phrasal non-heads in the PCs are not necessarily lexicalized, at least not in the lexicographer's sense of their meaning being greater than or different from the sum of the parts. They can, for instance, be used to describe any kind of attitude, such as *ég-er-svo-glöð svipurinn* 'the "I'm so happy" expression' and *oj barasta hvað þetta er leiðinlegt mómentið* 'the "ugh how boring this is" moment'. The semantics of these PCs would be an interesting topic for research, but as yet the Icelandic data is too scarce to warrant further speculation.

3.2.1 Nominative noun phrase and nominal head

The non-head of this construction is a noun phrase in the nominative, and as such a novel feature in Icelandic compounding although the dating of it is difficult for reasons of spelling and lack of analysis of older texts. The noun is followed by a prepositional phrase.

---

[18] Ásmundur Stefánsson, newscast on Icelandic Radio in the Nineties (Bjarnadóttir 1996[2005]).

(25) a. [maður   -á   -mann]   aðferð
    man.N.MASC.NOM.SG to.PREP man.N.MASC.ACC.SG method.N.FEM.SG
    'man-to-man method'

  b. [skref   -fyrir   -skref]
    step.N.NEUT.NOM.SG for.PREP step.N.NEUT.ACC.SG
    leiðbeiningar
    instructions.N.FEM.PL

    'step-by-step instructions'

  c. [poki   -í   -öskju]   kerfi
    bag.N.MASC.NOM.SG in.PREP box.N.MASC.DAT.SG system.N.NEUT.SG
    'bag in a box system'

  d. [korter   -í   -þrjú]   -náungi
    quarter.N.NEUT.NOM.SG to.PREP three.NUM.ACC guy.N.MASC.SG
    'a quarter to three guy'[19]

The nominalization of the non-head NPs in these PCs seems to be a possibility. This is supported by an anecdotal example from a fellow linguist quoting his young daughter, where the definite article is cliticized onto a noun phrase as a whole, e.g., *bland í poka* 'mixture in a bag' (of sweets bought by weight) becomes *bland-í-pokað mitt* 'my the "mix-in-a-bag"':[20]

(26) a. [bland   -í   -poka]NP   -ð
    mix.N.NEUT.NOM.SG in.PREP bag.N.NEUT.DAT.SG the.DEF.ART.NOM.SG
    mitt
    my.POSS.NEUT.NOM.SG
    'my mixture in a bag'

Similar PCs containing foreign noun phrases, mostly English, are easily found (27a–c), as are constructions containing adjectival or even verb phrases (27d–e):

(27) a. *coast-to-coast skautahlaup*   '"coast to coast" ice skating'
  b. *step-by-step bók*   'a "step by step" book'
  c. *point-in-time afritun*   'a "point in time" backup'

---

[19] A 'quarter to three guy' refers to the now expired closing hours of Icelandic bars, indicating a certain desperation. In the data used here, the head is *náungi*, but the synonym *gæi* is more frequent.

[20] Jón Hilmar Jónsson, The Árni Magnússon Institute for Icelandic Studies, personal communication.

    d. *all-in-one prentari*   'an "all in one" printer'

    e. *cut-to-fit skjákort*   'a "cut to fit" graphics adapter'

Needless to say, there is no agreement in the foreign phrases in the PC loanwords, but similar Icelandic PCs do exist, perhaps modelled on the loanwords. These show rather interesting agreement, as can be seen in the examples in (28a–b). The preposition *í* 'in' governs the dative of *einni/einu* 'one' in the non-heads of the PCs *allt-í-einni-tölva* 'all in one computer' and *allt-í-einu-tæki* 'all in one tool', but the gender is in agreement with the head of the PCs, the feminine *tölva* 'computer' in (28a) and the neuter *tæki* 'tool, instrument' in (28b).

(28)   a. [allt   -í   -einni]   -tölva
          all.NEUT.NOM.SG in.PREP one.NUM.FEM.DAT.SG computer.N.FEM.NOM.SG

          'all in one computer'

    b. [allt   -í   -einu]   tæki
          all.NEUT.NOM.SG in.PREP one.NUM.NEUT.DAT.SG tool.N.NEUT.NOM.SG

          'all in one tool'

Because of spelling issues, these PCs are elusive in texts, cf. (16) above.

3.2.2 Miscellaneous non-predicates

The remainder of the data for PCs discussed here contains a miscellany of words that are listed here for completeness, but the data is so scarce that any analysis is bound to be inconclusive. The non-heads of these PCs are seen to be adjectival phrases, with or without negation, and adverbial phrases. All the phrases contain full syntactic agreement; they are lifted straight from syntax and attached in front of nominal or adjectival heads, or "stuck in front of these words" in the rather informal wording straight from the mouth of a non-linguist.

(29)   I. AdjP + N:

        a. [ódýrari   -en -í -Frakklandi]   [net
           cheaper.ADJ than in France.N.NEUT.DAT Internet
           tenging]
           connection.N.FEM

           'A "cheaper than in France" Internet connection'

II. AdjP +N, with negation:

  b. [ekki- ofur- frjálsleg]   -kristni
     not   super free-like.ADJ.FEM.INDEF Christianity.N.FEM.INDEF
     '"not super liberal" Christianity'

  c. ekki- svo- fjarlæg   framtíð
     not so   distant.ADJ.FEM.INDEF future.N.FEM.INDEF
     'A "not so distant" future'

  d. ekki- svo- dapurlegi   -dagurinn
     not so   sad.ADJ.MASC.DEF day.N.MASC.DEF
     'the "not so sad" day'

III. AdvP/PP + Adj:

  e. klukkan -tíu -á -laugardegi   -skemmtilegur
     clock   ten on Saturday.N.MASC.DAT amusing.ADJ
     '"ten o'clock on a Saturday" amusing'

  f. inn-á-   hvert- einasta   -heimili   -s
     [into.PREP [every- one].NEUT.ACC.SG home.N.NEUT 's'.GEN]PP
     -frægur
     famous.ADJ
     'famous in every single home'

Two of the examples of PCIIs, *klukkan-tíu-á-laugardegi-skemmtilegur* '"ten o'clock on a Saturday" amusing' (29e), and *inn-á-hvert-einasta-heimilisfrægur*[21] 'in every single home famous' (29f), have adjectives as heads and thus contravene one of the properties in Trips (2016), where Germanic PCs are assumed to have only nominal heads (p.154). According to Meibauer (2007: 236–237), adjectival heads in PCs are marginal, as they seem to be in Icelandic where very few examples have been found (cf. §3.1.2 for an example of a PCI adjective). Speakers do seem to accept the PCIs above to the same degree as the other PCIIs in (29). More data is needed to establish the status of PC adjectives; as of now they seem to be as marginal in Icelandic as Meibauer found them to be in German.

---

[21] The PC *inn-á-hvert-einasta-heimilis -frægur* contains an unexpected *-s-* (marked with an * in (29f). This *-s-* is the correct genitive singular ending for the neuter noun *heimili*, which is out of place in this PC as the preposition takes the accusative. It could possibly be a linking phoneme, as *-s-* can be (Bjarnadóttir 1996[2005]). This PC is remarkable as it is the only example found to date of a prepositional phrase PC where the preposition does not take the genitive.

3.2.3 Predicates

The last group of Icelandic PCs listed here are verbal predicates, cf. Trips (2016) for similar constructions in English. As in the previous groups in this section, the data is scarce. The examples in this section are divided into four groups, i.e., imperatives, infinite, finite sentences, and questions. These PCs are generally found in blogs, and they are very spontaneous, easily understood, and considered to be more or less odd, incorrect, or at least very strange. These are attested examples, however, and as such seem to be within the capacity of the users, even if the selfsame users often treat them as jokes. It should be noted that the imperative in Icelandic can contain a subject pronoun cliticized onto the verbal form, i.e., *rugladu* (*rugla*.IMP *þú*2.PERS.PRON) Thus *rugladu mig*, lit. 'confuse you me'.

(30) Imperative (directives)

   a. [haltu   kjafti]   brjóstsykur
       hold+you.IMP mouth.N.MASC.DAT.SG candy.N.MASC

       '"hold your mouth" candy', i.e., "shut up" candy (because of size)

   b. [rugladu   -mig- í- hausnum] -mynd
       confuse+you.IMP me   in head.DEF movie

       'a "make me confused" movie'

   c. [gerðu-   það- sjálfur] -tónlist
       do+you.IMP it   yourself music

       '"do it yourself" music'

   d. [gettu   -betur-]   liðið
       guess+you.IMP better.ADV.COMP team.N.NEUT.DEF

       'the "guess better" team' (a quiz team)

   e. ['skrifaðu- í- gestabókina-   eða- ég- kýli- þig- í- andlitið'] dagur
       write+you in guest+book.DEF or   I   punch you in face.DEF   day

       'a "write in the guestbook or I'll punch you in the face" day'

One of the imperative PCs above is a common word, *haltukjaftibrjóstsykur* '"shut up" candy' (30a), used of a really large mouthful of candy that makes speech difficult. The parallel *haltukjaftityggjó* '"shut up" chewing gum' also exists. *Gettu-betur-liðið* 'the "guess better" team' (30d) is well known and used of the quiz teams taking part in a very popular television program called *Gettu betur* 'Guess better'. The other imperative PCs are nonce formations, and get gradually stranger the longer they are. The Icelandic PC imperatives have direct counterparts in English, according to Carola Trips' analysis (2016:160) of English directives.

The infinitive in (31) is awkward and included here for the sake of completeness, as other examples of this type of PC have not been found.

(31)   Infinitive
sprengja-   í- loft- upp lemja- vondu- kalla   -stórmynd
explode.INF in air up hit.INF bad   guys'.NP.ACC.PL.INDEF big-movie
'an "explode into air hit bad guys" blockbuster movie'

The PC in (31) could be a directive, as in *koma svo!* 'come on now', in which case it would have the meaning '"let's explode into the air & hit the bad guys" blockbuster movie'. The use of the infinitive with the function of a directive needs to be investigated. If the analysis holds up, the counterpart is found in Carola Trips' directives with *let* (2016:160).

As in Trips (2016: 159–160) for English, Icelandic PCs may have full clauses and questions as non-heads:

(32)   I. Question
a. hvers-vegna- ekki -samfélagið
why   not society.N.NEUT.SG,DEF
'the "why not" society'

II. Finite S
b. ég- verð- að- vita- hvað- gerist   -næst -bók
I   must to know what happens next book.N.FEM.SG.INDEF
'An "I must know what happens next" book'

c. ég- þoli-   ekki- illar- tölvur   -klúbburinn
I   tolerate not bad computers club.N.MASC.SG.DEF
'the "I cannot bear evil computers" club'

d. ég- rek- þau- í_gegnum- þig- horn
I   stick them through   you horns.N.NEUT.PL.INDEF
'the "I will stick through you" horns'

e. allt- er- list tímabilið
all is art [time-span]N.NEUT.SG.DEF
'the "everything is art" period'

f. ég- er- bara- einn- af- ykkur- strákunum-   brosið
I   am just one of you   boys.N.MASC.DEF smile.N.NEUT.DEF
'the "I am just one of you boys" smile'

All the examples in (32) are nonce formations. These constructions are not common, but they pose no burden of interpretation on native speaker recipient readers or listeners. More data would be helpful here, but as the spelling is completely unpredictable better tools are needed for automatic extraction.

4 Conclusion

In this study, PCs in Icelandic are divided into two groups; those that have formed a part of Icelandic since medieval times (PCIs), and constructions not attested until the 20th century (PCIIs). The first group, PCIs, contains only genitives or prepositional phrases with prepositions taking the genitive as non-heads, but the non-heads in the second group, PCIIs, vary widely, from noun phrases to full finite sentences. The one aspect all the PCs here have in common is that they contain full agreement and case assignment, with the exception of some PCs with foreign non-heads, as *"step-by-step" bók* '"step by step" book'. The Icelandic PCs do, for example, exhibit full genitive agreement in the non-heads of PCs such as *tveggjamannaherbergi* 'room for two', which is not the case in the German counterpart, *Zweibettzimmer*, according to Pafel (2015) (cf. §3.1.3).

The classification of the more complex PCIIs is in line with Carola Trips' analysis of English PCs, and all the PCII constructions here have a counterpart in her analysis of English. Due to scarcity of the Icelandic data, some of the English PC constructions are not found, despite seeming quite plausible. This could be the result of problems with spelling, which makes searching difficult. The only type of Icelandic PCIIs that seems to be unusual, in comparison with the English data, are PCs with adjectival heads, as in *klukkan-tíu-á-laugardegi-skemmtilegur* '"ten o'clock on a Saturday" amusing' (cf. §3.2.2), and *utanríkispólitískur* 'outside state political' (cf. §3.1.5).

As seen in §2, inflected word forms are also a feature of very many non-phrasal compounds in Icelandic. It is maintained here that non-head genitives and stems cannot be assumed to belong to specified layers of the morphology. Semantically, attempts to analyse them in this way result in bracketing paradoxes, as in *hör-vasa-klútur* 'linen pocket cloth', i.e., [N.STEM [N.GEN.PL N]] 'linen handkerchief' (the correct meaning) and [[N.STEM N]GEN.PL N] 'cloth in a linen pocket'. Splitting the analysis of morphological structure and semantics also seems counter-intuitive in the light of the fact that the choice of stems or genitives is to a large degree determined by the inflectional class of words. This has a bearing on the PCs. The traditional PCs (PCIs) always contain a genitive, either as a head of a non-head noun phrase, or as a part of a prepositional phrase. If there is no fundamental difference between stem and genitive non-heads in non-phrasal compounds, where do the genitive phrasal non-heads fit in? This question remains unresolved.

Although the more complex PCs are sometimes deemed outlandish, some PCs are totally acceptable on all levels to native speakers of Icelandic. This applies to the structures classified as PCIs in this study, i.e., the traditional ones. Words of this type are acceptable to the degree that very few people actually realize that they are structurally different from simpler structures, as in *milliþinganefnd* 'between sessions committee' [PP + N] and *efnahagsnefnd* 'financial matters committee' [[N.GEN N].GEN N]. Lexicalization does not seem to be a crucial point either, as most of the structures seem to be freely available for new formations, including nonce formations.

Now to the *gaman-væri-að-kaflinn* 'the "would-be-fun-to-do" section', i.e., thoughts on future work. This study is focussed on data. This data, however, is quite limited and should be expanded. Work on a large corpus of Modern Icelandic has just started at The Árni Magnússon Institute of Icelandic Studies, and that should produce extensive data, which will be analysed with a new version of our automatic compound splitter producing binary trees with full analysis of all constituents (cf. Daðason & Bjarnadóttir 2014). As Icelandic word formation exhibits interesting interaction between syntax and morphology, presenting this data seems a very worthwhile undertaking.

Acknowledgements

I would like to thank all the participants in the workshop on phrasal compounds in Mannheim on June 26th 2015, and especially the organizers Carola Trips and Jaklin Kornfilt for a most inspiring event. Thanks are also due to my colleagues, Jóhannes Bjarni Sigtryggsson, Jón Friðrik Daðason, Jón Hilmar Jónsson and Kristján Rúnarsson.

Abbreviations

ACC	accusative	ART	article
ADJ	adjective	DAT	dative
ADJP	adjectival phase	DEF	definite
ADV	adverb	DMII	The Database of Modern
ADVP	adverbial phrase		Icelandic Inflection

FEM	feminine	ONP	The Dictionary of Old Norse Prose
GEN	genitive		
IMP	imperative	PC	phrasal compound
INDEF	indefinite	PERS	person
INF	infinitive	PL	plural
MASC	masculine	POSS	possessive pronoun
N	noun	PP	prepositional phrase
NEUT	neuter	PREP	preposition
NOM	nominative	SG	singular
NP	noun phrase	SUP	superior degree
NUM	numeral	V	verb

References

Árnason, Kristján. 2011. *The phonology of Icelandic and Faroese.* Oxford: Oxford University Press.

Bjarnadóttir, Kristín. 1995. Lexicalization and the selection of compounds for a Bilingual Icelandic dictionary base. In *Nordiske studier i leksikografi*, vol. 3, 255–263.

Bjarnadóttir, Kristín. 2012. The database of modern Icelandic inflection. In *LREC 2012 Proceedings: Proceedings of "Language Technology for Normalization of Less-Resourced Languages", SaLTMiL 8 – AfLaT*, 13–18.

Bjarnadóttir, Kristín. 1996[2005]. *Afleiðsla og samsetning í generatífri málfræði og greining á íslenskum gögnum.* Reykjavík.

Bjarnadóttir, Kristín. 2002. *A Short Description of Icelandic Compounds.* The Website of The Institute of Lexicography. http://notendur.hi.is/~kristinb/compshort.pdf, accessed 2002-04-01.

Booij, Geert E. 1994. Against split morphology. *Yearbook of Morphology* 1993. 27–50.

Botha, Rudolf P. 1981. A base rule theory of Afrikaans synthetic compounds. In Michael Moortgat, Harry van der Hulst & Teun Hoekstra (eds.), *The scope of lexical rules*, 1–77. Dordrecht: Foris.

Daðason, Jón Friðrik & Kristín Bjarnadóttir. 2014. Utilizing constituent structure for compound analysis. *LREC 2014 Proceedings.* 1637–1641.

Hallsteinsdóttir, E., T. Eckart, C. Biemann, U. Quasthoff & M Richter. 2007. *Íslenskur Orðasjóður – Building a Large Icelandic Corpus. Proceedings of NODALIDA-07, Tartu, Estonia.*

Indriðason, Þorsteinn G. 1999. Um eignarfallssamsetningar og aðrar samsetningar í íslensku. *Íslenskt mál* 21. 107–150.

Indriðason, Þorsteinn G. 2014. Fallbeygðir fyrri liðir og tvær kenningar um orðhlutafræði. *Íslenskt mál* 36. 9–30.

Indriðason, Þorsteinn G. 1994. *Regluvirkni í orðasafni og utan þess. Um lexíkalska hljóðkerfisfræði íslensku.* Reykjavík.

Jónsson, Baldur. 1984. Samsett orð með samsetta liði. Fáeinar athuganir. 158–174.

Lieber, Rochelle. 1989. On percolation. In Geert Booij & Jaap van Marle (eds.), *Yearbook of morphology 2*, 95–138. Heidelberg: Springer.

Meibauer, Jörg. 2007. How marginal are phrasal compounds? Generalized insertion, expressivity, and I/Q-interaction. *Morphology* 17. 233–259.

Pafel, Jürgen. 2015. Phrasal compounds are compatible with Lexical Integrity. *Language Typology and Universals* 68. 263–280.

Perlmutter, David. 1988. The split morphology hypothesis: Evidence from Yiddish. In Michael Hammond & Michael Noonan (eds.), *Theoretical morphology.* 77–99. San Diego: Academic Press.

Rask, Rasmus Christian. 1811. *Vejledningen til det islandske eller gamle nordiske sprog.* Copenhagen: Schuboth.

Rögnvaldsson, Eiríkur. 1986. *Íslensk orðhlutafræði: Kennslukver handa nemendum á háskólastigi.* Reykjavík: Málvísindastofnun Háskóla Íslands.

Snædal, Magnús. 1992. Hve langt má orðið vera? *Íslenskt mál* 14. 173–207.

Svensén, Bo. 1993. *Practical lexicography. Principles and methods of Dictionary-Making.* Oxford: Oxford University Press.

Thráinsson, Höskuldur. 2007. *The syntax of Icelandic* (Cambridge Syntax Guides). Cambridge: Cambridge University Press.

Thráinsson, Höskuldur, Hjalmar P. Petersen, Jógvan í Lon Jacobsen & Zakaris Svabo Hansen. 2004. *Faroese. An overview and reference grammar.* Tórshavn: Føroya Fróðskaparfelag.

Trips, Carola. 2016. An analysis of phrasal compounds in the model of parallel architecture. In Pius ten Hacken (ed.), *The semantics of compounding*, 153–177. Cambridge: Cambridge University Press.

Websites

The Database of Modern Icelandic Inflection (Beygingarlýsing íslensks nútímamáls). http://bin.arnastofnun.is

Íslenskur orðasjóður (Wortschatz Universität Leipzig). http://wortschatz.uni-leipzig.de/ws_isl/

The Dictionary of Old Norse Prose. http://www.onp.ku.dk

Chapter 3

Compounding in Polish and the absence of phrasal compounding

Bogdan Szymanek

John Paul II Catholic University of Lublin

In Polish, as in many other languages, phrasal compounds of the type found in English do not exist. Therefore, the following questions are worth considering: Why are phrasal compounds virtually unavailable in Polish? What sort of structures function in Polish as equivalents of phrasal compounds? Are there any other types of structures that (tentatively) could be regarded as "phrasal compounds", depending on the definition of the concept in question? Discussion of these issues is preceded by an outline of nominal compounding in Polish. Another question addressed in the article is the following: How about phrasal compounds in other Slavic languages? A preliminary investigation that I have conducted reveals that, just like in Polish, phrasal compounds are not found in other Slavic languages. The only exception seems to be Bulgarian where a new word-formation pattern is on the rise, which ultimately derives from English phrasal compounds.

1 Introduction

In the Polish language, there are no phrasal compounds comparable to English forms like *a scene-of-the-crime photograph* etc., with a non-head phrase-level constituent. Instead, phrases are used. For instance:

(1)   a. a scene-of-the-crime photograph
          fotografia *(z)*   *miejsca*   *przestępstwa*
          photograph (from) scene.GEN crime.GEN
          'photograph from/of the scene of the crime'

Bogdan Szymanek. Compounding in Polish and the absence of phrasal compounding. In Carola Trips & Jaklin Kornfilt (eds.), *Further investigations into the nature of phrasal compounding*, 49–79. Berlin: Language Science Press. DOI:10.5281/zenodo.885119

    b. a "chicken and egg" situation (N+and+N) (Trips 2014: 44)

        i. *??sytuacja "kury   i   jajka"*
          situation   chicken.GEN and egg.GEN

          'a situation of a chicken and an egg'

        ii. *?sytuacja "kura   czy jajko?"*
          situation   chicken.NOM or   egg.NOM

          'a situation: "a chicken or an egg?"'

        iii. *sytuacja typu – co było pierwsze: kura czy jajko?*
           situation type.GEN what was first chicken or egg

           'a situation of the type – what was first: a chicken or an egg?'

    c. a "work or starve" philosophy (conjoined verbs) (Trips 2014: 44)
      filozofia   "pracuj   lub głoduj"
      philosophy work.IMP or starve.IMP

It can be seen, on the basis of these relatively simple examples of English phrasal compounds (PCs) that their Polish equivalents appear in a variety of phrasal and clausal forms (including more or less elaborate periphrasis). Occasionally the translation will allow for alternative renderings, sensitive to subtle lexical and stylistic differences. From the viewpoint of translation into Polish, the English orthographic convention of enclosing pre-head elements within quotation marks somehow looks more palatable (familiar) than its alternative, i.e. hyphenation. But still, a word-by-word rendering of the English PC *a "chicken and egg" situation*, i.e. as **„kura i jajko" sytuacja* is utterly impossible. As regards (1b) – the choice of the particular Polish form is not only a question of (syntactic) grammaticality but rather of semantic equivalence and faithfulness (in translation) as well as of the degree of stylistic appropriateness. The problems are then comparable to those we encounter when translating idioms.

In their "Introduction" to the special issue of STUF, entitled *Phrasal compounds from a typological and theoretical perspective*, Trips & Kornfilt (2015a: 236) point out that "there are no (comprehensive) studies [of phrasal compounds] available"„ for languages other than English, German or Turkish, while there are only "some brief discussions of aspects of phrasal compounds" for a few other languages (Trips & Kornfilt 2015a: 236). Clearly, in order to understand the status and scope of phrasal compounding in a cross-linguistic perspective, we need to examine the structures of a greater number of (typologically diverse) languages.

Polish is one such language for which there have been no reports in the literature concerning the category of phrasal compounds. That this is a non-issue in Polish linguistics is further suggested by the fact that an established term like *złożenie frazowe*, equivalent to English 'phrasal compound', simply is not available in Polish, in contradistinction to terms like *derywaty odfrazowe* '(de)phrasal derivatives' or *derywaty od wyrażeń syntaktycznych* 'derivatives from syntactic expressions', which suggests that Polish word-formation does operate on phrasal constituents, but only as long as they are inputs to affixal derivation. Therefore, it is argued in this paper that phrasal compounds (of the type found in English) do not exist in Polish.[1] Assuming the correctness of this prediction, the following questions are worth considering:

- Why are phrasal compounds virtually unavailable in Polish?

- What sort of structures function in Polish as equivalents of English phrasal compounds?

- Are there any other types of structures in Polish, that (tentatively) could be regarded as "phrasal compounds", depending on the definition of the concept in question?

- How about phrasal compounds in other Slavic languages?

2 An outline of nominal compounding in Polish

Generally speaking, compounding in Polish is much less productive than in a language like English.[2] The majority of the relevant data are compound nouns. Compound adjectives are also fairly common in contemporary Polish, while the formation of compound verbs is completely unproductive.[3] Below I focus on the class of compound nouns, their structural diversity and certain formal properties. Such a delimitation of the scope of this article is dictated not only by the fact that compound nouns outnumber compounds of other types in Polish, but also by our main topic, i.e. phrasal compounds, which are nouns.

Typically, a compound noun (or adjective) in Polish must involve a so-called linking vowel (interfix, intermorph, connective) which links, or separates, the

---

[1] Cf. Bisetto (2015: 395) for a similar claim concerning Italian and Romance languages in general.

[2] This section incorporates modified fragments from my article which originally appeared as Szymanek (2009).

[3] For the sake of completeness, it should be noted that there are a few older (often obsolete and lexicalized) compound verbs in present-day use; e.g. *lekceważyć* 'snub, disregard' < *lekce* 'lightly, little (obs.)' + *ważyć* 'weigh', *zmartwychwstać* 'rise from the dead' < *z* 'from' + *martwych* 'dead, gen. pl.' + *wstać* 'rise', etc.

two constituent stems. As a rule, the vowel in question is -*o*-, but there are other possibilities as well which surface in compound nouns incorporating some verbs or numerals in the first position. In the latter case, the intermorph is -*i*-/-*y*- or -*u*-, respectively (see Grzegorczykowa & Puzynina 1999: 458). Consider the following straightforward examples where the linking element appears in bold type, hyphenated for ease of exposition:[4]

(2) | Stem 1 | | Stem 2 | | Compound N |
|---|---|---|---|---|
| gwiazd·a 'star' | + | zbiór 'collection' | > | gwiazd-**o**-zbiór 'constellation' |
| siark·a 'sulphur' | + | wodór 'hydrogen' | > | siark-**o**-wodór 'hydrogen sulphide' |
| star·y 'old' | + | druk 'print, n.' | > | star-**o**-druk 'antique book' |
| żyw·y 'live' | + | płot 'fence' | > | żyw-**o**-płot 'hedge' |
| łam-a·ć 'break' | + | strajk 'strike' | > | łam-**i**-strajk 'strike-breaker' |
| mocz-y·ć 'soak, v.' | + | mord·a 'mug, kisser' | > | mocz-**y**-mord·a 'heavy drinker' |
| dw·a 'two' | + | głos 'voice' | > | dw-**u**-głos 'dialogue'[5] |
| dw·a 'two' | + | tygodnik 'weekly' | > | dw-**u**-tygodnik 'biweekly' |

Prosodically, the compounds are distinguished from phrases by the fact that they receive a single stress on the penultimate syllable (in accordance with the regular pattern of word stress in Polish). Thus, for instance, STA•ry•DRUK 'old print' (phrase) vs. sta•RO•druk 'antique book' (compound).

Morphologically, the typical presence of the interfix (usually -*o*-) does not exhaust the range of formal complications. In fact, there may be no interfix at all, in certain types of compounds. In some cases, the lack of an interfix seems to be

---

[4]Occasionally I will use hyphens to separate the elements of a compound, but it must be borne in mind that, according to the spelling convention, the majority of Polish compounds are written as one word, with no hyphen. Exceptions involve some coordinate structures like *Bośnia-Hercegowina* 'Bosnia-Herzegovina' or *czarno-biały* 'black and white'. Another boundary symbol, a raised dot, is used in some lists of examples to indicate the inflectional endings of words.

[5]The intermorph -*u*- is heavily restricted in its distribution and it mainly appears after the numerals *dwa* 'two' (*dwudźwięk* 'double note') as well as *sto* 'one hundred' (*stulecie* 'century'; exception: *stonoga* 'centipede').

lexically determined. For instance, most combinations involving the noun *mis-trz* 'master' as their head have no linking vowel (e.g. *balet-mistrz* 'ballet master', *kapel-mistrz* 'bandmaster', *zegar-mistrz* 'clockmaker'; but *tor-o-mistrz* 'railway specialist', *organ-o-mistrz* / *organ-mistrz* 'organ specialist'). In other cases, the omission of the intermorph seems to be due to the phonological characteristics of the input forms: if the final segment of the first constituent and/or the initial segment of the second constituent is a sonorant, the combination is likely to be realized without any intervening connective (e.g. *pół-noc* 'midnight', *trój-kąt* 'triangle', *ćwierć-nuta* 'quarter note, crotchet', *noc-leg* 'lodging, accommodation', *hulaj-noga* 'scooter' (see Kurzowa 1976: 68).

Another feature that blurs the picture is the frequent occurrence of co-formatives, i.e. morphological elements which, side by side with the interfix itself, contribute to the structure of a given compound. Thus, for instance, fairly common are compound nouns of the following structure: STEM1+interfix+STEM2+suffix, i.e. there is both an interfix and a suffix which jointly function as exponents of the category (hence the Polish traditional term: *formacje interfiksalno-sufiksalne*). Consequently, *nos-o-roż-ec* 'rhinoceros' incorporates the input forms *nos* 'nose' and *róg* 'horn' (with stem-final palatalization), followed by the obligatory noun-forming suffix *-ec* (cf. **nos-o-róg*). The compound is then structurally analogous to its counterparts in Czech and Slovak (*nosorožec*), while in Russian the equivalent is simply *nosorog*, with no suffix. Consider a few more Polish examples:

(3)	Stem 1	Stem 2	Compound N
	dług·i 'long'	dystans 'distance'	dług-o-dystans-owiec 'long-distance runner'
	obc·y 'foreign'	kraj 'country'	obc-o-kraj-owiec 'foreigner'
	drug·a 'second'	klas·a 'form'	drug-o-klas-ist·a 'second-form pupil'
	prac·a 'job'	daw-a·ć 'give'	prac-o-daw-c·a 'employer'
	gryź·ć 'bite'	piór·o 'pen'	gryz-i-piór-ek 'pen-pusher'

It may be seen that each of the compounds on the list ends in a suffix. The suffixes *-ec*, *-owiec*, *-ist·a*, *-c·a*, and *-ek* are quite common in this function, so that they may be said to do some of the formative work, as far as compounding is concerned, together with the linking vowel.

Various other Polish compounds end in a suffix, too, which has a fundamentally different status though, since it is inflectional. However, as we shall see, it may also have an important role to play, from the point of view of word-formation. Incidentally, it will be noticed that the examples of compounds given so far are all masculine nouns, which typically have no overt inflectional ending in the nominative sg. (thus e.g. *gwiazdozbiór·ø*, *nosorożec·ø*). Here the gender of the whole combination is inherited from gender specification on the head (in case it is nominal). Thus *gwiazdozbiór* is masculine because *zbiór* is masculine, etc. Yet, in quite a few compounds there is a gender-class shift, for instance from feminine to neuter or masculine, as in the following examples:

(4)	Stem 1	Stem 2	Compound N
	wod·a 'water'	głow·a 'head' [+feminine]	wod-o-głowi·e 'hydrocephalus' [+neuter]
	płask·a 'flat'	stop·a 'foot' [+feminine]	płask-o-stopi·e 'flat foot' [+neuter]
	czarn·a 'black'	ziemi·a 'earth' [+feminine]	czarn-o-ziem·ø 'black earth' [+masculine]

Thus, the compound status of *wodogłowie* (rather than **wodogłowa*) is signalled by two things: first, the presence of the usual connective -*o*- and, secondly, the gender-class modification, which results in a distinct paradigm of declension (cf. a few forms in the singular: *głow·a* NOM, *głow·y* GEN, *głowi·e* DAT vs. *wodogłowi·e* NOM, *wodogłowi·a* GEN, *wodogłowi·u* DAT, etc.). Thirdly, in fact, one could mention the characteristic palatalization of the stem-final consonant in the [+neuter] compounds above (throughout the paradigm). Due to this effect, the paradigmatic shift may be looked upon as a significant co-formative which, together with the intermorph -*o*-, defines the structure of the compound in question (hence the Polish term: *formacje interfiksalno-paradygmatyczne*). In fact, the shift of paradigm need not result in gender modification; for instance, the Slovak noun *slov·o* 'word' and the compound *tvar-o-slovi·e* 'morphology' are of the same gender, [+neuter], but their respective declensional paradigms are distinct. The same property is illustrated by the Polish compound *pust-o-słowi·e* 'verbosity' [+neuter] < *pust·y* 'empty' + *słow·o* 'word' [+neuter].

On some accounts, this formal type is extended to cover also masculine compounds which have a verbal root as their second element, with a zero marker of the nom. sg. For example: Polish *ręk-o-pis·ø* 'manuscript' < *ręk·a* 'hand' + *pis(-a·ć)* 'write'; likewise Russian *rukopis'*, Slovak and Czech *rukopis*. Further Polish examples are given below:

(5)	Stem 1	Stem 2	Compound N
	korek 'cork'	ciąg(-ną·ć) 'pull'	kork-o-ciąg·ø 'cork-screw'
	śrub·a 'screw, n.'	kręc(-i·ć) 'twist'	śrub-o-kręt·ø 'screwdriver'
	paliw·o 'fuel'	mierz(-y·ć) 'measure'	paliw-o-mierz·ø 'fuel indicator'
	piorun 'lightning'	chron(-i·ć) 'protect'	piorun-o-chron·ø 'lightning conductor'
	drog·a 'road'	wskaz(-a·ć) 'indicate'	drog-o-wskaz·ø 'signpost'
	długo 'long, adv.'	pis(-a·ć) 'write'	długo-pis·ø 'ballpoint pen'[6]

Taking into account the syntactic category of the input forms which participate in the coining of compound nouns in Polish, one needs to point out that, evidently, not all theoretically possible combinations are actually attested. To generalize, one can say for instance that only noun and verb stems may appear as second-position (final) constituents (see below). Alternatively, the verbal stems in question may be interpreted as (potential) nouns, too – products of verb-to-noun conversion. Incidentally, it is enough to distinguish between the first and second constituent, since nominal compounds in Polish hardly ever contain more than two elements (in obvious contradistinction to, for example, English compounds). In particular, recursion, which is perhaps evidenced by certain types of compound adjectives in Polish, is not really corroborated by the facts of N+N combination. To sum up, we list below the major syntactic types of compound nouns, with examples involving an intermorph only:

---

[6]Since adverbs do not inflect, the *-o* vowel in *długo-pis*, etc. may be interpreted not as an intermorph but rather as an integral element of the input form, at least in those cases where an adverb in *-o* exists.

(6)
Stem 1	Stem 2	Example
N	N	ocz-o-dół 'eye socket'
		(< oko 'eye' + dół 'pit')
V	N	łam-i-strajk 'strike breaker'
		(< łamać 'break' + strajk 'strike')
A	N	ostr-o-słup 'pyramid'
		(< ostry 'sharp' + słup 'pillar')
Num	N	dw-u-głos 'dialogue'
		(< dwa 'two' + głos 'voice')
N	V	wod-o-ciąg 'waterworks'
		(< woda 'water' + ciagnąć 'pull, draw')
Adv	V	szybk-o-war 'pressure cooker'
		(< szybko 'fast' + warzyć 'cook')
Pron	V	sam-o-lub 'egoist'
		(< sam 'oneself' + lubić 'to like')
Num	V	pierw-o-kup 'pre-emption'
		(< pierwszy 'first' + kupić 'buy')

However, as has been pointed out, the intermorph (interfix) need not be the only exponent of the compounding operation. It may co-occur with a derivational suffix, as a co-formative. Hence we get the following distributional pattern, illustrated below with compounds involving a noun in the head position ('plus' means presence and 'minus' means absence of an affix):

(7)
Interfix	Suffix	Example
+	+	nos-o-roż-ec 'rhinoceros'
		(< nos 'nose' + róg 'horn')
+	–	krwi-o-mocz 'haematuria'
		(< krew 'blood' + mocz 'urine')
–	+	pół-głów-ek 'halfwit'
		(< pół 'half' + głowa 'head')
–	–	balet-mistrz 'ballet master'
		(< balet 'ballet' + mistrz 'master')

As may be seen, the full range of theoretically available options is actually attested (although with different degrees of productivity). A complete formal classification would have to superimpose yet another feature, namely the presence or absence of the paradigmatic marker, often appearing in place of an overt suffix. Thus, for instance, *nos-o-roż-ec* contains the suffix *-ec* while, for example, *głow-o-nóg* 'cephalopod' has none; in the latter, the compounding operation is manifested by a paradigmatic (gender) shift: from [+feminine] (*nog·a* 'leg') to [+masculine].

When analysed from the functional perspective, the Polish noun compounds present themselves as a highly diversified class. First, there are a number of examples of co-ordinate structures like: *klubokawiarnia* 'a café that hosts cultural events' (< *klub* 'club' + *kawiarnia* 'café'), *kursokonferencja* 'training conference' (< *kurs* 'course, training' + *konferencja* 'conference'), *marszobieg* 'run/walk' (< *marsz* 'walk' + *bieg* 'run'), *chłoporobotnik* 'a peasant farmer who works in a factory' (< *chłop* 'peasant' + *robotnik* 'manual worker'), etc. It may be argued that a combination of the type in question is semantically headed by both constituents and hence their order is potentially reversible (cf. *?kawiarnioklub*, *?biegomarsz*; see Kurzowa 1976: 59). A formal variant within this class are juxtapositions like *klub-kawiarnia* 'a café that hosts cultural events' (cf. *klobokawiarnia* above) or *trawler-przetwórnia* 'factory trawler'. As may be seen, there is no intermorph here. Instead, both constituent nouns are hyphenated and they inflect.[7] The type is then formally similar to so-called copulative (dvandva) juxtapositions, evidenced by proper names like *Bośnia-Hercegowina* 'Bosnia-Herzegovina' or *Alzacja-Lotaryngia* 'Alsace-Lorraine'. Here, again, both constituents may inflect (cf. *Bośni-Hercegowiny*, gen., *Bośnią-Hercegowiną*, instr., etc.). Yet, in terms of headedness, the situation seems to be different here: neither constituent functions as the head.

However, the majority of Polish N+N or A+N compounds are hierarchically structured and subordinate, with the right-hand constituent functioning as the head. For example: *światłowstręt* 'photophobia', *gwiazdozbiór* 'constellation', *czarnoziem* 'black earth', *drobnoustrój* 'micro-organism'. All the examples on this list are endocentric, i.e. the compound may be interpreted as a hyponym of its head (thus, for instance, *światłowstręt* 'photophobia' means 'kind of phobia', etc.).[8] Exocentric combinations are also fairly common regardless of whether or not the compound incorporates an overt suffix. For instance, *nosorożec* 'rhinoceros' and *stawonóg* 'arthropod' denote 'kinds of animals' although their second constituents make reference to horns or legs, respectively (cf. *róg* 'horn', *nog-a* 'leg'). Other examples of the exocentric type: *trójkąt* 'triangle' < *trój-* 'three'

---

[7] A mixed pattern, formally speaking, is evidenced by co-ordinate structures like *chłodziarko-zamrażarka* 'cooler-freezer' where the first constituent is followed by the intermorph *-o-* so it does not inflect; yet the hyphen is obligatory here.

[8] Left-headed N + N compounds are truly exceptional (Grzegorczykowa & Puzynina 1999: 461); cf., however, *nartorolki* 'grass skis' when paraphrased as 'skis with (small) rollers/wheels'. In order to be consistent with the right-headed endocentric pattern, the form should rather be: (*) *rolkonarty*.

+ *kąt* 'angle', *równoległobok* 'rhomboid' < *równoległy* 'parallel' + *bok* 'side', *obcokrajowiec* 'foreigner' < *obcy* 'foreign' + *kraj* 'country'. Here the head of the compound is either unexpressed, as in *trój-kąt* '(a flat figure with) three angles' or is vaguely symbolized by the final suffix, as in *obc-o-kraj-owiec* 'a person from a foreign country, foreigner'. According to an alternative interpretation, the latter example might be viewed as endocentric rather than exocentric, assuming that the meaning of 'person' is directly encoded by the suffix *-owiec*. Structures of the kind just illustrated are also right-headed in themselves, since the first two constituents function as a complex, right-headed, modifier with respect to the implied head of the compound.

However, in exocentric compounds with a verbal element, this element mirrors the head of the corresponding verb phrase, regardless of whether it appears in the first or second position in the compound. This is illustrated with the following examples where the verb stem appears in bold face:

(8) V + N

łam-i-strajk 'strike breaker'
lit. 'sb. who breaks a strike'

baw-i-dam-ek 'ladies' man'
lit. 'sb. who amuses/entertains
ladies'

N + V

list-o-**nosz** 'postman'
lit. 'sb. who carries letters'

lin-o-**skocz**-ek 'tightrope walker'
lit. 'sb. who jumps (on) a
tightrope'

According to Nagórko (2016), left-headed structures (V + N), "albeit with some exceptions, are considered dated or humorous, cf. *gol-i-broda* 'barber; lit. shave-beard'[...], *najm-i-morda* 'legal counsel; lit. hire-mug'. Therefore, the Polish language is drifting, undoubtedly because of the foreign influence, towards the right-headed type of compounding."

The examples presented so far give the correct impression that the semantic structure of Polish nominal compounds is quite diversified and, at times, fairly complex and/or ambiguous. However, due to space limitations, it is hardly possible to give a full-fledged semantic classification of the data under discussion (for details, see Kurzowa 1976 or Grzegorczykowa & Puzynina 1999). Suffice it to say that, by and large, the semantic categories that are discernible are reminiscent of those normally established in the context of ordinary (e.g. affixal) derivation of Polish nouns. Thus, one can identify, for instance, formations that are agentive (*listonosz* 'postman', *dobroczyńca* 'benefactor'), instrumental (*gazomierz* 'gas meter'), locative (*jadłodajnia* 'eating place'), resultative (*brudnopis* 'rough draft'), attributive (*lekkoduch* 'good-for-nothing'), that denote activities (*grzybobranie* 'mushroom picking'), states/conditions (*płaskostopie* 'flat foot') or inhabitants

(*Nowozelandczyk* 'New Zealander'), etc. For a detailed interpretation of the semantics of Polish nominal compounds in terms of thematic relations, see Sambor (1976).

The examples of Polish compound nouns given so far are dictionary-attested. Most of them have been in use for quite some time (including quite a few old or obsolete combinations), as they represent the native Polish patterns of compound formation. Characteristically, there are a few lexical elements that have been abundantly exploited in native compounds. Consider the following list of attested nouns, each involving the verbal root *pis-* 'write' as the right-hand constituent: *brudnopis* 'rough draft' (*brudny* 'dirty'), *czystopis* 'fair copy' (*czysty* 'clean'), *dalekopis* 'teleprinter, telex' (*daleki* 'far'), *cienkopis* 'fine felt-tip pen' (*cienki* 'thin, fine'), *długopis* 'ballpoint pen' (*długi* 'long'), *rękopis* 'manuscript' (*ręka* 'hand'), etc.

However, the past few decades have witnessed the extension of the traditional Polish models of compound formation, mainly as a result of foreign influences and massive borrowing, especially from English. Two specific patterns, illustrating such recent developments, are worth noting here. Firstly, these are compounds involving initial combining forms and clipped modifiers. For example:[9]

(9)	eko-	ekoturystyka 'eco-tourism', ekorozwój 'eco-development'
	euro-	euroregion 'Euroregion', euroobligacja 'Eurobond'
	mikro-	mikromodel, 'micromodel', mikroksiążka 'microbook'
	pseudo-	pseudoartysta 'pseudo-artist', pseudouczony 'pseudo-scientist'
	spec-	speckomisja, specustawa 'special, i.e. extraordinary committee/law'
	tele-	telereportaż 'TV report'

Compositions of the type just illustrated do not contain the native linking vowel. However, the use of such combining forms is facilitated when they happen to end with the vowel -*o*, which is identical with the Polish default connective, and hence the type now often gives rise to hybrid combinations (e.g. *mikroksiążka* 'microbook').[10]

Secondly, there are N+N compounds which are due to borrowing from English; cf. *seksbiznes* 'sex business', etc. This has already led to a partial absorption and nativization of the English pattern, as well as to its gradual spread (see next section for more examples of this type).

---

[9]Further examples may be found, for instance, in Jadacka (2001: 94), Waszakowa (2015).

[10] It appears that at least some of the combining forms in question have actually acquired the status of prefixes.

Despite the new trends and foreign influences, the formation of compounds in Polish still preserves much of its original character. The fact is that, generally speaking, compounding in Polish is much less productive than in a language like English. Besides, quite apart from the question of phrasal compounds, there are a number of structural patterns and peculiarities of English compounds that simply do not exist in Polish (or they are highly limited). To sum up this section, one can mention just a few such points of difference:

- No recursiveness (with minor exceptions); moreover – virtually no N+N compounds with more than two constituents; hence:

- No structural ambiguity (cf. E. *California history teacher*)

- No modifier + head reversibility (cf. E. *flower garden* / *garden flower, radio talk* / *talk radio*)

- No identical-constituent compounds (cf. E. (*my*) *friend friend*)

- No plural modifiers in compounds (cf. E. *parks department* vs. the P. phrase *wydział*$_{NOM}$ *parków*$_{GEN\ PL}$), including phrasal modifiers with co-ordination (cf. E. [[*wines and spirits*] *department*] vs. the P. phrase *dział*$_{NOM}$ *win*$_{GEN\ PL}$ *i spirytualiów*$_{GEN\ PL}$).

3 Why are phrasal compounds virtually unavailable in Polish?

As far as Polish is concerned, it is hard to give any definitive reasons accounting for the lack of phrasal compounds of the type found in English. It is more obvious though why the process of Noun+Noun compounding is less vigorous and productive in Polish than in English. However, since the phrasal compounds investigated in the Germanic (and other) languages are nouns and have nominal heads, a closer examination of the peculiarities and structural restrictions governing the use of N+N composition in Polish may explain, albeit indirectly, the unavailability of the special XP+N pattern.[11]

The main reason why the class of N+N compounds in Polish (and Slavic in general) is not so numerous as in English is the fact that Polish grammar offers, and often imposes, alternative structural options for the combined expression of two nominal concepts. Where English frequently has a N+N compound, Polish may have (i) a noun phrase with an inflected noun modifier (usually in the genitive),

---

[11]On the affinity between N+N compounds and PCs, see Pafel (2015).

(ii) a noun phrase incorporating a prepositional phrase modifier, or (iii) a noun phrase involving a denominal (relational) adjective as a modifier, as is illustrated below:

(10)   a.   *telephone number*
             i. numer telefon·u
             ii. *numer do telefon·u
             iii. *numer telefon-icz-n·y

       b.   *computer paper*
             i. *papier komputer·a
             ii. papier do komputer·a
             iii. papier komputer-ow·y

       c.   *toothpaste*
             i. *past·a zęb·ów
             ii. past·a do zęb·ów
             iii. *past·a zęb-ow·a

Evidently, alternative structures are often available, cf. *papier do komputera* vs. *papier komputerowy* 'computer paper'. The kind of construction may depend on a variety of factors which need not concern us here. What is important is the fact that the Polish expressions just cited are syntactic objects, and that they may involve both inflection and derivation, but not compounding.[12] That is to say, there are no compounds like *komputeropapier* or *telefononumer*, to parallel the English counterparts. On top of this, there may be a suffixal derivative based on the modifier; see Ohnheiser (2015) for further details and generalizations concerning these options in various Slavic languages; see also ten Hacken (2013).

Consider additionally the following example where most of the structural options are actually attested, including a regular compound:

(11)   *steamship* (Polish *para* 'steam' + *statek* 'ship')
             i. *statek par·y (Genitive phrase)
             ii. statek na par·ę (N + PP)
             iii. statek par-ow·y (N + Relational Adjective)

---

[12]According to some Polish authors (see e.g. Jadacka 2005: 120), fixed nominal phrases like *pasta do zębów* 'toothpaste', *drukarka laserowa* 'laser printer', etc. ought to be viewed as a special type of a generally conceived category of compounding: the so-called 'juxtapositions' (P. *zestawienia*).

Bogdan Szymanek

iv. parowiec (suffixal derivative; cf. E. *steamer*)

v. parostatek (N-*o*-N compound; E. *steamship*)

The patterns illustrated above may partly explain why the number of dictionary-attested nominal compounds in Polish is significantly lower than in English. Quite simply, certain functions that are served by compounding in other languages tend to be realized by syntactic, inflectional and/or derivational means in Polish. Analogical patterns, though in different proportions, are exploited by other Slavic languages as well.

Another factor that seems to thwart the generation of phrasal compounds in Polish is purely formal and quite general: as a rule, Polish nominal compounds may involve only two lexical constituents. Thus, by virtue of this (fairly superficial) restriction alone, composites even remotely comparable to English PCs are ruled out, since the number of lexical elements in the modifier position of an English phrasal compound is usually three or higher, not to mention the head itself. This constraint ties up, of course, with another remarkable characteristics of Polish nominal compounding: there is no recursion.[13] By contrast, it is a well known feature of the English pattern of Noun+Noun compounding that it is recursive. In connection with the particular contrast noted here, one can speculate that, perhaps, there is some linkage here between (the possibility of) recursion and phrasal compounding, in a given language – in the sense that recursion might be a precondition for phrasal compounding.

Yet another remarkable factor is the fact that Polish does not offer any instances of literal borrowings of phrasal compounds, from languages like English or German, i.e. compositions which preserve the original lexical make up as well as the structural configuration of a PC in the source language. This seems to suggest that the characteristic structure of a PC is completely alien, from the viewpoint of Polish grammar and, accordingly, any foreign instances of PCs that need to be nativized or translated into Polish must be remodelled and encoded as prototypical phrasal constructions. This point may be illustrated with the following German examples adapted from Meibauer (2007: 250) and juxtaposed with corresponding expressions in Polish:[14]

---

[13]There are sporadic counterexamples suggesting that both constraints mentioned here, i.e. 'no recursion' and 'only two constituents', are (rarely) violated, as in the following example often quoted in grammar books: *Zwierzoczłekoupiór* [zwierz-o-człek-o-upiór] 'animal-man-ghost' (title of a novel by the Polish writer Tadeusz Konwicki). In contrast to Noun+Noun compounds, limited recursiveness (iteration) is allowed in the case of certain types of compound adjectives in Polish; cf. (*słownik*) *polsko-angielsko-niemiecko*(-...) -*rosyjski* 'a Polish-English-German(-...)-Russian (dictionary)'.

[14]The English glosses attached to the original German examples are not repeated after the Polish near-equivalents since they apply, by and large. However, the present-tense (1st person) form of the verb 'to buy', i.e. G. *kaufe* has been replaced by the future perfective form *kupię* in the

62

(12)   German (Meibauer 2007: 250)

  a. Autokärtchen
     car card.DIM
     P. autokarteczka

  b. Kaufkärtchen
     buy$_{V/N}$ card.DIM
     P. *kupkarteczka

  c. Kaufe-Ihr-Auto-Kärtchen buy.1.PS.SG.-your-car card.DIM
     P. *kupię-Twoje-auto-karteczka

  d. Kärtchen „Kaufe Ihr Auto"
     card.DIM buy.1.PS.SG. your car"
     P. karteczka „kupię Twoje auto"

  e. Kärtchen mit den Aufschrift „Kaufe Ihr Auto"
     card.DIM with the writing buy.1.PS.SG. your car"
     P. karteczka z napisem „kupię Twoje auto"

  f. Kärtchen, auf denen „Kaufe Ihr Auto" steht
     card.DIM on which „buy.1.PS.SG. your car" is written
     P. karteczka, na której jest napisane „kupię Twoje auto"

Meibauer (2007: 250) presents the German examples in this list as alternative modes of expression or "stylistic alternatives, some morphological, some syntactic"; cf., respectively, (12a–c) i.e. "complex words", as opposed to (12d–f), i.e. "syntactic constructions". The main focus is on case (12c), i.e. "an ad hoc phrasal compound with a CP as non-head" (Meibauer 2007: 249). Now, from the viewpoint of Polish morphology, this case (12c) is also significant, since it clearly demonstrates that a word-by-word rendering of the German PC is ruled out (as a matter of principle); cf. *kupię-Twoje-auto-karteczka*. The compound structure evidenced in (12b), i.e. a composition involving a verbal/nominal root followed by a (diminutive) noun is also rather unlikely in Polish, at least in this particular context and lexical configuration. As may be seen, what is freely available, both in German and in Polish, are various syntactic (periphrastic) modes of expression (cf. 12d–f). However, as far as Polish is concerned, the syntactic options actually emerge as the only viable choice, given the fact that – according to Meibauer (2007: 250) – a compound like G. *Autokärtchen* (cf. P. *autokarteczka*) is "underdetermined", in comparison to *Kaufe-Ihr-Auto-Kärtchen*. "The phrasal

---

Polish version as it seems more plausible in the given context. Besides, the diminutive G. form *Kärtchen* appears as P. *karteczka*, i.e. (formally) a double diminutive.

compound [*Kaufe-Ihr-Auto-Kärtchen*] is as explicit as the syntactic construction [*Kärtchen „Kaufe Ihr Auto"*], the main difference being that [the former] has a right-hand morphological head, whereas [the latter] shows a left-hand syntactic head." (Meibauer 2007: 250). Indeed, when we compare various German or English PCs and their renderings in Polish, the superficially visible difference is the reversal of the linear order of the major constituents; cf. for instance E. *a "work or starve" philosophy* vs. P. *filozofia "pracuj lub głoduj"*. It must be emphasized, though, that – underlyingly – these locutions differ in grammatical status: the English expressions are compounds, i.e. lexical objects, while the Polish ones are syntactic constructions.

As has been pointed out, literal borrowings of English or German PCs are hardly available in Polish. By contrast, the English type of ordinary Noun+Noun compounding (with a non-phrasal modifier) has been partially assimilated in present-day Polish, even though this type is not consistent with the default structure of a Polish nominal composition, where the linking vowel *-o-* should appear between two lexical constituents.[15] Consider a few examples of recent neologisms and loan adaptations:[16]

(13) biznesplan 'business project/plan'
      seksbiznes 'sex business'
      seksturystyka 'sex tourism'
      dres kod 'dress code'
      pomoc linia 'help line'
      Duda pomoc 'free-of-charge legal counselling offered, to ordinary people, by the presidential candidate Andrzej Duda and his staff' (lit. *Duda* <surname> + *pomoc* 'help')

These examples clearly suggest that the English pattern of N+N compounding is gaining ground in Polish. According to Jadacka (2001: 93), Polish neologistic compounds without an interfix (i.e. a linking element) have become increasingly common in the past few decades, even though a number of relevant examples

---

[15]However, as has been mentioned (cf. §2), a precedent already exists, in Polish morphology, for interfixless N+N compounds: there is the weak and now rather obsolete pattern of endocentric compositions, typically with the noun *mistrz* 'master' in head position, like in the following examples: *baletmistrz* 'ballet master', *kapelmistrz* 'bandmaster' (cf. G. *Kapellmeister*), *chórmistrz* 'choirmaster', *zegarmistrz* 'clock maker, watch maker', etc. However, this pattern is formally inconsistent: some other attested compounds with *-mistrz* do show up the regular interfix *-o-*; e.g. *ogniomistrz* 'artillery sergeant' (*ogień* 'fire'), *organomistrz* / *organmistrz* 'organ master' (cf. Kurzowa 1976 [2007]: 458).

[16]Such forms are more common in Russian; cf. Ohnheiser (2015).

are not yet dictionary-attested (cf. *Duda pomoc*, dated 2015). Also, the occasional presence of native nouns in such combinations (cf. *pomoc linia*) seems to suggest that this is now, indeed, a case of pattern borrowing.

Significantly, the spread of the foreign interfixless Noun+Noun pattern of compounding in Polish has not gone as far as in some other Slavic languages, for instance in Russian and Bulgarian. According to Bagasheva (2015), Bulgarian [N N] constructions "instantiate the grammaticalization of a new compound type in the language". The Bulgarian pattern in question extends to cover also cases where the prehead constituent of a compound is an initialism (just like in English); cf. *ФБР агент* 'FBI agent', *ДНК фактор* 'DNA factor'. In Polish, by contrast, such loan compounds are ruled out: the order of both constituents must be reversed so that the construction emerges as a phrase (here with an implicit (unmarked) genitive case on the modifying initialism); cf. P. **FBI agent* vs *agent FBI*, **DNA czynnik* vs. *czynnik DNA* 'DNA factor'. More importantly though, only in Bulgarian can we find examples of phrasal compounds modelled on the structure of English PCs (see §5 for examples).

To sum up, as we have seen, phrasal compounds of the type found in English or German are impossible in Polish, no matter whether they are actual borrowings or forced word-by-word translations, and this is regardless of whether a particular PC in the source language incorporates a phrasal or sentential prehead constituent, or just an initialism.[17] Incidentally, the behaviour of initialisms (and acronyms) in such constructions seems to offer a useful diagnostic here since – on the one hand – they are "lexical" because of their nounlike properties but – on the other hand – they are "phrasal" since they stand for fully fledged phrases (e.g. *the FBI* = *Federal Bureau of Investigation*, etc.). By using both phrasal compounds and initialisms/acronyms one can achieve greater text condensation. In English, we can actually use a construction involving two abbreviations, in the modifier and head positions; cf. *the SNP MPs* 'the Scottish National Party Members of Parliament'.[18] Again, no structure of this sort is possible in Polish.

Finally, it may be of interest to note that – even though phrasal prehead constituents are impossible in Polish compounds – the occurrence of phrasal bases in affixal derivation is completely unproblematic. In fact, according to the literature on Polish morphology, there are several distinct patterns of de-phrasal derivatives (see next section).

---

[17]It does not matter as well whether a given PC is quotative or non-quotative in character; cf. Pafel (2015) on the contrast between quotative and non-quotative PCs in German and English.
[18]Source of the example (spoken language): BBC Radio 4, *Friday Night Comedy*, May 15th, 2015.

4 Generalizing the concept of "phrasal compound": some relevant types of multi-word expressions in Polish

As has been pointed out, phrasal compounds of the kind found in English do not seem to exist in Polish. In particular, clausal and sentential modifiers appear to be completely ruled out in Polish compound nouns. But even phrases such as NP are rather unlikely in the prehead position. I have not been able to identify any convincing examples of the latter type of structure. Consider, however, the following recent example from the Internet,[19] which, characteristically, involves a multiword complex modifier with hyphenated constituents:

(14)   *elektryk-eks-prezydent-noblista pokojowy Lech Wałęsa*
       'electrician-ex-president-Nobel-peace(-prize laureate) Lech Wałęsa'

Superficially, i.e. orthographically, this expression may look deceptively similar to the category of phrasal compounds that we are interested in; cf. the multiple use of hyphens, conjoining the lexical items in the prehead position (which is a characteristic feature of many English phrasal compounds). However, the multiple use of hyphens certainly looks marked, odd, and eye-catching, from the viewpoint of the Polish orthographic convention. Besides, multiple hyphens are neither necessary nor sufficient as a formal diagnostic for identifying PCs, even in English (cf., for instance, Trips 2012: 323). Probably, the motivation for the multiple use of hyphens, in the above example, was to achieve greater expressiveness.[20] But, more importantly, it is doubtful if the expression under discussion is a phrasal compound by strictly grammatical criteria. It is not a determinative compound because the first element does not determine the second element semantically (cf. Trips & Kornfilt 2015b: 7: "PCs are always determinative compounds", according to Meibauer 2003). It is not a compound, to begin with. It rather appears that this is an instance of a non-restrictive appositional construction, using unconventional orthography (which makes a difference only in written language anyway); cf. the more usual spelling, with commas instead of hyphens:

---

[19]Piotr Cywiński, Szczucie na Komorowskiego i wściekła sfora Dudy, czyli jak *Gazeta Wyborcza* plewi chamstwo i pogardę w „szczujniach", www.wPolityce.pl , 4.03.2015. The phrase in question appeared in the following context: *Bo z pewnością znajdą się złośliwcy, którzy spytają, a gdzie był rzecznik bon-tonu, savoir vivre'u, niestrudzony bojownik dobrych manier, gdy np. elektryk-eks-prezydent-noblista pokojowy Lech Wałęsa mówił o urzędującej wówczas głowie państwa Polskiego: „mamy durnia za prezydenta"?*
[20]On the expressive nature of phrasal compounds, see e.g. Meibauer (2013), Trips (2014).

(15) *elektryk, eks(-)prezydent, noblista pokojowy Lech Wałęsa* 'id.'

If the notion of phrasal compounding is relaxed somewhat, so that the whole compound may correspond to a phrase, and not just its pre-head constituent, then certain examples in Polish may appear relevant. Consider, first, the structure of the noun *niezapominajka* 'forget-me-not':

(16) *niezapominajka* 'forget-me-not'
      nie zapominaj   -k   -a
      not forget.IMP.IPFV suff. suff.INFL

However, forms like *niezapominajka* are lexicalized and extremely rare in Polish.

It should be noted as well that the English noun *forget-me-not* is explicitly assigned to the category of English 'phrase compounds' by Bauer (1983: 206-207). To be more precise, the noun in question is given as an example of "exocentric phrase compounds", together with other plant names such as *love-in-a-mist*, and *love-lies-bleeding*. According to Bauer, apart from exocentric phrase compounds, there are also dvandva phrase compounds (e.g. *whisky-and-soda*) and, finally, endocentric phrase compounds, including right-headed structures with a phrase or sentence in the pre-head position (also left-headed structures like *son-in-law*). Evidently, the group of endocentric right-headed expressions (=phrasal compounds proper) is treated by Bauer as a subclass within his broad category of 'phrase compounds'.

If we apply this broad interpretation (in terms of 'phrase compounds') to the Polish data, then it may be argued that there are, perhaps, some other relevant patterns and examples, apart from the aforementioned noun *niezapominajka*. For instance, there is the unproductive pattern of so-called 'solid compounds' (P. *zrosty*), which are directly motivated by a syntactic phrase so that they appear without an interfix. Instead, the first constituent ends with the inflectional ending required by the structure of the original phrase (see Nagórko 1998: 195, 2016; Szymanek 2009: 471).

(17) 'Solid compounds' (P. *zrosty*) motivated by syntactic phrases (no interfix)

Phrase	>	*Compound*

ok·a   mgnieni·e
eye.GEN blink
(also: mgnienie oka – phrase)   okamgnieni·e
                                     'a blink of an eye'

czc·i   godn·y (Adj)
esteem.GEN worthy
(also: godny czci – phrase)   czcigodn·y
                                     'esteemed, honourable'

There is also a more numerous group of compound nouns made up of an adverb followed by a verbal root:

(18) 'Phrase compounds' of the type [[Adverb + Verb]$_{VP}$ (suff)]$_N$

Adverb	Verb	>	Compound N
cienko	pisać		cienkopis ø 'fine felt-tip pen'
'thinly'	'write'		
cicho	dawać (w ~ j)		cichodajka 'woman on the game, hooker'
'quietly'	'give'		(suff. -k)

The nouns given above may be regarded as 'phrase compounds' because they mirror a well-formed syntactic constituent, i.e. a type of VP (minus the thematic and inflectional characteristics on the verb). Importantly, the second element is not an attested deverbal noun (cf. *pis, *dajka), unlike in some other, similar forms (e.g. *dalekowidz* 'long-sighted person', *jasnowidz* 'clairvoyant', etc.).

To take another example, there is a class of (mostly expressive, often obsolete) exocentric compounds, whose internal structure reflects that of a VP they appear to be based on, where the VP is of the type [Verb+Noun]:[21]

---

[21] The verb governs the accusative case on the object noun; hence the ending *-ę* in the phrasal input, as opposed to the nominative (*-a*) in the compound. For more examples and discussion concerning this pattern, see Kurzowa (1976 [2007]: 440).

(19) 'Phrase compounds' of the type [[Verb + Noun]$_{VP}$]$_N$

Verb	Noun	>	Compound N
czyścić	but·y		czyścibut 'shoeshine (boy)'
'clean'	'shoe.ACC-PL'		
moczyć	mord·ę		moczymord·a 'heavy drinker'
'soak'	'mug, kisser.ACC'		
męczyć	dusz·ę		męczydusz·a 'bore, nudnik'
'torment'	'soul.ACC'		

However, it would be a risky move if we attempted to generalize, or extend any further, the notion of 'phrase compounds'. Because then we might soon find ourselves in a point of no return, i.e. where, for instance, synthetic compounds would be treated as being fundamentally phrasal in nature, just because they correspond to a licit phrase type in syntax (V NP); cf. P. *kredytobiorca* 'borrower, lit. credit-taker', *kredytodawca* 'lender, lit. credit-giver', etc. In other words, the generalization of the concept in question must have its limits.

It is a remarkable feature of the word-formation system in Polish (and other Slavic languages) that there are several other types of "multi-word expressions" which are based on (or which involve) phrasal constituents (see e.g. Martincová 2015; Ohnheiser 2015). Traditionally, the following phenomena have been interpreted, among others, as giving rise to de-phrasal lexical units:[22]

Derived nouns and adjectives based on phrases

Consider, respectively, the examples in (20) and (21):

(20) *Prepositional Phrase (P + Noun$_{Infl}$) > De-phrasal Noun*

bez 'without'	robot·y 'work.GEN'	bezroboci·e 'unemployment'
do 'to'	rzek·i 'river.GEN'	dorzecz·e 'river basin'
na 'on'	brzeg·u 'rim, bank.LOC'	nabrzeż·e 'embankment'
pod 'under'	dach·em 'roof.INSTR'	poddasz·e 'attic'
przed 'before'	wiosn·ą 'spring.INSTR'	przedwiośni·e 'early spring'

The derivatives on the above list share a characteristic grammatical property: they are all neuter gender nouns whose stem ends in a (functionally) palatalized consonant and hence they take the inflectional suffix ·*e* in the NOM.SG (the input

---

[22]See e.g. Szymanek (2010: 237) for more examples and discussion of derivations based on phrases in Polish.

noun may be MASC. (e.g. *bok* 'side') or FEM. (e.g. *rzek·a* 'river')). This characteristic pattern of inflection (together with the phonological effect on the stem-final consonant) may be looked upon as a co-formative which, apart from the preposition, spells out the derivational process in question. Accordingly, the de-phrasal nouns on the list are one instance of so-called paradigmatic derivation in Polish. However, for quite a few masculine nouns derived from prepositional phrases we do not observe any change in paradigm; for instance, *podtekst* 'implied meaning, subtext' and *tekst* 'text' are uniformly masculine (cf. **podtekście*, noun, neuter) and are declined according to the same paradigmatic pattern. Less commonly, the feminine paradigm is preserved; e.g. *troska* 'worry, care' – *beztroska* 'carefreeness'. In still other formations, the preposition co-occurs with an overt nominalizing suffix (most frequently *-ek/-k·a* or *-nik*): e.g. *podnóżek* 'footrest, footstool' vs. *noga* 'foot', *narożnik* 'corner (of a building, room, etc.)' vs. *róg* 'corner'.

The status of the nouns analysed here is complicated by the fact that the majority of native Polish prepositions have homophonous counterparts in various prefixes (the identity is not coincidental – it reflects a historical development: preposition > prefix). Therefore, some earlier studies of the data at hand stressed the prefixal character of the initial element, while others argued that the type is a specific instance of Preposition + Noun compounding. In more recent accounts (see Symoni-Sułkowska 1987: 10), a compromise solution is opted for: nouns like *podziemie* are viewed as a borderline phenomenon, between compounding and lexical derivation. Still, it is stressed that they are based on prepositional phrases; the prepositions (a syntactic category) that surface in the complex nouns acquire the secondary function of prefixes (a morphological category).

(21)   Prepositional Phrase (P + Noun$_{Infl}$) > De-phrasal Adjective

bez 'without'	robot·y 'work.GEN'	bezrobotn·y 'jobless'
między 'between'	wojn·ami 'war.INSTR.PL'	międzywojenn·y 'interwar'
pod 'under'	ziemi·ą 'earth, ground.INSTR'	podziemn·y 'underground'
przez 'through'	skór·ę 'skin.ACC'	przezskórn·y 'transdermal'

Here, again, the status of such "de-phrasal" formations is controversial. In fact, the exact mode of their derivation has received alternative accounts. The traditional view has it that the adjective *podziemny* 'underground' in, say, *podziemny wybuch* 'underground explosion' is derived from the prepositional phrase (P+N) *pod ziemią* 'under the ground' (minus inflection of the noun). Thus, the structure of the adjectival stem may be represented as follows: $[[[pod]_P [ziem-]_N]_{PP} -n-]_A$. This interpretation makes sense from the semantic viewpoint: the derived adjective and the corresponding phrase are functionally equivalent. One problem with this sort of analysis is that numerous Polish prepositions are, by and large, phonetically indistinguishable from common native prefixes. This may encourage an alternative analysis of *podziemny*: as a combination of a prefix (*pod-*) and the denominal adjective *ziemny* 'of earth, ground'. This analysis seems viable here since the adjective *ziemny* happens to exist as an independent word. In fact, in the majority of comparable structures a denominal adjective may be extracted. However, there are also cases like *pośmiertny* 'posthumous' where only the derivation from the prepositional phrase *po śmierci* 'after death' is likely, in view of the fact that the denominal adjective **śmiertny* (< *śmierć* 'death') does not exist (see Kallas 1999: 499). The third option, especially in cases like *pośmiertny*, would be to argue that the adjective is a product of parasynthetic derivation, with a simultaneous attachment of the prefix (*po-*) and the suffix (*-n·y*).[23] Details aside, the dominant view today is that we are dealing here with derivation from prepositional phrases. This view is said to be supported by the syntactic and semantic equivalence of the phrasal input and the derivational output (for details, see Kallas 1999: 500), i.e. by way of a purely formal, transpositional operation we get a lexical item corresponding to a syntactic phrase (Grzegorczykowa 1979: 71). According to some accounts (e.g. Wójcikowska 1991), derivation of adjectives from prepositional phrases is an instance of so-called 'univerbation' in Polish morphology (see below).

Univerbation

(22) Noun Phrase (N + Adj) > Derived Noun (id.)

kuchenka mikrofalowa	'microwave oven'	mikrofalówk·a	'id.'
szkoła zawodowa	'vocational school'	zawodówk·a	
sklep warzywny	'greengrocer's shop'	warzywniak	
statek kontenerowy	'container ship'	kontenerowiec	

From the semantic viewpoint, the derivatives listed in (22) above are based on the corresponding NPs, which have the status of set phrases (collocations). In a way, the head noun of the phrase is replaced by a nominal suffix, like *-k·a*,

---

[23]Parasynthetic derivation seems a viable solution also in certain cases where a prefixless adjective is actually attested; e.g. *mięsień* 'muscle' > *domięśniowy* 'intramuscular', *skóra* 'skin' > *przezskórny* 'transdermal', *ziemia* 'Earth' > *pozaziemski* 'extraterrestrial'.

-ak, owiec, (see Grzegorczykowa & Puzynina 1999: 419). Hence the process in question is described as univerbation or morphological condensation of a multi-word (phrasal) term (see Laskowski 1981: 113ff).

A somewhat different type of univerbation is evidenced by the following pairs:

(23) Noun Phrase (N + Adj) > Derived Noun (id.)

kuchenka mikrofalowa	'microwave oven'	mikrofal·a 'id.'
piłka nożna	'football'	nog·a
obraz olejny	'an oil painting'	olej
wódka żytnia	'rye vodka'	żyt·o
telefon komórkowy	'cellphone'	komórk·a
karta graficzna	'video card'	grafik·a

Again, on functional grounds, the derivative seems to be based on a NP, i.e. a noun modified by an attributive denominal adjective. However, in contradistinction to the previous group of examples, no nominal suffix appears in the derived noun, but rather the bare stem of the adjective; compare *kuchenka mikrofalowa* 'microwave oven' > *mikrofal·a* 'id.' vs. *mikrofalówk·a* 'id.'. Since most adjectives in the input phrases are denominal themselves, the product of the process is normally identical with the base-noun of the adjective (thus $olej_N$ 'oil' > $olej$-n-y_A 'of oil' / *obraz olejny* 'oil painting' > $olej_N$ 'id.'). However, other examples demonstrate that the situation may be more complicated (see Chludzińska-Świątecka 1979, Jadacka 2001: 137); cf., for instance, the following derivations involving non-native adjectives: *ogród zoologiczny* 'zoological garden' > *zoolog* 'id.' or *forma supletywna* 'suppletive form' > *supletyw* 'id.'. These colloquial creations demonstrate that, in formal terms, the mechanism that stands behind the derivatives under discussion is a sort of back-formation or desuffixation (neither *zoolog* nor *supletyw* exist as basic nouns).

Incidentally, it is worth pointing out that, in the Polish literature, there is a suitable and widely used term to denote coinages of the kind just illustrated, which incorporate a phrasal constituent as their base: *derywaty of wyrażeń syntaktycznych,* i.e. 'derivatives from syntactic expressions' or *derywaty odfrazowe* '(de)phrasal derivatives'.[24] However – as far as I know – there is no similar Polish term to denote the concept of "phrasal compounds" – *złożenia frazowe* sounds acceptable only as a literal rendering of the English, well-established term. The fact that, in the Polish linguistic terminology, there is just no name for the phenomenon of phrasal compounding, seems to suggest that the concept is not con-

---

[24]The latter term was used, for instance (many years ago), by Kreja (1971).

sidered worth naming, i.e. that phrasal compounds either do not exist or have not been identified as yet in the Polish morphological system.

5 How about phrasal compounds in other Slavic languages?

Antonietta Bisetto begins her contribution to the special issue of STUF on phrasal compounds with the following generalization: "Romance languages seem to lack phrasal compounds of the kind present in some Germanic languages" (Bisetto 2015: 395). I have conducted some preliminary research on this issue[25], as regards the situation in the Slavic languages, and – as far as I can see now – I think I can repeat Bisetto's generalization, with minor reservations (see below): Slavic languages – by and large –seem to lack phrasal compounds of the kind present in some Germanic languages.

My limited expertise and circumstantial evidence allows me merely to posit the above generalization as a working hypothesis. Further cross-linguistic research on this issue is necessary in order to verify this hypothesis so that it can be presented as a strong claim. A good example of the sort of research that is needed is the recent study by Körtvélyessy (2016), where the types and features of compounding (as well as affixation) in 14 Slavic languages are identified and compared. Crucially, "phrasal compounds" are not listed there among the major types of compounds in Slavic. This omission seems to imply that, to say the least, the category in question is not relevant for the Slavic languages at large (i.e. it may be inferred that either phrasal compounds do not exist in Slavic languages or they are truly marginal).

Indeed, one positive exception to this generalization may be Bulgarian. According to Boyadzhieva (2007), a recent phenomenon in Bulgarian "newspaper language" is the occasional use of structural equivalents of English phrasal compounds.[26] They have originated as literal translations of the corresponding English constructions, but then "they have gradually become quite frequent". The analysis is based on a small sample of 23 structurally varied expressions, most of which have been gleaned from the Bulgarian edition of the *Cosmopolitan* magazine. It appears that at least some of the examples on the list closely imitate the

---

[25] My thanks go to Pavol Štekauer for comments on Slovak and Czech as well as for soliciting relevant remarks from several other Slavic experts.

[26] Instead of the term 'phrasal compounding', Boyadzhieva uses the designation 'syntactic compounding'.

structure of phrasal compounds in English (unfortunately, English glosses are not provided).

However, Boyadzhieva (2007) points out as well that the "syntactic compounds" "are felt strange and untypical for the Bulgarian language". The recent occurrence of such structures is explained as a consequence of the fact that Modern Bulgarian shows a strong tendency towards analyticity, in comparison to other Slavic languages; however, Bulgarian is said to be less analytic than English.

Phrasal nominal compounds in Modern Bulgarian are also briefly discussed and illustrated in a paper by Bagasheva (2015). The type in question, which is said to constitute a new development in the language, is considered against the broader background of innovative "[N N] constructions", i.e. interfixless compounds like *bingo zala* 'bingo hall', *biznes obyad* 'business lunch', etc. The short list of "phrasal compounds" given by Bagasheva includes the following items:

(24) Phrasal compounds in Bulgarian (Bagasheva 2015)
    вземи-му-акъла-съвет [vzemi mu akâla sâvet]
    'take his mind away advice'
    море-слънце-пясък туризъм [more-sluntse-pjasuk turizum]
    'sea-sun-sand tourism'
    семейство и приятели номера [semejstvo i prijateli nomera]
    'family and friends tricks'
    завърти-му-ума-посрещане [zavârti mu uma posrešane]
    'take his mind away welcoming'
    промени-живота-си-предизвикателство [promeni života si predizvikatelstvo]
    'change your life challenge'

Except for the Bulgarian data, I have not found any examples, from other Slavic languages, that mirror the structure of phrasal compounds of the type found in English (or German). My informants mentioned only that rather different patterns of "syntactic" compounding may be involved, for instance, in certain surnames. For example:

(25) Czech
    Skočdopole lit. 'jump into field!'
    skoč   do pole
    jump.IMP to field
    Nejezchleb lit. 'don't eat bread!'

ne jez   chleb
not eat.IMP bread
Ukrainian
Nepiyvoda lit. 'don't drink water!'
ne pij   voda
not drink.IMP water
Polish
Nieznaj lit. 'don't (you) know!'
nie znaj
not know.IMP
Niechwiej lit. 'don't shake!'
nie chwiej
not shake.IMP

As can be seen, certain verb phrases in the imperative have been lexicalized to become proper nouns (surnames).

6 Conclusion

To sum up, when we compare the patterns and principles of compounding in Polish and English, it is easy to notice that there are quite a few structural options that are attested in English only (and vice versa). In this context, it should come as no surprise that phrasal compounding seems to be just another feature of this sort, i.e. it is not to be found in Polish, just like in many other languages.

But let us repeat the vital question: Why aren't there any compound nouns in Polish of the type that is found in English?

Here are some possible reasons that may conspire to produce the effect in question:

1. Compounding, as a general type of process in word-formation, is much less productive in Polish than in English.

2. Instead of the characteristic English N+N type of compounds, there are alternative and productive means in Polish grammar (particularly 'multi-word units') often used for the expression of a combination of two (or more) nominal concepts.

3. In contrast to English, the formation of compound nouns in Polish is not characterized by recursion or iteration. Moreover, there are virtually no

compound nouns with more than two constituents (regardless of the category of the first element). By this limitation alone, it is hardly possible to have a complex, multi-word modifier, in the form of a phrase.

4. While English phrasal compounds are determinative and right-headed, in Polish, some compounds are actually left-headed, with a considerable proportion of exocentric structures.

5. Perhaps the unavailability of phrasal compounding in Polish is also due to typological differences between English and Polish, i.e. the fact that Polish morphology is predominantly synthetic while English morphology is (more) analytic. It needs to be determined, on the basis of data from other languages, if a correlation of this sort exists and if it is significant; in other words, does the degree of synthesis in morphology correlate with the presence/absence of phrasal compounds, in various languages? Also, what is the role of language contact and borrowing in the spread of phrasal compounding?

References

Bagasheva, Alexandra. 2015. *On [N N] constructions in Bulgarian.* Paper presented at the Word-Formation Theories II / Typology and Universals in Word-Formation III Conference, Košice, 26th June – 28th June, 2015.

Bauer, Laurie. 1983. *English Word-Formation.* Cambridge: Cambridge University Press.

Bisetto, Antonietta. 2015. Do Romance languages have phrasal compounds? A look at Italian. *STUF–Language Typology and Universals* 68. 395–419.

Boyadzhieva, Ellie. 2007. Reflections on a new word-formation pattern in Bulgarian newspaper language. In Alexandra Bagasheva (ed.), *On Man and language. Papers in honor of Prof. Maya Pencheva on the occasion of her 60th anniversary,* 232–244. Sofia: University Publishing House "St. Kliment Ohridski".

Chludzińska-Świątecka, Jadwiga. 1979. *Rzeczowniki postadiektywne. Studium słowotwórczo-leksykalne.* Warsaw: Wydawnictwa Uniwersytetu Warszawskiego.

Grzegorczykowa, Renata. 1979. *Zarys słowotwórstwa polskiego. Słowotwórstwo opisowe.* Warsaw: Państwowe Wydawnictwo Naukowe.

Grzegorczykowa, Renata & Jadwiga Puzynina. 1999. Rzeczownik. In Renata Grzegorczykowa, Roman Laskowski & Henryk Wróbel (eds.), *Gramatyka współczesnego języka polskiego. Morfologia*, 389–468. Warsaw: Wydawnictwo Naukowe
PWN.

Jadacka, Hanna. 2001. *System słowotwórczy polszczyzny. 1945–2000*. Warsaw:
Wydawnictwo Naukowe PWN.

Jadacka, Hanna. 2005. *Kultura języka polskiego. Fleksja, słowotwórstwo, składnia*.
Warsaw: Wydawnictwo Naukowe PWN.

Kallas, Krystyna. 1999. Przymiotnik. In Renata Grzegorczykowa, Roman
Laskowski & Henryk Wróbel (eds.), *Gramatyka współczesnego języka polskiego*.
Morfologia, 469–523. Warsaw: Wydawnictwo Naukowe PWN.

Körtvélyessy, Lívia. 2016. Word-Formation in Slavic languages. *Poznań Studies in
Contemporary Linguistics* 52(3). 455–502.

Kreja, Bogusław. 1971. O specyficznych konstrukcjach typu *złoty* medalista. *Język
Polski* 51. 248–255.

Kurzowa, Zofia. 1976. *Złożenia imienne we współczesnym języku polskim*. Warsaw: Państwowe Wydawnictwo Naukowe. Reprinted in: Z. Kurzowa. 2007. *Z
przeszłości i teraźniejszości języka*. Kraków: Universitas, 429-527.

Laskowski, Roman. 1981. Derywacja słowotwórcza. In Jerzy Bartmiński (ed.),
Pojęcie derywacji w lingwistyce, 107–126. Lublin: Uniwersytet Marii Curie-
Skłodowskiej.

Martincová, Olga. 2015. Multi-word expressions and univerbation in Slavonic. In
Peter O. Müller, Ingeborg Ohnheiser, Susan Olsen & Franz Rainer (eds.), *Word-
Formation. An international handbook of the languages of Europe* (Handbücher
zur Sprach- und Kommunikationswissenschaft / Handbooks of Linguistics and
Communication Science 40.1), 742–757. Berlin: De Gruyter Mouton.

Meibauer, Jörg. 2003. Phrasenkomposita zwischen Wortsyntax und Lexikon.
Zeitschrift für Sprachwissenschaft 22. 153–188.

Meibauer, Jörg. 2007. How marginal are phrasal compounds? Generalized insertion, expressivity, and I/Q-interaction. *Morphology* 17. 233–259.

Meibauer, Jörg. 2013. Expressive compounds in German. *Word Structure* 6(1). 21–
42.

Nagórko, Alicja. 1998. *Zarys gramatyki polskiej (ze słowotwórstwem)*. Warsaw:
Wydawnictwo Naukowe PWN.

Nagórko, Alicja. 2016. Polish. In Peter O. Müller, Ingeborg Ohnheiser, Susan
Olsen & Franz Rainer (eds.), *Word-Formation. An international handbook of
the languages of Europe* (Handbücher zur Sprach- und Kommunikationswis-

senschaft / Handbooks of Linguistics and Communication Science 40.4), 2831–2852. Berlin: De Gruyter Mouton.

Ohnheiser, Ingeborg. 2015. Compounds and multi-word expressions in Slavic. In Peter O. Müller, Ingeborg Ohnheiser, Susan Olsen & Franz Rainer (eds.), *Word-Formation. An international handbook of the languages of Europe* (Handbücher zur Sprach- und Kommunikationswissenschaft / Handbooks of Linguistics and Communication Science 40.1), 757–779. Berlin: De Gruyter Mouton.

Pafel, Jürgen. 2015. Phrasal compounds are compatible with Lexical Integrity. *Language Typology and Universals* 68. 263–280.

Sambor, Jadwiga. 1976. Kompozycje rzeczownikowe dwunominalne i nominalno-werbalne w tekstach współczesnego języka polskiego. In M. R. Mayenowa (ed.), *Semantyka tekstu i języka*, 239–256. Wrocław: Ossolineum.

Symoni-Sułkowska, Jadwiga. 1987. *Formacje rzeczownikowe utworzone od wyrażeń przyimkowych.* Wrocław: Ossolineum.

Szymanek, Bogdan. 2009. I-E, Slavonic: Polish. In Rochelle Lieber & Pavol Štekauer (eds.), *The Oxford handbook of compounding*, 464–477. Oxford: Oxford University Press.

Szymanek, Bogdan. 2010. *A panorama of Polish Word-Formation.* Lublin: Wydawnictwo KUL.

ten Hacken, Pius. 2013. Compounds in English, in French, in Polish, and in general. *SKASE Journal of Theoretical Linguistics* 10(1). 97–113.

Trips, Carola. 2012. Empirical and theoretical aspects of phrasal compounds: Against the 'syntax explains it all' attitude. In Angela Ralli, Geert Booij, Sergio Scalise & Athanasios Karasimos (eds.), *Online Proceedings of the eighth Mediterranean Morphology Meeting*, 322–346. Patras: University of Patras.

Trips, Carola. 2014. How to account for the expressive nature of phrasal compounds in a conceptual-semantic framework. *SKASE Journal of Theoretical Linguistics* 11(1). 33–61.

Trips, Carola & Jaklin Kornfilt. 2015a. Introduction. *STUF – Language Typology and Universals* 68(3). 233–240.

Trips, Carola & Jaklin Kornfilt. 2015b. Typological aspects of phrasal compounds in English, German, Turkish and Turkic. *STUF – Language Typology and Universals* 68(3). 281–322.

Waszakowa, Krystyna. 2015. Foreign word-formation in Polish. In Peter O. Müller, Ingeborg Ohnheiser, Susan Olsen & Franz Rainer (eds.), *Word-Formation. An international handbook of the languages of Europe* (Handbücher zur Sprach- und Kommunikationswissenschaft / Handbooks of Linguistics and Communication Science 40.3), 1679–1696. Berlin: De Gruyter Mouton.

Wójcikowska, Elżbieta. 1991. *Formacje atrybutywne typu podgórski, nadludzki w języku polskim.* Warsaw: Wydawnictwa Uniwersytetu Warszawskiego.

Chapter 4

On a subclass of nominal compounds in Bulgarian: The nature of phrasal compounds

Alexandra Bagasheva
Sofia University

The paper focuses on the study of a rarity in the Bulgarian language – phrasal compounds (PCs). Although not recorded in the Bulgarian National Corpus (BulNC), such compounds have successfully infiltrated the language of lifestyle magazines and the jargon of tourism. Although it does not attempt to provide a quantitative study, this paper reviews the properties of PCs in Bulgarian against a checklist of cross-linguistically recognised properties of PCs, gleaned from the growing body of literature on this type of compound. An explanation for the appearance and nature of PCs in Bulgarian is sought in their being offshoots of the recent accommodation in the language of a novel subordinative, modifying $[N_1N_2/N_2N_1]_N$ compound type. From lexical or "matter" borrowing, root $[N_1N_2/N_2N_1]_N$ of a determinative type established themselves as a new strategy within compounding, recognisable as structural or "pattern" borrowing via upward strengthening, and paved the way for PCs.

1 Introduction

The literature on morphology has recently abounded with discussions of linguistic phenomena that bear the label *phrasal* (e.g. phrasal names - Booij 2009a, phrasal lexemes - Masini 2009, and phrasal compounds - Lieber 1992; Pafel 2015; Trips 2016; Bağrıaçık & Ralli 2015, to name but a few). Though not coterminous, the three items of interest share two properties that seriously challenge the Lexical Integrity Hypothesis: they have a naming and not a descriptive function and they contain syntactic objects, phrases, in their structural makeup. They all seem

Alexandra Bagasheva. On a subclass of nominal compounds in Bulgarian: The nature of phrasal compounds. In Carola Trips & Jaklin Kornfilt (eds.), *Further investigations into the nature of phrasal compounding*, 81–117. Berlin: Language Science Press. DOI:10.5281/zenodo.885121

to pose serious questions concerning the architecture of language, the nature of compounding, the nature of the lexicon (if this is assumed to be a separate component), the essence of the syntax-morphology interface (in a modular conception of language), etc.

Without aiming at providing answers to such ambitious questions as the above, the current paper focuses on the nature and status of the non-homogenous group of compounds in which the non-head can host a constituent at phrase-level or above in a Slavonic language – Bulgarian. Acknowledging that studying the nature of an atypical linguistic element (for the specific language) will probably raise more questions than answer fundamental existing ones, the objectives of the paper are twofold: a) to analyse the properties of phrasal compounds at a stage in their development in a typologically specific language when they are considered a novelty and b) to provide a plausible scenario for the appearance of such constructions.

Phrasal compounds are recognised as characteristic of Germanic languages (Trips 2012; 2016) and opinions have been voiced that some can be found in Romance languages (at least in Italian, e.g. Bisetto 2015). They have also been discussed as standard elements of the lexicon (as syntactic or morphological objects) in Turkish and Greek (Bağrıaçık & Ralli 2015; Ralli 2013a,b), but have been deemed virtually non-existent in Slavonic languages (Ohnheiser 2015). In relation to these claims, the paper traces the appearance and features of phrasal compounds in Bulgarian in an attempt to see whether they share any characteristics with well-studied and established phrasal compounds in English and German. An explanation is sought for their appearance and nature in the language and their restricted use (in terms of domains).

In view of the set objectives the paper is structured as follows: part one reviews the findings of previous research on phrasal compounds in English and German; part two presents the adopted analytical framework; in part three the features of phrasal compounds in Bulgarian are checked against a summative list of properties of phrasal compounds in other languages; in part four an analysis and tentative explanation of the data are provided; and part five concludes.

2 Phrasal compounds – what we know so far

In the literature dealing with phrasal compounds it has been unanimously recognised that they differ from root nominal compounds in that the non-head member can be a phrase, a clause or even a clause complex[1] (see Trips 2012, 2016). This property of phrasal compounds seems to have attracted the greatest attention since it challenges basic postulates of standard, generative or at least modular approaches to language with the debate focusing on the interface between morphology and syntax (Bağrıaçık & Ralli 2015, Botha 1981, Lieber 1988, Ralli 2013a,b). Numerous researchers have tried to reconcile this fact with received postulates, such as the Lexical Integrity Hypothesis (e.g. Lieber & Scalise 2006), or with incessant competition between the modules of morphology and syntax (Ackema & Neeleman 2004), others have postulated the existence of two types of PCs depending on their properties and locus of generation, i.e. they recognise morphological PCs and syntactic PCs (Bağrıaçık & Ralli 2015, Botha 1981, Lieber 1988) or have postulated two distinct mechanisms of clause/phrase to word conversion, which leads to the creation of two different types of PCs – pure quotative phrasal compounds and pseudo-phrasal compounds or non-quotative PCs (Pafel 2015). Attempts have also been made to explain away the nature of phrasal compounds by lexicalisation of the non-head constituent (Bresnan & Mchombo 1995). Others have analysed these compounds from alternative perspectives (e.g. Jackendoff's parallel architecture – Trips 2012; 2016; Construction Grammar - Hein 2015; etc.) laying the emphasis on the semantics, pragmatics and usage patterns of phrasal compounds, besides the obvious structural features (e.g. Meibauer 2007; 2015).

There seems to be unanimous agreement, irrespective of the theoretical framework, that PCs have a single, unified meaning as a naming unit. This is achieved by reducing the structural complexity of PCs through downgrading, quoting or conversion to a word status. Alternatively, PCs are denied lexicalisability and are identified as metacommunicative (e.g. Hohenhaus 2007). To be even more specific, Pafel (2015) clearly states that the non-head constituent in genuine, quotative phrasal compounds is a noun. He argues that quotative phrasal compounds are morphologically and semantically regular NN compounds and they do not contain syntactic phrases. The scholar admits that non-quotative, pseudo-phrasal compounds can have only nouns as heads, while in quotative compounds the head can also be adjectival. If this criterion of the nature of the head is to be taken as diagnostic, then in Bulgarian only quotative phrasal compounds exist. This possibility will be explored in part three.

Among the general points of agreement seems to be the headedness of phrasal compounds. The prevalent opinion is that such constructions are right-headed.

---

[1] The term *clause complex* is taken from Halliday's Systemic Functional Grammar (Halliday 1994, Halliday & Matthiessen 2014) and is considered co-extensive with the standard maximal XP extension, i.e. a CP. The term is chosen to avoid any theoretical commitment.

In her paper Trips (2012: 322) writes,

> [w]hat makes these compounds so special is that the left-hand member is a complex, maximal phrase: as in the examples given above, it can be a whole sentence like an IP (or CP depending on the analysis), which clearly sets them apart from NNCs, the left-hand member of which is non-phrasal and thus an entity on the word level.

It logically follows that the head constituent is the rightmost member of the construction. However, the assumption that PCs are invariably right-headed is somewhat premature as will be shown in part three. Suffice it here to say that just as there are both left- and right-headed nominal compounds of the same type in Bulgarian, e.g. *очи-череши* [oči-čereši, 'eyes-cherries', *large, beautiful eyes*] vs. *гайтан-вежди* [gaytan-veždi, 'woollen braid', *well-shaped eyebrows*], in the same manner PCs in Bulgarian can easily have the nominal head on the left-hand side.

The last almost unanimously recognised feature of PCs that distinguishes them from subordinative (determinative, modifying) nominal compounds relates to recursion. As Trips (2012) and Trips (2016: 286) maintain, "[i]t is well-known that the rule for building determinative nominal compounds can be applied to the product of this rule infinitely [...], while such recursion is ill-formed in phrasal compounds".

To sum up, from the growing literature on phrasal compounds the following features of PCs undoubtedly characterise them crosslinguistically:

1) they behave like words both in terms of distribution (syntactic behaviour) and in terms of meaning;

2) they have a non-disputed naming function;

3) they have a stereotyping effect;

4) while they can have a variable structural head, they are mostly nominal;

5) they do not tolerate recursion;

6) they are (mostly) right-headed.

Besides these recognised features of PCs, their status as lexicalised/lexicalisable or nonce formations has also attracted the attention of scholars, with opinions on the matter still divided (e.g. Bresnan & Mchombo 1995; Hohenhaus 1998;

Meibauer 2007; Trips 2012, 2016; etc.). The two diametrically opposed views are represented by Bresnan & Mchombo (1995), who maintain that phrases which function as constituents of words are always lexicalised, and Hohenhaus (1998), who contends that PCs are non-lexicalisable context-dependent nonce formations. In between these extremes, Trips (2012; 2016) and Meibauer (2007) admit the existence of both lexicalised PCs and those produced on the fly.

The overview presented here of findings relating to phrasal compounds cross-linguistically is far from exhaustive but it will suffice as a checklist to be used in describing PCs in Bulgarian.

3 The analytical framework

As Booij (2010: 93) maintains, if instead of recognising abstract rules, we subscribe to an analogy-based approach recognising constructional schemas, we could pay due attention to semantic specialisations and apply the adequate degree of granularity of analysis (generalisation) to be able to describe a wide variety of word-formation data.

Admittedly, a constructionist approach to language renders void the controversy over the distinction between compounds that are morphological formations as in Modern Greek (Ralli (2013b,a)) and compounds that are syntactic formations such as those in Turkish (Bağrıaçık & Ralli 2015; Ralli 2013a; etc.). However, the choice of this framework is not simply a matter of convenience. It is motivated by three separate considerations: first, constructions can have varying degrees of complexity and schematisation, without compromising the uniformity of pairing meaning and form characteristic of the constructicon[2]. Second, as demonstrated by various pieces of research, Booij's Construction Morphology (Booij 2007, Booij 2009a) has sufficient explanatory power to analyze schemas of varying degrees of complexity and abstractness. Third, as Fried (2013: 2) claims,

> The constructional approach is also proving itself fruitful in grappling with various broader analytic challenges, such as accounting for seemingly unmotivated syntactic patterns that do not easily fit in a synchronically attested grammatical network for a given language, or that present a typologically odd and inexplicable pattern.

---

[2] Within constructionist approaches to language, there is no dividing line between grammar and the lexicon. Language (or the constructicon) is conceived of as a lexicon-syntax continuum or a complex network of constructions of varying degrees of complexity held together by inheritance relations (Goldberg 2003, Hoffmann & Trousdale 2013).

For the reasons stated above, the answers to the research questions are provided in the general framework of constructional approaches to language and language change (Booij 2009b, 2010, Croft 2001a, Goldberg 2006, Hilpert 2015, Traugott & Trousdale 2013, among others) and the onomasiological approach to word-formation (Štekauer 1998; 2005), where the naming needs and active role of speakers are duly recognised. Various offshoots of constructionalism with idiosyncratic views and analytical procedures have arisen in recent years (for relevant overviews see Croft 2007, Sag et al. 2012), yet they all share a set of assumptions which allow for the non-differentiated adoption of a constructionalist analytical stance. The basic tenet of constructionalism adopted here holds that language is a constructicon, a set of taxonomic networks where each construction constitutes a node in the network that forms a continuum from the fully concrete to the highly schematic. The relations between constructions are ones of inheritance and motivation. A construction itself is a conventionalised pairing of meaning and form. The constructicon is acquired via language use and innovated via neoanalysis and analogisation (Traugott & Trousdale 2013). Both processes are localized within constructions, or more precisely in actualized constructs. A construction is instantiated in actual language use by specified constructs that are fully phonetically specified and have contextually sensitive meaning, based on their conventionalised meaning or any appropriate extension thereof. A shift in any dimension of the construct might be strengthened via propagated use across the speech community into a modified or novel construction depending on the degree of dissimilarity from the initial one(s). The general model of a construction captures constructions that vary along at least three significant dimensions: type of concept, schematicity and complexity. Type of concept specifies the conventional meaning associated with the construction in terms of its contentfulness or procedural characteristics, i.e. whether it could be used referentially or whether it encodes intralinguistic relations. The dimension of schematicity is related to formal (phonological) specificity and degree of abstraction of a token construct, and classifies constructions into substantive (fully specified), schematic (abstract), and intermediate or partial (at least one constituent is specified). The dimension of complexity captures the internal constituency of a construction and distinguishes between atomic, complex and intermediate. Within this constructicon, constructionalisation, defined as "the creation of $form_{new}$-$meaning_{new}$ (combinations of) signs" that constitute "[...] new type nodes, which have new syntax or morphology and new coded meaning, in the linguistic network of a population of speakers" (Traugott & Trousdale 2013: 22) is achieved incrementally via constructional changes, defined as shifts along one of the dimensions of a construction (Traugott & Trousdale 2013: 26). Constructionalisation is one of the ways in which language change is actualised. At the same time it has long been recognised that "languages can undergo structural change as a result of contact" (Heine & Kuteva 2006: 48). In the case of Bulgarian, the influx of lexical or "matter" (MAT) borrowing from English characteristic of the last decades of the 20th century (Krumova-Cvetkova et al. 2013, Radeva 2007, etc.) brought about the establishment of a new subordinative, nominal compound type, which proved fruitful ground for the accommodation of PCs. The establishment of this compound type involved the structural or "pattern" (PAT) borrowing of the abstract construction schema $[N_1N_2]_N$, where N_1 modifies N_2 or restricts its interpretation, filled out with native linguistic material exclusively.

With the understanding of constructionalisation within the constructionalist approach and the notion of grammatical replication we are able to analyse in a smooth and uniform manner the nativisation of a borrowing (more specifically lexical borrowing from English such as *бинго маниак* [bingo maniak, *bingo maniac*] and the pattern borrowing of the subordinative, modifying nominal compound construction $[N_1N_2]_N$) and their constructionalisation into a new node type or a newly boosted pattern. Simply put, this framework makes it possible to identify the stabilisation of the $[N_1N_2]_N$ pattern in Bulgarian as the constructionalisation of a compound type, a new strategy within compounding, which paved the way for the advent of phrasal nominal compounds in the language. As Arcodia et al. (2009) claim, phrasal constituents are only possible with subordinative compounds, so it naturally follows that the establishment of the determinative $[N_1N_2/N_2N_1]_N$ compound type in Bulgarian serves as a prerequisite for the spread of phrasal compounds. Present-day $[N_1N_2]_N$ compounds in Bulgarian (recognized as atypical of Slavic languages, but characteristic of Germanic languages) came into the language under foreign influence. In the Bulgarian word-formation literature there is unanimous agreement that the new-found instigated productivity and the fixation of the pattern in terms of both form and meaning potential have been achieved under the influence of English (Krumova-Cvetkova et al. 2013, Murdarov 1983, Radeva 2007, etc.), i.e. as the result of language contact. From an influx of lexical borrowing the pattern has grown into a structure accommodating exclusively native constituents (e.g. *чалга певец* [čalga pevec, 'pop folk singer'], *чалга изпълнител* [čalga izpâlnitel, 'performer of pop folk music'], *тото пункт* [toto punkt, 'lottery kiosk']).

The onomasiological approach to language (Štekauer 1998), and more specifically to word-formation, acknowledges the active agency of speakers in creating new lexical items. For onomasiologists the desire of members of a speech community to come up with the most appropriate (with appropriateness measured by the minimax effect, i.e. minimal cognitive effort, maximum communicative effect, operationalisable as degrees of explicitness) name for a conceptualized piece of extralinguistic reality is the driving force behind word-formation. When the conceptualisation is novel for the cultural context, borrowing is not a neglected resource. In other cases, all the resources of a language (constructicon) can be creatively employed for encoding the intended conceptualisation. It is in the minds and mouths of speakers that the establishment and use of a new name lie (with a host of factors playing a crucial role, purely conceptual, sociolinguistic, cognitive, etc., which will not be commented on for lack of space. For the interplay and different roles of the various relevant factors see Štekauer 2005).

Combining the two analytical perspectives (constructionalisation as both a mechanism and the result of language change, and MAT developing into PAT borrowing) leads to the following understanding of the appearance of phrasal compounds in Bulgarian, with the ₙ always being the categorial head (for inflection purposes):

(1) a. $[X_R Y]_N$ – construction schema of nominal compounds

b. $[N_1 N_2/ N_2 N_1]_N$ – construction schema of determinative, root nominal compounds

c. $[X_{phrase/clause} N/ N X_{phrase/clause}]_N$ – construction schema of phrasal compounds

R – is the implicit intracompound relation between the constituents of the compound. As in English, this relationship is multifarious. It captures both modifying and thematic relations. As far as intracompound relations are concerned, Bulgarian $[N_1N_2]$ determinative compounds display the whole array of compound internal relations recognized in the literature (including psycholinguistic accounts, e.g. Bauer & Tarasova 2013, Gagné & Shoben 1997, Ryder 1994).

The schematic representation of productive constructions above captures the specific portion of the compounding network in which the newly established subordinative, modifying type of compound in Bulgarian found its place. The three levels of abstraction (1a, 1b, and 1c) represent the hierarchy of the nominal compound network: (1a) represents the most abstract schema of all nominal compounds whose instantiations can vary significantly in terms of constituents (e.g. [NN_{deverbal, suffixed}]: *родоотстъпник* [rodootstâpnik, 'clan-departer', *traitor*]), [VN]: *нехранимайко* [nehranimajko, 'not-feed-mother', *scoundrel/ good-for-nothing*], [NN_{deverbal,suffixless}]: *изкуствовед* [izkustvoved, 'art-know-er',

art critic/expert], etc. (1b) represents the schema of the newly established determinative, root compound type (e.g. *чалга изпълнител* [čalga izpâlnitel, 'pop
folk performer']) whose accommodation in the language made possible the appearance of phrasal compounds, whose generalised construction schema is represented by (1c).

Determinative and phrasal compounds differ along two parameters – the modifying constituent (noun vs. phrase/clause) and the nature of $_R$ which in the case
of $[N_1 N_2/ N_2 N_1]_N$ compounds can be quite specific, though invariably diverse,
including thematic relations between the two constituents. In the case of phrasal
compounds the simplest way to define $_R$ is to acknowledge that it is a severely
underspecified relationship which accounts for the meaning 'N is a type characterised by the stereotypical properties of X'. Even this difference, however, does
not pose a problem for uniform treatment of the two subtypes of nominal compounds since Bauer & Tarasova (2013) recognise a grossly semantically underspecified adnominal modification relationship in various types of constructions,
even ones not restricted to different types of compounds.

In the remainder of the paper it is assumed that all the analysed phrasal compounds are instantiations of the construction schema hierarchy presented above.

4 Phrasal compounds in Bulgarian

4.1 Bulgarian in comparison to Germanic languages

Since phrasal compounds are acknowledged as characteristic of Germanic languages (more specifically English and German), and their existence is denied for
Bulgarian, at the outset a rough typological sketch of the language under investigation is in order. In terms of analyticity the three languages might be ordered
along a cline, with English being the one with the greatest degree of analyticity, Bulgarian occupying a middle position (with heavy inflectional paradigms
for verbs, but virtually none for nouns) and German taking the last position. All
three languages are remotely genealogically related as they belong to different
groups of the same family. All three languages can be identified as nominative-
accusative.

Applying the typology associated with syntactic harmony (Hawkins 1983), the
following summative facts can be presented (see Table 1).

If the typologically relevant features are anything to go by, then one would
not predict any major differences between the three languages with regard to the

Table 1: A typological sketch of Bulgarian, English and German

	Bulgarian	English	German
Canonical word order	SVO	SVO	SVO, but also SOV in some types of embedded clauses
Prepositions vs. postpositions	Prepositions	Prepositions	Prepositions Postpositions (marginally)
Modifier-head (including Numeral-Noun, Demonstrative-Noun, Possessive pronoun-Noun, Adjective-Noun)	Modifier-head	Modifier-head	Modifier-head
Genitive-noun	Both orders (G-N, N-G) possible	Both orders (G-N, N-G) possible	Both orders (G-N, N-G) possible
Head-relative clause	H-R	H-R	Both orders (H-R, R-H) possible
Case system (nouns)	No	No (barring the Genitive)	Yes
Affixation	Highly productive	Highly productive	Highly productive
Compounding	Less productive	Highly productive	Highly productive

behaviour of (phrasal) compounds in the three languages. However, Ohnheiser (2015: 1824) claims that

> in Slavic languages the formation of compounds including a verbal modifier is impossible.

This would suggest that phrasal compounds containing full predication are ruled out for Bulgarian. Admittedly, as a Slavonic language, Bulgarian is characterised by more productive affixation, rather than compounding. As Olsen (2015: 911) claims,

> the Romance and Slavic languages are not highly compounding languages (especially if the default case of lexical combinations of basic stems without formatives or functional categories are the focus of attention).

Yet, synthetic (e.g. *въжеиграч* [vâžeigrač, 'rope-play-er', *tight-rope walker*]; *факлоносец* [faklonosec, 'torch-bear-er', *torchbearer*]; *земевладелец* [zemevladelec, 'land-own-er', *landowner*]) and coordinative nominal (e.g. *вагон-ресторант* [vagon-restorant, 'wagon-restaurant', *dining car*], *къща-музей* [kâša muzey, *house museum*], *страна-членка* [strana-členka, *member state*]) and adjectival compounds (e.g. *патил препатил* [patil prepatil, 'having suffered having suffered too much', *experienced*], *кървавочервен* [kârvavočerven, *blood red*], *тревнозелен* [trevnozelen, *grass green*]) are abundant in the language. What Bulgarian is claimed to lack are verb compounds and root or primary nominal compounds of a subordinative, modifying type. In the nominal field (where the input and the output of the process are nouns, albeit in the input often they are deverbal nouns), composition proper resulting in nominal compounds is mostly based on thematic relations between head and non-head and yields synthetic or parasynthetic compounds.

Nonetheless, the emergence of many new composite substantives without a linking vowel between the two components in Bulgarian is a sign that the language is developing towards more pronounced analyticity (Avramova & Osenova 2003: 73) and this tendency concerns mainly the nominal system (Vačkova & Vačkov 1998: 100). Not surprisingly, it is precisely new types of nominal compounds that have been emerging steadily in the language, namely subordinative, modifying nominal compounds (with a subtype containing abbreviations as a modifying constituent) and phrasal compounds. Phrasal compounds of the type *on-the-spot creations, will-she-or-won't-she-get-the-guy comedy,* etc. were in fact nonexistent in Bulgarian before the 1990s and this model of hyphenated compound phrases has certainly been imported.

Alexandra Bagasheva

4.2 Phrasal compounds in Bulgarian

Phrasal compounds in Bulgarian are special in several respects: a) they appear mostly in writing[3]; b) they seem to be text type and genre specific – at present they appear systematically in the Psychology, Friends and Advice sections of the Bulgarian edition of Cosmopolitan; c) they can be spelled with hyphens, in quotation marks or a combination of the two (besides, hyphenation sometimes includes the head, while enclosure in quotation marks never does) and d) they can be left- or right-headed, with left-headedness being characteristic of non-lexicalised ones exclusively (without any other correlation observed between headedness and the type of PC involved, i.e. predication vs. non-predication or quotative vs. pseudo-phrasal compounds). Concerning the PCs marked by hyphens or quotation marks, none of the phrasal non-heads are lexicalised (i.e. they are not listed in any available lexicographic source and are not attested in the BulNC). Without reading too much into spelling conventions, we have to note that quoting is perceived as a stereotyping strategy, as can be gleaned from example (22) in the Appendix, in which we have a well-formed relative clause which is quoted apart from the relativiser. The quoting achieves the effect of creating a special type or category of well-wishers (without describing well-wishers actually interested in someone's thoughts).

The very few lexicalised PCs in Bulgarian are restricted to the jargon of tourism. They are either hybrid formations or sound like loan translations (even though the specific non-head phrases are not attested in the alleged source language, English). They are recorded in specialised dictionaries in the field.

Comparing the list of Bulgarian PCs with the set of properties defined above, we get the following picture:

1) they behave like words both in terms of distribution (syntactic behaviour) and in terms of meaning – they can be premodified by adjectives, e.g. *направи-си-сам-проблеми-в-офиса ситуация* [napravi-si-sam-problemi-v-ofisa situaciya, 'create-your-own-problems-at-the-office situation'] много трудна *направи-си-сам-проблеми-в-офиса ситуация* [mnogo trudna ~, 'very difficult ~']; they can be marked for definiteness, e.g. *направи-си-сам-проблеми-в-офиса ситуация*та от вчера [~ situaciyata ot včera, 'the ~ from yesterday']; they can be marked for plurality, e.g. множество *направи-си-сам-проблеми-в-офиса ситуации* [množestvo ~ situacii, 'a lot of ~ situations'], etc.;

---

[3] For lack of a reliable corpus of spoken Bulgarian the appearance of phrasal compounds in oral communication is not discussed in the current paper.

2) they have a non-disputed naming function – *вземи-му-акъла-съвет* [vze-mi-mu-akâla-sâvet, 'blow-his-mind-away-advice'] names a specific piece of advice which prescribes an easily identifiable course of action;

3) they have a stereotyping effect – *напрежението ето-че-моментът-най-сетне-настъпи* [napreženieto eto-če-momentât-nay-setne-nastâpi, the-tension there-the-time-has-finally-come'] names a very specific kind of tension which everyone is liable to a long-awaited moment has finally arrived;

4) while they can have a variable structural head, they are mostly nominal – all examples in Table 2 are nouns;

5) they do not tolerate recursion – It is impossible to recursively expand in either direction any of the compounds in Table 2;

6) they are (mostly) right-headed – this is not necessarily the case. As will become evident from Table 2, phrasal compounds in Bulgarian have no marked headedness preference. 14 out of 29 compounds are right-headed, while 15 have the categorial and semantic head on the left. All 29 are endocentric compounds and resemble determinative, modifying nominal compounds in the language in all respects but two – the structural make-up of the non-head constituent and the relationship between the head and the non-head constituent. In the constructionist framework adopted here, these differences are of no relevance, since at the highest level of generalisation of the corresponding construction they are collapsed into a single, governing abstract schema.

Before presenting the most important features of PCs in Bulgarian in table format (Table 2), we need to comment on two issues relating to the last two properties in this list.

As in other languages, PCs in Bulgarian do not tolerate recursion in the non-head position (for other languages see above). Bauer (2009: 350) states that "[w]e do not have sufficient information to see whether recursion or lack of recursion in compounds is the default, or whether either of these correlates with any feature of compounding, though it would be something worth checking." Recursion is excluded for all types of compounds in Bulgarian in general (e.g. *груборазтуриколиба* [gruborazturikoliba, 'brutally tear-down-hut', *brutal adulterer*], *лошовестоносец* [lošovestonosec, 'bad-news-bring-er', *harbinger*], *изящноизкуствовед* [izyaštnoizkustvoved, 'fine art leader', *fine art critic*]

*нова чалга певец [nova čalga pevec, *new pop folk singer*]). What is allowed
is independent coordination within the non-head constituent only (e.g. *авто и
мототехника* [avto i mototehnika, 'technical equipment for cars and motorcy-
cles']). But as Plag (2003: 84) notes, this phenomenon is characteristic of both
affixation and compounding and is not indicative of any peculiar features of
(nominal) compounds – or as Bell (2011: 157) concludes, coordination data has
no bearing on the (morphosyntactic) nature of nominal compounds. It is reasonable to propose, with Trips (2016: 286), "that this restriction is subject to extra-
grammatical factors like limitations of processing". However, the fact that recursion is excluded as a possibility for PCs does not render them different from other
compounds in Bulgarian (none of which permits recursion) and does not reveal
that "phrasal compounds do not behave like normal compounds" as suggested by
Trips (2016). Rather, at least in Bulgarian, phrasal compounds behave very much
like subordinative nominal compounds. What is more, Arcodia et al. (2009: 11)
note that "having a phrasal constituent is possibly a unique property of subordinate compounds." To cut a long story short, phrasal compounds do not tolerate
recursion but this does not set them apart from other nominal compounds in the
language.

Just as the non-admission of recursion does not mark out phrasal compounds
as unique in Bulgarian, neither do their properties in relation to headedness. Extant $[N_1N_2/N_2N_1]_N$ compounds without a linking component are either considered appositive, as in *вагон-ресторант* [vagon-restorant, 'dining car'], *замест-
ник-директор* [zamestnik-direktor, 'deputy director'], *кандидат-студент* [kan-
didat-student, 'student applicant'] (Radeva 2007: 56-58), or are interpreted as a
group in their own right (with a variety of labels attached to them by different authors, see Kirova 2012, Murdarov 1983, Radeva 2007, etc.) with a semantic opera-
tor of implicit comparison (Radeva 2007: 58) as in *очи-череши* [oči-čerešhi, 'eyes-
cherries', *large, beautiful eyes*], *гайтан-вежди* [gaytan-veždi, 'woollen braid',
well-shaped eyebrows], *снага-топола* [snaga-topola, 'body-poplar', *slender body*],
etc.

The problems in the classification and analysis of NN compounds stem from
the fact that they occur with variable semantic heads (on the parametrised treatment of the concept of head in compounding see Guevara & Scalise 2009; Scalise
& Guevara 2006). In *очи-череши* [oči-čerešhi, 'eyes-cherries', *large, beautiful
eyes*] and *снага-топола* [snaga-topola, 'body-poplar', *slender body*] the element
that is being described appears on the left and the meaning of the whole suggests
that it is the semantic anchor: eyes like cherries and a body like a poplar. In the
exocentric *гайтан-вежди* [gaytan-veždi, 'woollen braid', *well-shaped eyebrows*],

it is the rightmost member that names the entity being described and the first constituent introduces the comparative attribute. In terms of categorial headedness the first two compounds have two categorial heads (as both constituents will be inflected), while in the third instance categorial and semantic head coincide. The way out of the analytical conundrum is to acknowledge that all such compounds (including the influx of endocentric subordinative nominal compounds) are determinative, modifying compounds with variable semantic and/or categorial head.

Likewise we need to allow for both left- and right-headed phrasal compounds, in which the position of the head does not affect the set of remaining properties of the respective compounds. Thus, *да-се-почувстваш-добре ефект* [da-se-počuvstvaš-dobre efekt, 'to-start-feeling-well effect'] is right-headed, while *напрежението ето-че-моментът-най-сетне-настъпи* [napreženieto eto-če-momentât-nay-setne-nastâpi, 'the-tension there-the-time-has-finally-come'] is left-headed but no ensuing predictions can be made as to the remaining properties of the compounds. In fact, the two compounds share all their properties – they contain fully-fledged declarative predications, they are both quotative and the head in both cases is of the same semantic type, namely Attitude.

And last but not least, Trips's (2012) claim that the most frequent PCs (in her empirical study of PCs in English based on data from the BNC) are quotative PCs holds true for Bulgarian PCs (as evidenced in the table below). The table presents a summary of the outstanding properties of phrasal compounds in Bulgarian and their classification in accordance with recognised classificatory criteria (Pafel's (2015) quotative and pseudo PCs, Trips's (2016) predicational and non-predicational PCs and their semantic types).

Table 2: Phrasal compounds in Bulgarian

Example in Bulgarian[4] (semantic type[5] of the head of the PC)	Transliteration	Meaning	Type in relation to the predication status of the non-head (structural make-up)	Quotative or pseudo	Headedness
свали-го-съвет (attitude/utterance/medium conveying utterance)	svali-go-sâvet	hit-on-him-advice	full predication (imperative)	quotative	right
вземи-му-акъла-съвет (attitude/utterance/medium conveying utterance)	vzemi-mu-akâla-sâvet	blow-his-mind-away-advice	full predication (imperative)	quotative	right
завърти-му-ума-посрещане (action)	zavârti-mu-akâla-posrešane	make-his head-spin-welcoming	full predication (imperative)	quotative	right
промени-живота-си-предизвикателство (action)	promeni-života-si-predizvikatels-tvo	change-your-life-challenge	full predication (imperative)	quotative	right
прочети-му-мислите съвет (attitude/utterance/medium conveying utterance)	pročeti-mu-mislite sâvet	read-his-thoughts advice	full predication (imperative)	quotative	right
предизвикай-го-да-говори-съвет (attitude/utterance/medium conveying utterance)	predizvikay-go-da-govori-sâvet	coerce-him-into-talking-advice	full predication (imperative)	quotative	right
типа който-пръв-ще-успее-да-пъхне-лед-в-ризата-на-другия +(action)	+típâ koy-prâv-še-uspee-da-pâhne-led-v-rizata-na-drugiya	the-type-who-will-first-succeed-in-putting-some-ice-down-the-shirt-of-the-other	full predication (interrogative)	quotative	left
+(thing)	+[6] tip-ne-e-za-izpuskane-nezawisimo-ot-cenata	type-it-is-not-to-be-missed-no-matter-the-price	full predication (existential)	quotative	left

Example in Bulgarian[4] (semantic type[5] of the head of the PC)	Transliteration	Meaning	Type in relation to the predication status of the non-head (structural make-up)	Quotative or pseudo	Headedness
тип не-е-за-изпускане-независимо-от-цената факта Боже-не-може-да-бъде! (conceptual entity)	fakta Bože-ne-može-da-bâde!	the fact Oh-God-this-cannot-be-true!	full predication (existential)	quotative	left
разновидност 'Боже-сетих-ли-се-да-изключа-котлона-днес' +(conceptual entity)	+raznovidonost 'Bože-setih-li-se-da-izklyuča-kotlona-dnes'	variety 'Oh-God-did-I-remember-to-switch-off-the-cooker?'	full predication (interrogative)	quotative	left
вариант 'ей-тази-седмица-наистина-май-ще-ме-уволнят-или-зарежат-или-и-двете' +(conceptual entity)	+variant 'ey-tazi-sedmica-naistina-may-še-me-uvolnyat-ili-zarežat-ili-i-dvete'	option 'wow-this-week-I-will-really-get-fired-or-ditched-or-both"	full predication (coordinated clause complex)	quotative	left
да-се-почувстваш-добре ефект (attitude)	da-se-počuvstvaš-dobre efekt	to-start-feeling-well effect	full predication (da-construction)	quotative	right
напрежението ето-че-моментът-най-сетне-настъпи (attitude)	napreženieto eto-če-momentât-nay-setne-nastâpi	the-tension there-the-time-has-finally-come	full predication (declarative)	quotative	left
направи-си-сам-проблеми-в-офиса ситуация (action)	napravi-si-sam-problemi-v-ofisa situaciya	create-your-own-problems-at-the-office situation	full predication (imperative)	quotative	right

Example in Bulgarian[4] (semantic type[5] of the head of the PC)	Transliteration	Meaning	Type in relation to the predication status of the non-head (structural make-up)	Quotative or pseudo	Headedness
развръзка за-вечни-времена (action)	razvrâzka-za-večni-vremena	denouement for-eternal-times	non-predicational (N-prep-Adj-N)	pseudo	left
навика с-цигара-в-ръка (property)	navika-s-cigara-v-râka	the-habit-with-cigarette-in-hand	non-predicational (N-prep-N-prep-N)	pseudo	left
предъвкването-между-другото (action)	predâvkvaneto-meždu-drugoto	the-chewing-over-casually-among-other-things	non-predicational(N-prep-N)	pseudo	left
стърчащо-услужливо-дълго-нокътче (thing)	stârčašo-uslužlivo-dâlgo-nokâtče	the-sticking-out conveniently-long-nail_dim	*7 non-predicational (Adj-Adv-Adj-N)	pseudo	right
иначе-любимия-човек (individual)	inače-lyubimiya-čovek	the-otherwise-beloved-person	non-predicational (Adv-Adj-N)	pseudo	right
намек "има нещо помежду им" (medium conveying an utterance)	namek "ima nešo pomeždu im"	hint "there is something going on between them"	full predication (existential)	quotative	left
колежките-кобри-по-душа (individual)	koležkite-kobri-po-duša	the-female-colleagues-real-cobras-in-their-hearts	non-predicational (N-N-prep-N)	pseudo	left
просто-независеща-от-него-странност (property)	prosto-nezaviseša-ot-nego-strannost	a-simply-not-depending-on-him-foible	*non-predicational (N-Adj-prep-ProN-N)	pseudo	right
обикаляне-без-купуване решение (action)	obikalayane-bez-kupuvane rešenie	window-shopping-without-buying decision	non-predicational (N-prep-N-N)	pseudo	right

Example in Bulgarian[4] (semantic type[5] of the head of the PC)	Transliteration	Meaning	Type in relation to the predication status of the non-head (structural make-up)	Quotative or pseudo	Headedness
доброжелатели, които „само искат да знаят какво мислиш за бъдещето си" (individual)	dobroželateli, koito "samo iskat da znayat kakvo misliš za bădešteto si"	well-wishers who "just want to know what you are thinking about your future"	#[8] full predication (declarative)	quotative	left
функцията „На този ден" (utterance/medium conveying utterance)	funkciyata "Na tozi den"	the function "On that day"	non-predicational (N-prep-ProN$_{dem}$-N)	quotative	left
статус „Обичам мазни, потни чичковци" (utterance/medium conveying utterance)	status "Običam mazni, potni čičkovci"	status "I love sleazy, sweaty old guys"	full predication (declarative)	quotative	left
reach-in /roll-in /walk-in хладилници (thing)	reach-in hladilnici	reach-in refrigerators	*non-predicational (V-prep-N)	pseudo	right
roll-in хладилници (thing)	roll-in hladilnici	roll-in refrigerators	*non-predicational (V-prep-N)	pseudo	right
walk-in хладилници (thing)	walk-in hladilnici	walk-in refrigerators	*non-predicational (V-prep-N)	pseudo	right
море-слънце-пясък туризъм (thing)	more-slânce-pyasâk turizâm	sea-sun-sand tourism	non-predicational (N-N-N)	pseudo	right
ски-слънце-сняг туризъм (thing)	ski-slânce-snyag turizâm	ski-sun-snow tourism	non-predicational (N-N-N-N)	pseudo	right

4.3 An interpretation of phrasal compounds in Bulgarian

In view of the fact that the two editions of the Dictionary of New Words and Meanings in Bulgarian (2001 and 2010) register nominal compounds of the determinative type with nouns and abbreviations as non-head constituents and that the only available piece of research on PCs on Bulgarian reports on a corpus harvested from printed and electronic media for the period 2004–2005, it is plausible to conclude that the development of PCs in Bulgarian runs closely behind the establishment of the NN determinative compound type.

The establishment of the $[N_1N_2/N_2N_1]_N$ root compound type with determinative, modifying intracompound relations in Bulgarian paved the way for the emergence of phrasal compounds. Once established, the $[N_1 \ N_2]_N$ schema in the constructicon of Bulgarian provided the grounds for tolerance of various kinds of linguistic elements in the N_1 slot (phrases and abbreviations, e.g. *жп възел* [žp vâzel, *railway junction*], *ЕС лидер* [ES lider] 'EU leader', *МВР център* [MVR centâr, 'centre of the Ministry of the Interior'], *СДВР шеф* [SDVR šef, 'boss of the Sofia Directorate of the Interior'], etc.). In other words, the semantics of the pattern – N_2 of a type somehow related to N_1 – warrants the on-the-spot creation of non-lexicalised phrasal compounds.

For the time being phrasal compounds are most frequent in lifestyle magazines and in the jargon of tourism. Their establishment in the language is far from complete and results from very specific sociocultural parameters in a weak contact situation. As argued here, what resulted from contact was the establishment of the $[N_1N_2]_N$ pattern whose successful constructionalisation led to the diversification of the construction into phrasal compounds (PCs) and abbrevia-

---

[4]Punctuation and capitalisation are given as they appear in the original sources.

[5]The semantic labels used are those proposed and defined by Trips (2016: 161). It appears that they are applicable cross-linguistically and can be of value in future contrastive studies. In Bulgarian there are not (at present) PCs with heads of the type Time.

[6]+ The semantic labels associated with these phrasal compounds are derived from the noun which their heads elaborate, be it appositively or via a preposition. The actual semantic motivating nouns can be seen in the Appendix.

[7]* These examples are based on deverbal (*-ing*) or constituents used as adjectives with an initial verbal element in the derivation. The syntactic status of the non-head constituent in the hybrid constructions is not unequivocal.

[8]# This example stands apart from all the others in containing a fully-fledged relative clause. The relative clause is extremely strange – it is quoted and thus acquires a stereotyping/typifying effect. All deictic properties of the constituents of the relative clause are cancelled or suspended and the well-wishers are not described as actually experiencing a desire at a particular time t_0 but are classified as members of a particular type or category. This example might be indicative of the way in which protosyntactic packaging or condensing leads to phrasal compounding.

tion compounds (ACs), as we have just seen with the examples above. The users of the language who utilise PCs freely constitute special small speech communities in the sense of Lipka (2002) and Hohenhaus (2005) in relation to vocabulary knowledge and use.

None of the examples analysed here has been recorded in the BulNC to date. Although this is not a fact that can be capitalised on in a conclusive way, it appears that PCs in Bulgarian do not have listeme status (to the exclusion of those found in the jargon of tourism). They appear mostly in writing, with the genres and text types restricted to the Psychology, Friends and Advice sections of popular lifestyle magazines. On the basis of these facts it could be argued that the appearance of such structures is a contact phenomenon in its infancy.

The same used to apply to NN determinative compounds that have been termed "an Anglo-Americanism in Slavic morphosyntax" (Vakareliyska & Kapatsinski 2014: 277). The authors contend that

> since 1990, most of the South and East Slavic languages have independently adopted, to varying extents, English loanblend [N[N]] constructions, in which an English modifier noun is followed by a head noun that previously existed in the language, for example, Bulgarian ekšân geroi 'action heroes' (ibid.).

Yet, as argued by Croft (2001b) from lexical[9] (or MAT) borrowing as in *поп идол* [pop idol, *pop idol*], via hybrid formations (or loanblends) such as *екшън герой* [ekšân geroy, *star from an action movie*], exclusively native root $[N_1N_2]_N$s of a determinative type such as *ужас-трѫпка* [užas trâpka, *horror vibe*] and *чалга певец* [čalga pevec, *pop folk singer*] established themselves as a new strategy within compounding (or PAT borrowing) via upward strengthening. The abstraction of a new pattern from lexical borrowings gave rise to constructional changes in two networks, namely modification and compounding, leading to the constructionalisation of a new compounding strategy. The lexical replication of item-specific borrowings, e.g. *екшън филм* [ekšân film, *action movie*] grew into grammatical replication as defined by Heine & Kuteva (2006: 49). This has led to the appearance of one novel type of nominal compound in Bulgarian with three subtypes, marked by an asterisk in Figure 1. The remaining two types are the bahuvrihi $[V N]_N$ and the synthetic and parasynthetic ones $[NV]$ +/- suff N characteristic of Slavonic languages.

---

[9] A description of the process of lexical (MAT) borrowing going structural (PAT) and the establishment of a new constructional type is provided in §5.2 below.

$$[XY]\ N_{[-dyn;\ -rel]} \longrightarrow [N_1+N_2]_N$$
$$\longrightarrow {}^*[Abbr\ N]_N$$

$[VN]_N \qquad [NV]_{+/-\ suff}\ N \qquad {}^*[N_1N_2/N_2N_1]_N \qquad {}^*[X_{phrase/clause}\ N/NX_{phrase/clause}]_N$

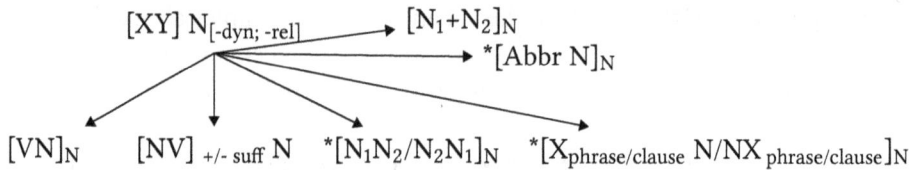

Figure 1: Types of nominal compound in Bulgarian

The constructional network of compounds is represented in Figure 1. at just two levels of abstraction and the highest node within nominal compounding can only be instantiated by one of the types it sanctions. The first node (from left to right) at the lower level of abstraction $[VN]_N$ denotes the type constituted by exocentric nominal compounds such as *развейпрах* [razveyprah, 'scatter-dust', *idler*], *размуриколиба* [razturikoliba, 'tear-down-hut', *adulterer*]; *загоритен-джере* [zagoritendžere, 'burn-pan', *a person with no sense of time*]. The second, [N V] $_{+/-\ suff}$ N, is actualised by two subtypes: suffixal and suffixless synthetic compounds (which may be semantically endo- or exocentric), e.g. suffixal *гласопо-давател* [glasopodavatel, 'voice-giver', *voter*]; *гробокопач* [grobokopač, 'grave-dig-er', *gravedigger*]; *данъкоплатец* [danâkoplatec, 'tax-pay-er', *taxpayer*]. The suffixless subtype comprises such compounds as *животновъд* [životnovâd, 'an-imal-breed', animal breeder]; *езиковед* [ezikoved, 'language-know-er', *linguist*], etc. The third node, $[N_1N_2/N_2N_1]_N$, branches into subordinative (root) nominal compounds exemplified by the right-headed *бинго зала* [bingo zala, *bingo hall*], *фитнес салон* [fitnes salon, *fitness centre*] and the left-headed *гора закрилница* [gora zakrilnica, 'forest protector', *a forest to hide out in*]. The fifth node, [Abbr N]$_N$, captures invariably right-headed compounds in which the first constituent is an abbreviation as in *ФБР агент* [FBR agent, *FBI agent*], *МВР акция* [MVR akciya=Ministry of the Interior action, *police operation*], *ВиК части* [ViK časti, *plumbing parts*], *жп възел* [žp vâzel, *railway junction*], etc. The sixth node is a schematic representation of the construction actualising coordinative nominal compounds such as *плод-зеленчук* [plod-zelenčuk, 'fruit-vegetable', greengro-cer's] and *архитект-проектант* ['arhitekt-proektant', architect-designer].

Within this nominal network, phrasal compounds in Bulgarian bear all the hallmark characteristics that Heringer (1984: 9) ascribes to *episodic compounds*, in circulation mainly within small groups, such as the readership of the Bulgarian Cosmopolitan.

5 Phrasal compounds in Bulgarian: some generalisations

5.1 The semantics of phrasal compounds in Bulgarian

On the basis of their semantics phrasal compounds should be recognized as composites within the constructicon. As Lampert (2009: 62-63) contends,

> two categories relevant for linguistic representations at all levels [...] must [...] be kept apart: First, those that result from an 'additive' (or: computational) combination of semantically and/or formally simplex items, yielding [...] compositions of variable complexities in accordance with combinatorial rules; second, there are composites, which cannot readily be analyzed in terms of a 'simple' (additive) computation of their formal constituents and/or semantic components, but only as 'wholes' or Gestalts.

This understanding of composites is fully in keeping with the constructionist understanding of schemas at a medium level of complexity and specificity, and captures two of the outstanding properties of phrasal compounds which warrant them a unique type status among compounds. First, they are not constituted by atomic elements and second, there is no uniform, straightforward computational mechanism which can represent the generation of their meaning (the relation between the constituents cannot be formulated in a linear, descriptive manner). The semantic generalisations concerning the meaning of PCs necessarily employ some marked mechanism, e.g. metonymy (Trips 2016), heavy pragmatic inferencing (Meibauer 2015), metacommunicatively executed stereotyping (Hohenhaus 2007), fictive interaction, encyclopedic and episodic knowledge (...) (Pascual et al. 2013). Phrasal compounds in Bulgarian display the same semantic complexities as PCs in other languages.

For Pafel (2015) quotative PCs behave exactly like $[N_1N_2]_N$ compounds, i.e. their semantics is computable on the basis of an intracompound modification relation as in determinative nominal compounds. According to Heine & Kuteva (2009: 145) there are crosslinguistically four basic types of compound structures with recognised internal relations:

1) modifying (tatpurusha) compounds where N_1 is a modifier of N_2 (e.g. *dog house, бинго зала* [bingo zala, 'bingo hall']);

2) appositive (karmadharaya) compounds where the reference of N is the intersection of N_1 and N_2 (e.g. *singer-songwriter, архитект-проектант* [arhitekt-proektant, 'architect-designer']);

3) additive (dvandva) compounds where N encompasses the meanings of both N₁ and N₂ with the latter being distinct referents of N (e.g. *speaker-listener*, *плод-зеленчук* [plod-zelenčuk, 'fruit-vegetable', *greengrocer's*]); and

4) alternative (bahuvrihi) compounds where the meaning of N lies outside the combination of N₁ and N₂ on the basis of metonymy (e.g. *hunchback*, *загоритенджера* [zagoritendžere, 'burn-pan', *a person with no sense of time*]).

Analysing the semantics of PCs in Bulgarian indicates that they behave like modifying compounds. The lexicalised *море-слънце-пясък туризъм* [more-slân-ce-pyasâk turizâm, 'sea-sun-sand tourism'] names a specific type of relaxation or tourism associated with summertime and specific activities relating to the availability of all three prerequisites, sea, sun, and sand. The same semantic interpretation applies to *walk-in хладилници* [walk-in hladilnici, 'walk-in refrigerators'] which denotes a specific type of refrigerating facility where one can walk in and pick out the required foodstuffs. The modifying relationship is fairly straightforward and these PCs look a lot like ordinary modifying nominal compounds except as regards the structure of the non-head constituent. Their semantics can be explained by what Trips (2016: 171) suggests "R(x1,x2)", i.e. "[t]he only thing which is specified is that there is a relation between" the head and the non-head constituent. The only qualification to make is that unlike in English, in Bulgarian the type of relation involved is easily read off the compound. It is likely that the further spread and expected heightened productivity of PCs in Bulgarian the nature of the relation (R) will become as diversified and underdetermined as in English.

Non-lexicalised PCs, such as *предизвикай-го-да-говори-съвет* [predizvikay-go-da-govori-sâvet, 'coerce-him-into-talking-advice'] or *напрежението ето-че-моментът-най-сетне-настъпи* [napreženieto eto-če-momentât-nay-setne-nas-tâpi, 'the-tension there-the-time-has-finally-come'] and *направи-си-сам-проблеми-в-офиса ситуация* [napravi-si-sam-problemi-v-ofisa situaciya, 'create-your-own-problems-at-the-office-situation'], irrespective of the variation in headedness (left- or right-headed) and the semantic type of the head element (Attitude and Action), display the same semantics, i.e. name a specified or stereotyped type of the head. The listener/reader will understand the tension in *напрежението ето-че-моментът-най-сетне-настъпи* [napreženieto eto-če-momentât-nay-setne-nastâpi, 'the-tension there-the-time-has-finally-come'] as a specific type of tension that one experiences in the typified circumstances. The presumption that comprehension of the PC depends on the "hearer's knowledge of context, background, stereotypes, etc., adhering to pragmatic principles such as Gricean maxims" (Meibauer, quoted after Trips 2016: 169) seems to be sufficient for explaining the functioning of Bulgarian PCs in context. However, from the speaker's perspective, this cannot explain how PCs are produced on the fly. Adopting Trips's (2016: 172-176) account of the semantics of predicational PCs in English provides a plausible explanation for the meaning computation of PCs in Bulgarian from the speaker's perspective. The "IS-A" relationship and metonymy-based type-shifts account in a satisfactory manner for the semantics of predicational PCs. As Trips (2016: 174) specifies "the phrasal non-head is an utterance which undergoes one (or more) typeshift(s) either from UTTERANCE to THING [...] or from UTTERANCE to EVENT(UALITY)." In this manner the necessary stereotyping of the situation described in the phrasal non-head is achieved.

A detailed semantic analysis of PCs in Bulgarian was beyond the objectives and scope of the current paper, yet in the process of checking their properties against established compounds in other languages, an analysis of meaning generating principles was inevitable and this led to the conclusion that the elements in the modifier slot function as situational proverbs. They name situations or event types but do not describe a discourse-anchored situation. The non-predicational ones denote entities of well-specified types.

5.2 Can phrasal compounds in Bulgarian be the result of pattern borrowing?

The similarities between subordinative, modifying nominal compounds and PCs seem to go beyond their semantics. Like subordinative, nominal compounds, phrasal compounds have arisen as the result of language contact. As Ohnheiser (2015: 1856) has noted,

> to a significant extent the increase of new vocabulary in the modern Slavic languages feeds on borrowings and loan translations or hybrid formations, a large part of which consist of *compound patterns* and compound elements of foreign origin (Ohnheiser 2015: 1856; emphasis added).

Both subordinative, modifying $[N_1N_2/N_2N_1]_N$ compounds and phrasal nominal compounds in Bulgarian probably result from this recognised influx of foreign compound patterns.

In contact linguistics it has become common to make a distinction between direct borrowing of lexical and phonetic material and structural borrowing or grammatical replication. As Sakel (2007: 15) claims,

we speak of MAT-borrowing when morphological material and its phonological shape from one language is replicated in another language.

Similarly Heine & Kuteva (2006: 49) differentiate between lexical and grammatical replication on the basis of borrowing or not of form or phonetic sub-
stance. Grammatical replication for them is recognised when a replica language
"creates a new grammatical structure (Rx) on the model of some structure (Mx)
of another language" (Heine & Kuteva 2006: 49). For Sakel (2007: 15),

> PAT describes the case where only the patterns of the other language are
> replicated, i.e. the organisation, distribution and mapping of grammatical
> or semantic meaning, while the form itself is not borrowed.

Whichever terminology we adopt, it appears that from the perspective of constructionalism the development of atypical constructions should be recognised
as PAT borrowing or grammatical replication. Crucially, it may be the case that
in borrowing constructions of medium complexity the two types of borrowing
are merely successive steps in the process of constructionalisation.

When we combine the understanding of constructionalisation as a kind of language change with the typology of borrowing it transpires that the establishment
of root, subordinative nominal compounds in Bulgarian is an example par excellence of constructionalisation in a contact situation. In keeping with Traugott
& Trousdale's (2013) postulations, the emergence of constructional nodes with
schematic slots is what is captured with the term "grammatical constructionalisation". In the development of $[N_1N_2]_N$ constructions in Bulgarian exactly this
process is observed: upward strengthening of a construction with schematized
nodes. Importantly, Traugott & Trousdale (2013: 22) emphasise that constructionalisation is associated with the emergence of a new node in a constructional
network, or more specifically "[...] when constructs begin to be attested which
could not have been fully sanctioned by pre-existing constructional types." As the
compounding network in Bulgarian did not tolerate root, subordinative $[N_1N_2]_N$s
before the influx of lexical borrowings from English (Brezinski 2012, Krumova-
Cvetkova et al. 2013, Murdarov 1983, Radeva 2007, etc.), it is natural to conclude
that the rapid spread of $[N_1N_2]_N$s in the language and their development from
lexical borrowing via loanblends into fully integrated constructions with native
constituents is an illustration par excellence of MAT borrowing gone PAT (Sakel
2007). The real question is whether phrasal compounds in the language follow
the same scenario or whether they resulted from the further diversification of
the already nativised compound pattern.

While $[N_1N_2]_N$s have already firmly developed into PAT borrowing (hundreds of them being found with purely native constituents and duly recorded in lexicographic reference books), PCs are still a borderline phenomenon (in view of their restricted genre and text type appearance). However, the attested PCs in Bulgarian cannot be interpreted as direct lexical borrowings or calques as no corresponding potential English sources easily suggest themselves. This suggests that the paths of development of root, subordinative nominal compounds and PCs in the language differ.

Hilpert (2015: 116) contends that

> whereas in grammaticalization, the experience of a linguistic unit leads to the progressive entrenchment of a more schematic construction, situated at a higher level in the constructional network, constructional change can manifest itself in the strengthening of several more specific sub-schemas, at lower levels of the constructional network. This proposal will be called the upward strengthening hypothesis.

Following this hypothesis, the establishment of the new root, subordinative compound type in Bulgarian $[N_1N_2]_N$ should be interpreted as the result of upward strengthening, while that of PCs is the result of constructional change. The newly established compound type acted as fertile soil in which phrasal compounds could be planted. The planting was aided by the peculiar formal and functional properties of phrasal compounds and the general meaning underspecification of nominal modification (Bauer & Tarasova 2013).

To go a step further, we can specify that both subordinative, modifying nominal compounds and PCs are the result of pattern borrowing, not process borrowing. The distinction between the two types of borrowing, according to Renner (2015), is based on the degree to which the borrowing affects the receptor or replicator language's extant constructions. Renner defines "contact-induced morphostructural change as all contact-induced morphological changes beyond the copying of a morpheme, i.e. the novel availability or increased profitability of a WF process or pattern caused by language contact" (Renner 2016). The novel availability of a word-formation process he dubs process borrowing, while the increased profitability of a word-formation process or model is recognised as pattern borrowing. The latter results in moderate structural change, with the core of the receptor language's system remaining unaffected. The borrowing of subordinative nominal compounds from English into Bulgarian did not lead to the introduction of a novel word-formation process, but enhanced the profitability of the existing but marginal $[N_1N_2/N_2N_1]_N$ compound pattern.

Admittedly, this scenario for the appearance of PCs is in keeping with the development of nominal compounds as suggested by Heine & Kuteva (2009). It is possible that in the grammaticalisation chain of the combination of nouns another step may have to be added – after the fixation of the pattern into a compound, the modifying, non-head slot may tolerate other structural constituents which have been functionally downgraded (without any suggestions as to the nature of the downgrading mechanism) to acquire noun-like properties. This possibility does not violate or compromise the nature of compounding, since as Gaeta & Ricca (2009: 35) suggest compounds may be analyzed "by treating the properties of being a lexical unit and being the output of a morphological operation as independent". Moreover, compounding has been recognised as a 'pocket phenomenon' in language (Bauer 2001; Jackendoff 2009), where the rules of syntax do not apply.

Another plausible scenario, driven by economy principles and the minimax effect in language functioning is the condensation of phrasal/clausal constituents to elements of word building. In this case, the ratio of explicitness/implicitness is manipulated, so that a large amount of descriptive information is left out and delegated to pragmatic inferencing to achieve a labelling effect (the result of stereotyping/typifying).

Both scenarios are compatible with the understanding of language as a constructicon. After all, there seem not to be any restrictions as to the size or complexity of a construction (to the exclusion of psycholinguistic considerations of processing limitations), which allows for the existence of phrasal compounds which collapse features of different traditional structural elements.

6 Concluding remarks

One of the basic functions of word-formation objects, i.e. words, is the categorising function (Schmid 2007), tightly interwoven with the entrenchment of concepts. This is further supported by Bolozky's belief that "lexical formation is first and foremost semantically based and concept driven" (Bolozky 1999: 7).

Conceding that phrasal compounds have a unanimously acknowledged naming function leads to recognising their concept-creating or at least strongly typifying function, which is cognitively speaking tantamount to establishing a category. In the words of Hohenhaus (2005: 356) "Hypostatization is a side-effect of the naming function of word-formation, whereby the existence of a word seems to imply for speakers the existence in the real world of a single corresponding 'thing' or clearly delimited concept."

In a nutshell, the greatest driving force behind the (still limited) advent of phrasal compounds in Bulgarian is their type-creating power, be it metacommunicative, metonymy-driven or fictive. The pattern has been established and its instantiations share all properties of standard phrasal compounds in English and German, to the exclusion of headedness variability, which is characteristic of Bulgarian phrasal compounds only. Their smooth accommodation in the compounding network of the language can easily be explained in terms of the ratio between explicitness and implicitness which they provide as subschema instantiations of the subordinative, modifying constructional node within the compounding network.

In parallel to Ray Jackendoff and Eva Wittenberg's interlinguistic hierarchy of grammars (Jackendoff & Wittenberg 2012), we propose that there is a similar intra-language hierarchy of meaning packaging options whose choice depends on at least the following variables: genre, immediate situational context, speaker's preferences and linguistic background and the mode of interaction between interlocutors, which would determine the degree of explicitness necessitated in a given communicative exchange. Standard phrasal syntax and compounds are seen as alternative modes of packaging following different internal logics. In keeping with Jackendoff's (2009) contention that in compounds protosyntactic combinatorial patterns prevail, we believe that the syntax of a language has only an indirect influence on the shape and types of compounds in a given language mediated by the part-of-speech system with the concomitant inflectional morphology. Proto-syntax, as the alternative name for "a simpler grammar", is characterized according to Jackendoff (2009) and Jackendoff & Wittenberg (2012: 1) as an expression system which puts "more responsibility for understanding on pragmatics and understanding of context. As the grammar gets more complex, it provides more resources for making complex thoughts explicit." Even though Jackendoff & Wittenberg define the "hierarchy of grammars" as a continuum along which the grammatical systems of languages with different degrees of complexity can be arranged, we assume that it is possible for the different resources of a single language to be arranged into a grammar hierarchy, where different patterns for packaging meaning display properties that can be arranged along the scales of complexity and explicitness. When a compound is used, the relation of what is explicitly expressed to possible interpretations is effected by pragmatics and general experiential knowledge.

Answers to the questions raised in the introduction can only be provided after a longitudinal or cross-sectional study of PCs in Bulgarian is conducted within a decade and hopefully this is a promising continuation of the ongoing research

Alexandra Bagasheva

reported here.

Appendix: Phrasal compounds in Bulgarian in context

The majority of examples (21 to be precise) have been taken from Boyadžieva (2007) which presents a corpus study of Cosmopolitan BG for the period 2004-2005 is presented.

(2) Свали-го-съвет [Cosmopolitan, BG, March 2005: 113]

(3) Вземи-му-акъла-съвет [Cosmopolitan, August 2005: 45]

(4) Завърти-му-ума-посрещане [Cosmopolitan, BG, www]

(5) Промени-живота-си-предизвикателство [Cosmopolitan, BG, www]

(6) Прочети-му-мислите съвет [Cosmopolitan, BG, September 2004: 60]

(7) Предизвикай-го-да-говори-съвет [Cosmopolitan, BG, December 2004: 62]

(8) Често си спретват игри от типа
кой-пръв-ще-успее-да-пъхне-лед-в-ризата-на-другия.
[Cosmopolitan, BG, February 2005: 72]

(9) Тя може да те спаси в кризисни моменти – от неотложна нужда за посещение на зъболекар до внезапната поява на блуза, тип не-е-за-изпускане-независимо-от-цената. [Cosmopolitan, BG, www]

(10) Това определено не се простира отвъд факта
Боже-не-може-да-бъде!, харесвате едни и същи ястия и филми. [Cosmopolitan, BG, September 2004: 53]

(11) Ако си една средностатистическа жена, няма как стресът да не е станал второто ти Аз – без значение дали става дума за лаката му разновидност 'Боже-сетих-ли-се-да-изключа-котлона-днес' или за язво-формиращия вариант 'ей-тази-седмица-наистина-май-ще-ме-уволнят-или-зарежат-или-и-двете. [Cosmopolitan, BG, www]

(12)   Този антидепресант повишава нивото на допамин в мозъка, като по този начин осигурява един от най-коварните ефекти на цигарите – да-се-почувстваш-добре ефект. [Cosmopolitan, BG, July 2004: 129]

(13)   Така се елиминира напрежението ето-че-моментът-най-сетне-настъпи. [Cosmopolitan, BG, September 2005: 63]

(14)   Изпускането на парата твърде скоро може да е равносилно на направи-си-сам-проблеми-в-офиса ситуация . [Cosmopolitan, BG, December 2004: 105]

(15)   Как да доведеш нещата до щастлива развръзка за-вечни-времена. [Cosmopolitan, BG, www]

(16)   Целта е да преодолееш тютюнджийската абстиненция, докато се откачиш от навика с-цигара-в-ръка. [Cosmopolitan, BG, December 2004: 104]

(17)   Едва ли си даваш сметка, до каква степен лошият режим на хранене и предъвкването-между-другото на разни дреболии пречат на диетата ти. [Cosmopolitan, BG, September 2005: 119]

(18)   Като начало, молим ви, не си отглеждайте стърчащо-услужливо-дълго-нокътче на кутрето. Поддържайте ноктите си добре подрязани и чисти. [Grazia, BG, September 2004: 49]

(19)   Забелязала ли си, че ти се иска да си купиш нещо почти веднага след скандал с иначе-любимия-човек? [Cosmopolitan, BG, September 2005: 73]

(20)   Даже в по-либералните фирми и най-дребният намек "има нещо помежду им" кара колежките-кобри-по-душа да изпълзят от леговищата си.[Cosmopolitan, BG, December 2004: 104]

(21)   Просто-независеща-от-него-странност [COSMO men, August 2005: 4]

(22)   Ако шопингът все пак ти действа като мощна доза антидепресанти, има решение и то се нарича обикаляне-без-купуване решение. [Cosmopolitan, BG, September 2005: 73]

(23) След всички мнения какво трябва и не трябва да правиш, когато си на 20, главата ти се замайва и ти иде да се скриеш далеч от всички тези съветници и доброжелатели, които „само искат да знаят какво мислиш за бъдещето си" (http://www.cosmopolitan.bg/cosmo-zapovedi/11-neshta-za-koito-da-ne-se-obviniavash-na-20-18537.html, Cosmolitan BG 2016, last accessed 14 July 2016)

(24) Функцията „На този ден" е създадена, само за да те излага. (http://www.cosmopolitan.bg/svetut-okolo-teb/16-feisbuk-problema-koito-20-godishnite-sreshtat.html, Cosmolitan BG 2016, last accessed 14 July 2016)

(25) За съжаление дори възрастните понякога си правят детински шегички и нищо чудно да осъмнеш със статус „Обичам мазни, потни чичковци". (http://www.cosmopolitan.bg/svetut-okolo-teb/16-feisbuk-problema-koito-20-godishnite-sreshtat.html, Cosmolitan BG 2016, last accessed 14 July 2016)

(26) reach-in хладилници (Horeva, Ph.D., manuscript, Sofia University, 2015)

(27) roll-in хладилници (Horeva, Ph.D., manuscript, Sofia University, 2015)

(28) walk-in хладилници (Horeva, Ph.D., manuscript, Sofia University, 2015)

(29) море-слънце-пясък туризъм (Horeva, Ph.D., manuscript, Sofia University, 2015)

(30) ски-слънце-сняг туризъм (Horeva, Ph.D., manuscript, Sofia University, 2015)

References

Ackema, Peter & Ad Neeleman. 2004. *Beyond morphology: Interface conditions on word-formation*. Oxford: Oxford University Press.
Arcodia, Giorgio F., Nicola Grandi & Fabio Montermini. 2009. Hierarchical NN compounds in a cross-linguistic perspective. *Rivista di Linguistica* 21(1). 11–33.
Avramova, Cvetanka & Petya Osenova. 2003. Отново по въпроса за границата между сложна дума и словосъчетание (върху материал от най-новата българска лексика [Once again on the issue of the boundary between a compound and a phrase]. *Bulgarian* 1. 68–75. [In Bulgarian].

Bağrıaçık, Metin & Angela Ralli. 2015. Morphological vs. Phrasal compounds: Evidence from Modern Greek and Turkish. *STUF–Language Typology and Universals* 68. 323–357.

Bauer, Laurie. 2001. Compounding. In Martin Haspelmath, Ekkehard König, Wulf Oesterreicher & Wolfgang Raible (eds.), *Language typology and language universals*, 695–707. Berlin: de Gruyter.

Bauer, Laurie. 2009. Typology of compounds. In Rochelle Lieber & Pavol Štekauer (eds.), *The Oxford handbook of compounding*, 343–356. Oxford: Oxford University Press.

Bauer, Laurie & Elizaveta Tarasova. 2013. The meaning link in nominal compounds. *SKASE Journal of Theoretical Linguistics* 10(3). 1–18.

Bell, Melanie. 2011. At the boundary of morphology and syntax. Noun noun constructions in English. In Alexandra Galani, Hicks Glyn & George Tsoulas (eds.), *Morphology and its interfaces*, 137–167. Amsterdam/Philadelphia: John Benjamins Publishing Company.

Bisetto, Antonietta. 2015. Do Romance languages have phrasal compounds? A look at Italian. *STUF–Language Typology and Universals* 68. 395–419.

Bolozky, Shmuel. 1999. *Measuring productivity in word formation: The case of israeli Hebrew* (Studies in Semitic languages and linguistics). Leiden: Brill.

Booij, Geert E. 2007. *The grammar of words*. 2nd edn. Oxford: Oxford University.

Booij, Geert E. 2009a. Phrasal names: A constructionist analysis. *Word Structure* 2(2). 219–240.

Booij, Geert E. 2009b. Phrasal names: A constructionist analysis. *Word Structure* 2(2). 219–240.

Booij, Geert E. 2010. *Construction morphology*. Oxford et al.: Oxford University Press.

Botha, Rudolf P. 1981. A base rule theory of Afrikaans synthetic compounds. In Michael Moortgat, Harry van der Hulst & Teun Hoekstra (eds.), *The scope of lexical rules*, 1–77. Dordrecht: Foris.

Boyadžieva, Elly. 2007. Reflections on a new word-formation pattern in Bulgarian newspaper language. In Alexandra Bagasheva (ed.), *On Man and language. A festschrift to maya pencheva*, 232–244. Sofia: Sofia University Publishing House "St. Kliment Ohridski".

Bresnan, Joan & Sam Mchombo. 1995. The lexical integrity principle: Evidence from Bantu. *Natural language and linguistic theory* 13. 181–254.

Brezinski, Stefan. 2012. *Bulgarian speech and writing: How to speak and write correctly*. Sofia: Iztok-Zapad. [In Bulgarian].

Croft, William. 2001a. *Radical Construction Grammar: Syntactic theory in typological perspective.* Oxford: Oxford University Press.

Croft, William. 2001b. Radical construction grammar: Syntactic theory in typological perspective. In Lívia Körtvélyessy, Pavol Štekauer & Salvador Valera (eds.), *Word-formation across languages*, 1–29. Newcastle upon Tyne: Oxford University Press.

Croft, William. 2007. Construction grammar. In Dirk Geeraerts & Hubert Cuyckens (eds.), *The Oxford handbook of cognitive linguistics*, 463–508. Oxford: Oxford University Press.

Fried, Mirjam. 2013. Principles of constructional change. In Thomas Hoffmann & Graeme Trousdale (eds.), *The Oxford handbook of construction grammar*, 419–437. Oxford: Oxford University Press.

Gaeta, Livio & Davide Ricca. 2009. Composita solvantur: Compounds as lexical units or orphological objects? *Italian Journal of Linguistics* 21. 35–70.

Gagné, Christina & Edward Shoben. 1997. Influence of thematic relations on the comprehension of modifier-noun combinations. *Journal of Experimental Psychology: Learning, Memory, and Cognition* 23(1). 71–87.

Goldberg, Adele E. 2003. Constructions: A new theoretical approach to language. *Trends in Cognitive Sciences* 7. 219–224.

Goldberg, Adele E. 2006. *Constructions at work: The nature of generalization in language.* Oxford: Oxford University Press.

Guevara, Emilio & Sergio Scalise. 2009. Searching for universals in compounding. In Elisabetta Magni Scalise Sergio & Antonietta Bisetto (eds.), *Universals of language today*, 101–129. Berlin: Springer.

Halliday, Michael. 1994. *Introduction to functional grammar. 2nd ed.* London: Edward Arnold.

Halliday, Michael & Christian Matthiessen. 2014. *Halliday's introduction to functional grammar, 4th ed.* London / New York: Routledge.

Hawkins, John A. 1983. *Word order universals.* New York: Academic Press.

Hein, Katrin. 2015. *Phrasenkomposita im Deutschen. Empirische Untersuchung und konstruktionsgrammatische Modellierung* (Studien zur Deutschen Sprache 67). Tübingen: Narr.

Heine, Bernd & Tanya Kuteva. 2006. *The changing languages of Europe.* Oxford: Oxford University Press.

Heine, Bernd & Tanya Kuteva. 2009. The genesis of grammar: On combining nouns. In Rudie Botha & Henriette de Swart (eds.), *Language evolution: The view from restricted linguistic systems*, 139–177. Utrecht: LOT.

Heringer, Hans Jürgen. 1984. Wortbildung: Sinn aus dem Chaos. *Deutsche Sprache* 12. 1–13.

Hilpert, Martin. 2015. From hand-carved to computer-based: Noun-participle compounding and the upward strengthening hypothesis. *Cognitive Linguistics* 26(1). 113–147.

Hoffmann, Thomas & Graeme Trousdale. 2013. Construction grammar: Introduction. In Thomas Hoffmann & Graeme Trousdale (eds.), *The Oxford handbook of construction grammar*, 1–14. Oxford: Oxford University Press.

Hohenhaus, Peter. 1998. Non-lexicalizability as a characteristic feature of nonce word formation in English and German. *Lexicology* 4(2). 237–280.

Hohenhaus, Peter. 2005. Lexicalization and institutionalization. In Pavol Štekauer & Rochelle Lieber (eds.), *Handbook of Word-Formation*, 353–373. Berlin: Springer.

Hohenhaus, Peter. 2007. How to do (even more) things with nonce words (other than naming). In Judith Munat (ed.), *Lexical creativity, texts and contexts*, 15–38. Amsterdam/Philadelphia: John Benjamins Publishing Company.

Jackendoff, Ray. 2009. Compounding in the parallel architecture and conceptual semantics. In Rochelle Lieber & Pavol Štekauer (eds.), *The Oxford handbook of compounding*, 105–129. Oxford: Oxford University Press.

Jackendoff, Ray & Eva Wittenberg. 2012. http://ase.tufts.edu/cogstud/incbios/ RayJackendoff/recentpapers.htm, accessed 2016-07-14.

Kirova, Lyudmila. 2012. On a model of complex nomination entering Bulgarian via Turkish borrowings and its contemporary development. *LiterNet* 5. 1–7.

Krumova-Cvetkova, Liliya, Diana Blagoeva, Emiliya Pernishka Kolkovska & Maya Bozhilova. 2013. *Българска лексикология* [Bulgarian Lexicology]. Sofia: Akademichno izdatelstvo "Prof. Marin Drinov". [In Bulgarian].

Lampert, Martina. 2009. *Attention and recombinance. A Cognitive-Semantic investigation into morphological compositionality in English.* Frankfurt am Main: Peter Lang.

Lieber, Rochelle. 1988. Phrasal compounds and the morphology-syntax interface. *Chicago Linguistic Society* II Parasession on agreement in grammatical theory(24). 202–222.

Lieber, Rochelle. 1992. *Deconstructing morphology. Word formation in syntactic theory.* Chicago: University of Chicago Press.

Lieber, Rochelle & Sergio Scalise. 2006. The lexical integrity hypothesis in a new theoretical universe. *Lingue e Linguaggio* 5. 7–32.

Lipka, Leonard. 2002. *English lexicology.* Tübingen: Gunter Narr.

Alexandra Bagasheva

Masini, Francesca. 2009. Phrasal lexemes, compounds and phrases: A constructionist perspective. *Word Structure* 2(2). 254–271.

Meibauer, Jörg. 2007. How marginal are phrasal compounds? Generalized insertion, expressivity, and I/Q-interaction. *Morphology* 17. 233–259.

Meibauer, Jörg. 2015. On "R" in phrasal compounds – a contextualist approach. *Language Typology and Universals* 68(3). 241–261.

Murdarov, Vladko. 1983. *Съвременни словообразувателни процеси* [Contemporary Word-Formation Processes]. Sofia: Naouka i izkustvo. [In Bulgarian].

Ohnheiser, Ingeborg. 2015. Compounds and multi-word expressions in Slavic. In Peter O. Müller, Ingeborg Ohnheiser, Susan Olsen & Franz Rainer (eds.), *Word-Formation. An international handbook of the languages of Europe* (Handbücher zur Sprach- und Kommunikationswissenschaft / Handbooks of Linguistics and Communication Science 40.1), 757–779. Berlin: De Gruyter Mouton.

Olsen, Susan. 2015. Composition. In Peter Müller, Ingeborg Ohnheiser, Susan Olsen & Franz Rainer (eds.), *Word-Formation: An international handbook of the languages of Europe, vol. I*, 364–385. Berlin & Boston: Mouton de Gruyter.

Pafel, Jürgen. 2015. Phrasal compounds are compatible with Lexical Integrity. *Language Typology and Universals* 68. 263–280.

Pascual, Esther, Emilia Królak & Theo Janssen. 2013. Direct speech compounds: Evoking socio-cultural scenarios through fictive interaction. *Cognitive Linguistics* 24(2). 345–366.

Plag, Ingo. 2003. *Word-formation in English*. Cambridge: Cambridge University Press.

Radeva, Vasilka. 2007. *В света на думите* [In the World of Words]. Sofia: Sofia University Publishing House "St. Kliment Ohridski". [In Bulgarian].

Ralli, Angela. 2013a. Compounding and its locus of realization: Evidence from Greek and Turkish. *Word Structure* 6. 181–200.

Ralli, Angela. 2013b. *Compounding in Modern Greek* (Studies in Morphology 2). Dordrecht: Springer.

Renner, Vincent. 2015. *Extending the domain of contact-induced change in lexical morphology: A focus on pattern and process borrowing. Paper presented at the Workshop on Morphological Borrowing, Gothenburg, Sweden, 10-11 December 2015.*

Renner, Vincent. 2016. *Contact-induced morphostructural change: An overview. Paper presented at the 13th ESSE Conference, Galway, Ireland, 22-26 August 2016.*

Ryder, Mary Ellen. 1994. *Ordered chaos: The interpretation of English Noun-Noun compounds* (University of California Press Publications in Linguistics 123). Berkeley: University of California Press.

Sag, Ivan A., Hans C. Boas & Paul Kay. 2012. Introducing sign-based construction grammar. In Hans C. Boas & Ivan Sag (eds.), *Sign-Based construction grammar*, 1–29. Stanford, CA: CSLI Publications.

Sakel, Jeanette. 2007. Types of loan: Matter and pattern. In Yaron Matras & Jeanette Sakel (eds.), *Grammatical borrowing in crosslinguistic perspective*, 15–29. Berlin, New York: Mouton de Gruyter.

Scalise, Sergio & Emilio Guevara. 2006. Exocentric compounding in a typological framework. *Lingue e Linguaggio* 5(2). 185–206.

Schmid, Hans-Jörg. 2007. Entrenchment, salience and basic levels. In Dirk Geeraerts & Hubert Cuyckens (eds.), *The Oxford handbook of cognitive linguistics*, 117–138. Oxford: Oxford University Press.

Štekauer, Pavol. 1998. *An onomasiological theory of English Word-Formation*. Amsterdam/Philadelphia: John Benjamins.

Štekauer, Pavol. 2005. *Meaning predictability in Word-Formation*. Amsterdam/Philadelphia: John Benjamins.

Traugott, Elizabeth Closs & Graeme Trousdale. 2013. *Constructionalization and constructional changes*. Oxford: Oxford University Press.

Trips, Carola. 2012. Empirical and theoretical aspects of phrasal compounds: Against the 'syntax explains it all' attitude. In Angela Ralli, Geert Booij, Sergio Scalise & Athanasios Karasimos (eds.), *Online Proceedings of the eighth Mediterranean Morphology Meeting*, 322–346. Patras: University of Patras.

Trips, Carola. 2016. An analysis of phrasal compounds in the model of parallel architecture. In Pius ten Hacken (ed.), *The semantics of compounding*, 153–177. Cambridge: Cambridge University Press.

Vačkova, Kalina & Vasil Vačkov. 1998. Словообразуване и аналитизъм. Типологична обусловеност на някои словообразувателни процеси в съвременния български език Word-formation and analyticity. Typological conditioning of some word-formation processes in the Bulgarian language. *Slavic Philology* 22. 95–101. [In Bulgarian].

Vakareliyska, Cynthia & Vsevolod Kapatsinski. 2014. An Anglo-Americanism in Slavic morphosyntax: Productive [N[N]] constructions in Bulgarian. *Folia Linguistica* 48(1). 277–311.

Chapter 5

Modeling the properties of German phrasal compounds within a usage-based constructional approach

Katrin Hein

Institut für deutsche Sprache, Mannheim

This paper discusses phrasal compounds in German (e.g. "Man-muss-doch-über-alles-reden-können"-Credo, 'one-should-be-able-to-talk-about-everything motto'). It provides the first empirically based investigation and description of this word-formation type within the theoretical framework of construction grammar. While phrasal compounds pose a problem for "traditional" generative approaches, I argue that a usage-based constructional model (e.g. Langacker 1987; Goldberg 2006) which takes into consideration aspects of frequency provides a suitable approach to modeling and explaining their properties. For this purpose, a large inventory of phrasal compounds was extracted from the *German Reference Corpus* (DeReKo) and modeled as pairings of form and meaning at different levels of specificity and abstractness within a bottom-up process.

Overall, this paper not only presents a new and original approach to phrasal compounds, but also offers interesting perspectives for dealing with composition in general.

1 Introduction

This paper discusses so-called "phrasal compounds" (PCs) (e.g. *"Man-muss-doch-über-alles-reden-können"-Credo*, 'one should be able to talk about everything motto') or *"Second-Hand-Liebe"*, 'second-hand love'), which can be defined as "complex words with phrases in modifier position" (Meibauer 2003: 153; cf. Lawrenz 2006: 7). They are largely ignored in the research literature, although the study

Katrin Hein. Modeling the properties of German phrasal compounds within a usage-based constructional approach. In Carola Trips & Jaklin Kornfilt (eds.), *Further investigations into the nature of phrasal compounding*, 119–148. Berlin: Language Science Press. DOI:10.5281/zenodo.885123

of PCs is worthwhile in theoretical terms alone and sheds an important light on the process of composition in general.

Hein (2011) has shown that this word-formation type poses a problem for "traditional" generative approaches which assume a modular architecture of grammar and do not allow for "syntax *in* morphology". And even the approaches which can handle the formal generation of PCs because they provide for a non-linear, i.e. a recursive, interaction between morphology and syntax, fail to explain *why* a speaker chooses a PC instead of a prototypical N-N-compound like *Baumhaus* ('tree house').[1]

This paper argues that a usage-based constructional model (e.g. Langacker 1987; Goldberg 2006) which entails direct pairings of form and meaning ("constructions") and takes into consideration aspects of frequency, provides a suitable approach to modeling and explaining the properties of PCs. For this purpose, the findings of a broad empirical, construction-grammatical investigation are presented.

To gain new insights into the functioning of this word-formation type, I extracted a large number of German PCs from the *Deutsches Referenzkorpus* (DeReKo) (Institut für Deutsche Sprache 2011) in a first step. In a second step, an inventory of 1,576 individual nominal PCs was analyzed and modeled as pairings of form and meaning ("constructions") at different levels of specificity and abstractness within a bottom-up process. In addition, I will also relate the posited constructions within a so-called "constructicon" (e.g. Ziem & Lasch 2013: 95) to each other.

As neither an empirically based investigation nor a description of PCs within the theoretical framework of construction grammar has been provided so far, I will present a new and original approach to the word-formation type that offers interesting perspectives for dealing with composition in general.

---

[1] An exception is Meibauer (2007) who tries to give an explanation for the expressivity of PCs by adapting Levinson's (2000) "Theory of Generalized Conversational Implicatures". Moreover, Trips (e.g. Trips 2012; 2016) provides an analysis of PCs within Jackendoff's model of Parallel Architecture which allows her "to gain further insights into the question of why PCs are built at all by speakers/writers and why they are sometimes preferred over other options" (Trips 2012: 322).

2 The bottom-up model

2.1 Data – empirical basis

The data for my study has been extracted from the *German Reference Corpus* (DeReKo) (Institut für Deutsche Sprache 2011) which at that time comprised 5.4 billion words and "constitutes the largest linguistically motivated collection of contemporary German texts" (*Corpus Linguistics Programme Area* 2016: 2). Therefore, this investigation is based on written text. While DeReKo contains fictional, scientific and newspaper texts as well, I concentrated only on newspaper texts.

2.1.1 Data extraction

Technically speaking, the extraction of PCs from the corpus was done with the help of a perl script containing different types of regular expressions. This method has led to the extraction of 1,182,720 strings; as it is synonymous with searching for certain *surface forms*, it is clear that the search results did not only contain PCs, but also a large number of word strings which only *look like* PCs (e.g. street names consisting of three words with dashes between them). See Hein (2015: Chapter III.1) for a detailed explanation of how PCs can be found and extracted from DeReKo and for an overview of the complete corpus that has been compiled for my study.

2.1.2 Data selection and grouping

As the conducted bottom-up process or rather the underlying analyses are very complex, it was not possible to consider every single genuine PC comprised in the results extracted from DeReKo. In fact, I worked with an inventory of 1,576 nominal PCs (types), arguing that this inventory can be seen as an acceptably representative sample of the potential spectrum of nominal phrasal compounding.[2]

What criteria were applied for the compilation of this inventory, i.e. the corpus of the study? First, I attempted to consider the widest possible range of PCs. Second, I had to bear in mind the targeted bottom-up process: In order to model the properties of the word formation pattern within a bottom-up process, it is important to be able to work with different groups of compounds which share

---

[2] Only nominal PCs have been considered in the study. (See Hein (2015: Chapter III.2)) for a detailed description and a discussion of the analyzed inventory.

certain formal and/or semantic properties. As a starting point for compiling the corpus and its subgroups, I chose the properties of the head constituent.[3]

Overall, four different types of nominal heads – and consequently four main types of PCs – were considered:

1. PCs with a non-derived head noun;

2. PCs with a deadjectival head noun;

3. PCs with a desubstantival head noun;

4. PCs with a deverbal head noun.

Within those four main groups, I also tried to consider a variety of head constituents with different semantic/formal properties. This is why each main group of PCs is separated into several subgroups. Tables 1 to 4 try to illustrate the principle of compiling different PC-groups and PC-subgroups according to the properties of the head. (Note that the following lists are not complete – a detailed description of grouping and selecting the data can be found in Hein 2015: Part III).

Table 1: Group 1: PCs with a non-derived head noun

Subgroup[4]	PC-examples[5]
Concrete noun (absolute)	*Working-Class-Junge* ('working-class boy')[6] *Jeans-und-T-Shirt-Mädchen* *Zweite-Wahl-Obst*
Concrete noun (relative)[7]	*No-name-Vater* ('no-name father') *Kleine-Leute-Sohn* *Take-That-Kollege*
Abstract noun for the description of a point of view	*Entweder-Oder-Credo* ('either-or motto') *"Das-Boot-ist-voll"-Parole* *"Wer-macht-den-meisten-Lärm"-Devise*

---

[3] §2.4 will explain why it is plausible to start from the properties of the head when compiling the corpus and its subgroups.

Table 2: Group 2: PCs with a deadjectival head noun

Subgroup	PC-examples
Nomen Qualitatis	*Mir-doch-egal-Leichtigkeit* ('I-don't-care ease') *50er-Jahre-Naivität* *Trinkmilchjoghurt-mit-Erdbeergeschmack–Rosa* *Frau-Holle-Blau*
Denomination of a person	*Formel-1-Liebling* ('Formula 1 favorite') *"Im-fremden-Bett-schlaf-ich-immer-schlecht-* *Sensibelchen"*
Valent noun	*Prinz-Harry-Besessenheit* ('Prince Harry obsession') *Zwölf-Minuten-Länge*

Table 3: Group 3: PCs with a desubstantival head noun

Subgroup	PC-examples
Denomination of a person	*High-Society-Fräulein* ('high-society lady') *"Morgens-Fango/Abends-Tango-Rentner"* *Bad-Taste-Komiker*
Collective noun	*Zwei-Klassen-Menschheit* ('two-class mankind') *Vor-68er-Studentenschaft*
Relative noun	*Ost-West-Freundschaft* ('East-West friendship') *Cosa-Nostra-Häuptling* *Schütze-des-Fünf-zu-null-Mutti*

---

[5]Depending on the properties of the head.

[6]All the examples used in this study are taken from DeReKo (Institut für Deutsche Sprache 2011) and are cited in their original writing (hyphens, type and position of quotation marks, etc.). See Hein (2015: Chapter III.2.2) for a discussion of criteria linked to the PC-status (e.g. the underlying concept of phrases and sentences).

[7]In this as well as the following tables only the first example of each type of PC is translated into English.

[8]For each PC-main-type I have tried to consider valent/relative and non-valent head nouns.

Katrin Hein

Table 4: Group 4: PCs with a deverbal head noun

Subgroup	PC-examples
Nomen Agentis	*Tour-de-France-Kenner* ('Tour-de-France expert') *Rote-Rosen-Verkäufer* *Immer-mal-wieder-Raucher*
Nomen Loci	*Dreieinhalb-Zimmer-Bleibe* ('three-and-a-half-room apartment') *60er-Jahre-Siedlung*
Nomen Actionis	*Heile-Welt-Bedürfnis* ('rosy-world desire') *"Dumme-Jungen-Gequatsche"* *"Null Bock"-Verhalten* *Ich-habe-es-ja-gesagt-aber-ihr-habt-nicht-auf-mich-gehört-Gerede*
Nomen Acti	*Kain-und-Abel-Tat* ('Cain-and-Abel deed') *"Habemus Papam"-Rede*

2.2 Scheme of analysis

To understand the bottom-up process, not only is the arrangement of the data (cf. the previous §2.1) important, but also the scheme of analysis which was used to classify the PCs from the corpus and to describe them as pairings of form and meaning requires a brief explanation.[9]

Overall, a variety of formal and semantic properties of PCs is involved, e.g. syntactic and pragmatic properties of the nonhead constituent, valence properties of the head constituent as well as the semantic relation between the two constituents, i.e. the semantic role adopted by the nonhead. Many of these properties are also relevant for the description of prototypical compounds like *Baumhaus* ('tree house') – thus the innovativeness of my approach is not caused by creating completely new categories, but by the way those categories are combined with each other.

In accordance with the theoretical background of my work – i.e. the construction grammatical framework – PCs are described as direct pairings of form and

---

[9] In this paper I can only give a brief *simplified* overview over the categories I used. Cf. Hein (2015: Chapter III.2.2) for a more elaborated description.

meaning.[10] This is why the levels and categories of analysis are divided into two
groups: properties for the description of the form side vs. properties for the description of the meaning side of PCs. Tables 5 and 6 list the levels of analysis
in accordance with this distinction and give some *examples* for corresponding
categories and PCs.

Table 5: Description of the *form side* of PCs

Level of analysis	Category (examples)	PC (examples)
Syntactic properties of the nonhead	Phrase_NP	*Sechseinhalb-Tage-Woche* ('six-and-a-half-day week'); *Harte-Jungs-Gerede; Söhne-Mannheims-Jahr;*
	Sentence_declarative	*Ich-esse-alles-Geplapper*
	...	('I-eat-everything talk')
Phraseological properties of the nonhead	Lexicalized freely formed	*Tour-de-France-Monat Schmeiß-keine-Plastiktüten-in-den-Wald-Gerede*
	...	
Pragmatic properties of the nonhead	= Communicative minimal unit (in the sense Zifonun et al. 1997: 86)	*Alles-oder-Nichts-Devise* ('all-or-nothing slogan'); *"Soldaten sind Mörder"-Jahr*
	≠ Communicative minimal unit	*"Zwei-Minuten-Sache"* ('two-minute affair'); *Kaffee-und-Kuchen-Rentner*
Valence properties of the head	valent/relational	*Ost-West-Freundschaft* ('East-West friendship'); *Stop-and-Go-Tauglichkeit*
	non-valent	*60er-Jahre-Siedlung*
	...	('1960s-housing')

---

[10] Note that my study is based on a wide understanding of meaning which includes semantic
aspects as well as pragmatic aspects. This is in line with the construction grammatical rejection
of the strict separation between semantics and pragmatics (cf. Kay 1997: 123).

[11] The specific semantic relations/roles are divided into four more abstract groups ("rough patterns") which Eichinger (2000: 36 f.; 118 ff; 184) developed for prototypical N-N-compounds. I

Table 6: Description of the *meaning side* of PCs

Level of analysis	Category (examples)	PC (examples)
Semantics (1): How can the meaning of the PC be accessed? / Is its interpretation influenced by valence properties of the head?	Synthetic compound	*Zehn-Minuten-Länge* ('ten-minute duration'); *Alles-mögliche-Verkäufer* *Last-Minute-Verkäufer* ('last-minute seller')
	Non-synthetic compound	*Lange-Frisch-Milch*
Semantics (2): Specific description of the relation between the two constituents and the role taken by the nonhead	1) subject-orientated[11]	1) *Ein-Mann-Zuständigkeit* ('*one-man responsibility*') (Agens)
	2) object-orientated	2) *"Ernte 23"-Raucher* ('*Ernte 23 smoker*') (Patient)
	3) adverbial	3) *Drei-Wochen-Mitgliedschaft* ('three-month membership') (temporal); *Auf-der-Bank-Schläfer* (local);
	4) attribute-like	4) *"Pretty Woman"-Phänomen* ('pretty-woman phenomenon') (theme); *200-Häuser-Siedlung* (constitutional); *Trinkmilchjoghurt-mit-Erdbeergeschmack-Rosa* (comparative); "Früher-war-alles-besser"-Gerede (explicative)

2.3 Theoretical assumptions

As noted above, the aim of my study is to model the properties of PCs within a usage-based constructional approach. For these purposes, the 1,576 PC-types of the corpus (cf. §2.1) are modeled as constructions at different levels of specificity and abstractness within a bottom-up process. Which theoretical assumptions are crucial for this undertaking?

The basic idea for my approach is formed by Booij's (2010: 3) observation "that word formation patterns can be seen as abstractions over sets of related words". This means that complex words – like PCs – are licensed by abstract schemata/ patterns. Between a complex word and the scheme that allows for its formation, a relation of "instantiation" is assumed.

Moreover, it is important to underline that I adopt the central assumption of usage-based theories that frequency aspects have an influence on the development of such abstract patterns (e.g. Ziem & Lasch 2013: 38). This assumption is, among others, based on the psychological phenomenon of "entrenchment" that refers to the development of "cognitive routines" (Langacker 1988: 130): "The occurrence of psychological events leaves some kind of trace that facilitates their re-occurrence. Through repetition, even a highly complex event can coalesce into a well-rehearsed routine that is easily elicited and reliably executed." Therefore, a linguistic structure that is "pre-packaged" because of its entrenchment can be perceived as a holistic unit (Langacker 2000: 3f).

According to the significance ascribed to frequency, I adopt Goldberg's (2006: 5) definition of the notion "construction" in which non-predictability is not the only crucial criterion anymore:[12]

> Any linguistic pattern is recognized as a construction as long as some aspect of its form or function is not strictly predictable from its component parts or from other constructions recognized to exist. In addition, patterns are stored as constructions even if they are fully predictable as long as they occur with sufficient frequency.

The extent to which the pattern "phrasal compounding" fulfills this criterion of frequency and productivity (cf. Booij 2010: 51f) has been shown in Hein

---

will refer to those abstract groups in §3.1. A detailed description of the assignment of semantic roles/relations to those abstract groups can be found in Hein (2015: Chapter III.2.2.2.2).

[12] Cf. Hein (2015: Chapter II.2) for a detailed discussion of different definitions for the notion of construction and their applicability for PCs.

(2015)[13]: While it is only *theoretically hypothesized* in the literature that phrasal compounding is a productive word formation pattern (c.f. Lieber 1992, Meibauer 2003), I conducted an empirical study to check whether PCs have hapax-status in my corpus. The latter is a productivity measure proposed by Baayen (1992); so-called "hapax legomena" are defined as the "the number of once-words" (Tuldava 2005: 28) within a specific textual context. This measure indicates if "the language user comes across new types from time to time" (Booij 2010: 52; cf. Ziem & Lasch 2013: 106).

The results of my productivity study can only be presented briefly at this point (cf. Hein 2015: Chapter III.3.2 for the complete study): Counting the absolute frequencies of the 1,576 PC-types from the corpus, i.e. counting the number of tokens for each type in the corpus, showed that 75% have the status of hapaxes. Although 25% of the PC-types occur more than once in my corpus, one can conclude that phrasal compounding is a productive word formation pattern for two reasons: Taking a closer look at the words which occur more than once in my corpus shows that among them are many completely lexicalized forms like *35-Stunden-Woche* ('35-hour week') (4.485 tokens) – it should be clear that completely lexicalized PCs can't be "new types". Moreover, the high frequency types do not have a large scattering across different head nouns (here again, a dominance of the head noun *Woche* can be stated).

All in all, the empirical investigation of productivity indicates that it is plausible to ascribe the theoretical status of a construction to the general pattern 'phrasal compounding' within a usage-based constructional approach.

2.4 Modeling of the data

Finally, I will show how the empirically gained data and its subcategorization, the scheme of analysis and the theoretical assumptions work together in the bottom-up process.

Generally speaking, the bottom-up process takes the 1,576 individual complex words as a starting point. At first, each of them is described as a direct pairing of form and meaning properties, applying the scheme of analysis that has been explained in §2.2. I then attempt to make generalizations across groups of PCs that share some of the crucial formal/semantic properties of their head constituent (cf. §2.1.2). The underlying working hypothesis is that PCs with an identical or formal/semantic comparable head possess commonalities on their meaning

---

[13] To what extent PCs fulfill the criterion of non-predictability is discussed in Hein (2015: Chapter II.2.2.3).

side which can be captured via constructions. This hypothesis is plausible insofar as the head is crucial for the basic semantic interpretation of determinative
compounds (e.g. Fandrych & Thurmair 1994: 38) in general.[14] At this point it
becomes clear why the properties of the head were chosen as a starting point for
the compilation of different PC-subgroups (cf. §2.1) in my study.

On the one hand, the procedure sketched out allows me to posit a variety
of semantically orientated sub-constructions. On the other hand, I will try to
stipulate an abstract construction for the word-formation type by generalizing
about the posited sub-constructions. This means that at the highest point of the
bottom-up model, an abstract representation for phrasal compounding is carved
out on the basis of the individual words and the generalizations that are possible
within the PC-main-groups and the PC-subgroups.

According to the theoretical assumptions which have been discussed in the
previous section (cf. §2.3), it is important to underline that aspects of frequency
play an important role for the identification of strong form-meaning-correlations
in the data. Therefore in this study, constructions are only posited for such correlations which occur with a sufficient frequency.[15] As becomes evident in §3,
the absolute frequency is not the only aspect crucial in this context. In addition,
the productivity of observable form-meaning-correlations has to be considered
(i.e.: Are certain patterns limited to a very special type of head noun, or are they
instantiable for different types of heads?).

What does the concrete application of the process described above look like?
After the division of the corpus data into the four main groups (non-derived vs.
de-adjectival vs. desubstantival vs. deverbal head, cf. §2.1.2), all PCs with the
same lexeme in head position (e.g. all PCs with the head noun *Rot*) are analyzed
according to the scheme of analysis sketched out in §2.2 in a first step. In doing
so, similarities on the meaning side can be carved out and captured within more
abstract generalizations.

In a second step, this procedure is transferred to groups of PCs with a semantically similar head noun (e.g. all PCs with a nonhead describing a color /all PCs
with a Nomen Qualitatis head). In a third step, I am trying to generalize over *all*
members of one main group (i.e. all PCs with a de-adjectival nominal head). This
means that I am asking whether all PCs from one main group display a) generaliz-

---

[14] From my point of view, it is beyond doubt that PCs are word formation products, i.e. genuine
compounds (cf. Schlücker 2012: 12 for a comparable argumentation).

[15] In consideration of the fact that "real language" is characterized by variation and special cases,
the applicability of this "frequency criterion" is not always easy. In short, it's the question of
what can count as "enough frequent" to stipulate a construction which is crucial here. Cf. Hein
(2015) for a critical discussion of the applicability of this frequency criterion on authentic data.

able commonalities and b) display certain distinctive form-meaning-correlations that are characteristic for this special group.

The fourth – and last – step is to explore whether it is possible to stipulate one (or more) form-meaning pairings that can likewise display the properties of *all* PCs from my corpus.

3 Results

In this section, the main *results* of the bottom-up process described in the previous section are carved out. First of all, it is important to underline that it was indeed possible to structure the empirically gained, broad inventory of 1,576 PCs with the help of pairings of form and meaning at varying degrees of abstraction (cf. §4 for theoretical implications of this finding). Due to the lack of space, I cannot provide a complete reproduction of all results gained in Hein (2015). Rather, I will focus on three main aspects: First, I will present some central universal patterns of phrasal compounding (§3.1). In this context, I will discuss quite specific constructions as well as more abstract constructions. Moreover, the most central representation for the pattern phrasal compounding is carved out (§3.2). Finally, I will sketch out how the stipulated constructions can be related to each other (§3.3).

3.1 Universal patterns of phrasal compounding

3.1.1 Fine-grained generalization

The corpus-based investigation points out that there are various, non-restricted possibilities concerning the meaning side of PCs: All the semantic roles/relations (cf. the examples in table 6) which play a role for prototypical determinative compounds like *Baumhaus* ('tree house') seem to be instantiable in the pattern "phrasal compounding", too.[16] At the same time, it becomes apparent that there are a very limited number of specific meaning types which can be labeled as particularly universal/established for phrasal composition. Being universal/established is justified in two respects within a usage-based approach: First, in the corpus there are a high number of concrete instantiations for the patterns listed below. Second, those patterns of meaning are productive insofar as there are no

---

[16] The form side of nominal PCs is likewise principally open. My investigation clearly shows that phrasal compounding is open to all types of phrases/sentences in nonhead position (cf. Hein 2015: Chapter III.3.1.2).

or almost no restrictions for their instantiation. This means that those meaning patterns are not limited to constituents with very specific properties.

Talking about universal patterns of phrasal compounding under the perspective of fine-grained generalization, the reading "explicative" has to be mentioned in the first place. Crucial for this pattern is the complete (semantic) spelling out of the constituent B through the constituent A. For example, *Alles-oder-Nichts-Devise* ('all-or-nothing slogan') is a Devise which is characterized by the attitude 'Alles oder nichts'. Figure 1 illustrates how the formal and semantic properties of the PCs with a corresponding reading can be captured via a construction:

Explicative-Construction
[[Sentence/Sentence-ellipt /Sentence-Scheme-ellipt /Verb Group$_{+CM}$/Phrase$_{+CM}$]-Proper Name – [Substantive]$_{+/-valent}$]$_{N; PC}$

e.g. *Alles-oder-Nichts-Devise* ('all-or-nothing slogan')
"Im-fremden-Bett-schlaf-ich-immer-schlecht-Sensibelchen"
"Schaun-wir-mal-Franz"
"Zu mir oder zu dir"-Gequatsche
Wer-kriegt-wen-Albernheit
Coca-Cola-trink-Unterhaltungs-Freundschaft
Work-in-Progress-Dings
Zurück-zu-den-Grundsätzen-Rede
Keine-Drogen-Geschwätz
Sowohl-Als-auch-Verhalten
Ich-will-mir-was-Gutes-Tun-Bedürfnis
"Vater ist der Beste"-Stolz
Is-was?-Dreistigkeit

Figure 1: Explicative-Construction

This reading becomes manifest in PCs whose first constituent is an entire sentence (e.g. *Ich-will-mir-was-Gutes-Tun-Bedürfnis*, 'I-want-to-do-something-good-for-me need'), an elliptical sentence (*"Zu mir oder zu dir"-Gequatsche*, 'To-me-or-to-you talk'), an elliptical sentence scheme (e.g. *Sowohl-Als-auch-Verhalten*, 'both-sides-of-the-coin behavior'), a verb group in the sense of Zifonun et al. (1997) (e.g. *Coca-Cola-trink-Unterhaltungs-Freundschaft*, 'Coca-Cola-drinking-discussion friendship') or a phrase which has the status of a communicative minimal unit (CM) (e.g. *Keine-Drogen-Geschwätz*, 'no-drugs talk').[17]

---

[17] Cf. Hein (2015: Chapter III.2.2.1.2) for an explanation of the underlying phrase concept.

Moreover, this reading occurs in *all* four main groups (cf. §2.1.2), i.e. in PCs whose second constituent is a non-derived noun (e.g. *"Schaun-wir-mal-Franz"*, 'let's-see-what-happens Franz'), a deadjectival noun (*"Vater ist der Beste"-Stolz*, 'father-is-the-best pride'), a desubstantival noun (*Coca-Cola-trink-Unterhaltungs-Freundschaft*) or a deverbal noun (*Sowohl-Als-auch-Verhalten*). This variety of formal types linked to an explicative reading underlines the productivity of the pattern. The cognitive plausibility of the form-meaning pair stipulated in Figure 1 is also strengthened by the fact that 331 of the 1,576 PCs from my corpus are instantiations of this construction; only the reading "theme" (cf. Figure 3) is more frequent in my investigation. Moreover, the Explicative-Construction is a very strong construction insofar as it displays an *inevitable* correlation between form and meaning, e.g. all PCs with the illustrated form have an explicative meaning. In my investigation, this is a unique feature of the Explicative-Construction.

There are two more specific readings which occur in all four main groups, i.e. which are not restricted to specific types of head nouns and can therefore be labeled as universal patterns of phrasal compounding: the reading "domain" and the reading "theme". Instead of an inevitable form-meaning correlation, the corresponding constructions in Figures 2 and 3 display form-meaning correlations which can be regarded as very probable if one considers aspects of frequency and productivity.

The reading "domain" is characterized by the creation of a reference field for the head noun B through the first constituent A and occurs 205 times in the corpus. Its form side is converse to the form side of the Explicative-Construction: It is limited to phrases without CM-status and sentences that are proper names.

The semantic reading "theme" is the most frequent reading in the corpus (405 instantiations) and is characterized by the slogan-like spelling out of a communicative or artistic concept in B through the first constituent A.

3.1.2 Coarse-grained generalization

At the center of this section are universal patterns of phrasal compounding that are gained through coarse-grained generalization over the observable form-meaning correlations in the corpus.

They can be understood as the result of generalizing over the more specific form-meaning correlations of the type presented in the previous section. While the meaning side of the constructions in Figures 1 to 3 was described with the help of specific semantic relations/roles, I will work with more abstract semantic descriptions below: As already mentioned in §2.2 ("scheme of analysis"), I assign the specific semantic relations/roles to four more abstract groups ("rough

Domain-Construction

[[Phrase-CM/Sentence+Proper Name] – [Substantive]+/-valent]N; PC

e.g. *Upper-Class-Mädchen* ('upper-class girl')
Tour-de-France-Woche
Berlin-Mitte-Phänomen
Take-That-Kollege
"Big-Brother"-Liebling
Kopf-Rumpf-Länge
Au-pair-Fräulein
Trimm-Dich-Verhalten

Figure 2: Domain-Construction

Theme-Construction

[[Phrase-CM/Infinitive-coordinated/Verb Group-CM /Sentence+Proper Name] – [Substantive]+/-valent]N; PC

e.g. *Happy-Mosel-Jahr* ('Happy Mosel Year')
"La Bohème"-Jahr
Don-Quijote-Sujet
Kosten-Nutzen-Devise
"Holy-Bandits"-Motto
Vorher-nachher-Peinlichkeit
Wild-West-Sportler
Wald-und-Wiesen-Italiener
Fast-Food-Zeugs
Achse-des-Bösen-Rede
"Stop-and-Go"-Verhalten
"Hilfe-Such-Verhalten"

Figure 3: Theme-Construction

patterns") that Eichinger (2000: 36 f.; 118 ff.; 184) developed for prototypical compounds:

1. subject-orientated patterns;

2. object-orientated patterns;

3. adverbial patterns;

4. attribute-like patterns.

Two questions are crucial in this context: Is there a distinguishing abstract pattern for each of the four main groups of PCs, i.e. is it crucial for the meaning side if the head-noun is non-derived, deadjectival, desubstantival or deverbal? And which of Eichinger's "rough patterns" can count as the most established pattern for phrasal compounding?

First of all, it has to be emphasized that there are instantiations for all four "rough patterns" in the corpus of this investigation[18] – as already stated in §3.1.1, phrasal compounding is open for the realization of all semantic relations that one can find in prototypical determinative compounds. Thus, the following form-meaning correlation has to be stated at the highest point of the bottom-up model:

Subject-orientated - / Object-orientated - / Adverbial - / Attribute-like -Construction

$[[Syntagma] – [Substantive]]_{N; PC; +/-SynthC}$[19]

Figure 4: Subject-orientated - / Object-orientated - / Adverbial - / Attribute-like -Construction

While the pattern in Figure 4 illustrates all *potentially formable* meaning-types of PCs, the realization of one semantic pattern – attribute-like – has to be labeled as particularly likely and universal. This becomes clear when one looks at the frequencies in the corpus: 1,315 of the 1,576 PC-types are instantiations of the "rough pattern" attribute-like. However, the attribute-like-reading is not only frequent, but also productive insofar as there seem to be no restrictions for its instantiation: It is instantiated in all four main groups, i.e. this reading occurs

---

[18] For example, the Explicative-Construction stipulated in Figure 1 is an instantiation of the more abstract Attribute-like-Construction.

[19] "SynthC" is used as abbreviation for "synthetic compound".

for all types of nominal heads. Moreover, it is also the most frequent reading when one looks at the four subgroups separately. Last but not least, there are instantiations of this pattern in each single subgroup (e.g. concrete vs. abstract noun etc.) within the four main groups (cf. the description of data grouping in §2.1.2). All in all, those observations about the frequency, the productivity and the balanced distribution of this "rough pattern" within the corpus make it plausible to stipulate the following construction:

Attribute-like-Construction

Form   [[Syntagma] – [Substantive]_{non-derived, de-adjectival, de-substantival}
or de-verbal; +/-valent] N; PC

Meaning Comprises semantic relations/roles like "domain", "explicative", "theme", "constitutional" etc.

e.g. *Wild-West-Sportler* ('wild-west athlete')
"Im-fremden-Bett-schlaf-ich-immer-schlecht-Sensibelchen"
Is-was?-Dreistigkeit
Take-That-Kollege
Zweite-Wahl-Obst

Figure 5: Attribute-like-Construction

With the lowest probability, the rough pattern "adverbial" becomes manifest in PCs: The corpus comprises only 50 types with this reading. Moreover, adverbial readings occur only in two of the four main groups in exemplary fashion, i.e. with sufficient frequency and balanced distribution. As can be seen in Figure 6, my investigation points out that an adverbial relation between the two constituents is predominantly restricted to PCs with desubstantival or deverbal nominal head.[20] The construction in Figure 6 is also less universal than the construction in Figure 5 insofar as adverbial readings are restricted to a few quite specific semantic heads within the two main groups "desubstantival" and "deverbal".

---

[20] This doesn't mean that there is absolutely no evidence for PCs with an adverbial reading and a non-derived or de-adjectival head noun. Rather the number of such cases is so rare that it is not justifiable within a usage-based-approach to integrate this possible correlation into a representation that raises the claim to reflect established form-meaning correlations.

Katrin Hein

Adverbial-Construction

Form   [[Phrase] – [Substantive]de-substantival/deverbal]N; PC; +/-SynthC
Meaning   Comprises semantic relations/roles like "temporal", "local",
              "causal" etc.

e.g. *Drei-Wochen-Mitgliedschaft* ('three-week membership')
Open-Air-Schläfer

Figure 6: Adverbial-Construction

Though the form-meaning pairing is not completely universal, its status as a construction is supported by a very distinct, homogeneous form side – only phrases, but no sentences can occur in the non-head position.

What conclusions can be drawn from the bottom-up model about the instantiation of subject- and object-orientated semantic patterns?

At first glance, subject-orientated readings seem to be quite common in phrasal compounding: With 128 corresponding PCs, subject-orientated readings occur at the second-most in the corpus, followed by object-orientated readings with 83 corresponding PCs. As it is assumed that in determinative compounds the exploitation of the subject-position is less common than the exploitation of the object-position as a matter of principle (cf. Eichinger 2000: 131), this is a surprising finding. But a closer look at the results shows that the frequency of subject-oriented readings is caused by a high-frequent occurrence in two specific subgroups within the main group "non-derived noun" (abstract nouns which describe a point of view; relational concrete nouns). For this reason, the frequency of subject-orientated readings in my corpus should not be overrated.

Nonetheless, subject-orientated readings occur in all four main groups, i.e. there are no restrictions for the head-noun. However, as represented in Figure 7, PCs with a subject-orientated reading predominantly exhibit a *valent* head noun, i.e. a head noun which has a clearly agentive component (e.g. *Maxime* in *Blaue-Reiter-Maxime*, 'Blaue-Reiter maxim').

The instantiation of the object-orientated pattern is blocked for PCs with a non-derived head noun in my study, while it is very rare (only 3 corresponding forms in the corpus) in PCs with desubstantival head nouns. This explains why in Figure 8 the object-orientated pattern is correlated to compounds with deadjec-

---

Subject-orientated-Construction

Form   [[Syntagma]-CM – [Substantive]+valent/agentive]N; PC; +/- SynthC

Meaning   Comprises semantic relations/roles like "Agens", "Experiencer", "Possessor" etc.

e.g. *Vater-Sohn-Freundschaft* ('father-son friendship')
Ein-Mann-Zuständigkeit

Figure 7: Subject-orientated-Construction

Object-orientated-Construction

Form   [[Syntagma]-CM – [Substantive]de-adjectival/deverbal; +valent]N; PC; SynthC

Meaning   Comprises semantic relations/roles like "Patient", "Co-Patient", "Stimulus" etc.

e.g. *Rote-Rosen-Verkäufer* ('red-roses seller')
"Don Quichotte"-Dichter

Figure 8: Object-orientated-Construction

tival or deverbal head noun. In other words, this meaning predominantly occurs in PCs whose head noun is not an "originary substantive" (cf. Hölzner 2007: 235). Considering the valence properties of this type of nouns, this outcome is to be expected.

In conclusion, it has to be stated that there are two kinds of PCs where the maximal meaning potential (cf. Figure 4) is realized in an exemplary manner: PCs with desubstantival and PCs with deverbal head noun. PCs with deadjectival head noun occur with a relatively broad meaning spectrum, but they are excluded from the exemplary realization of adverbial patterns. The biggest limitations have to be posited for PCs with a non-derived head noun: Such forms are excluded from the exemplary realization of adverbial and object-orientated readings.

Overall, these findings show that the abstract properties of the head noun are crucial for the meaning potential which can be realized in a PC. Moreover, taking the formal and semantic properties of the head as starting point for the bottom-up model (cf. §2.1.2) appears to be particularly suitable to explain the formal and semantic spectrum of PCs systematically.

Therefore, the working hypothesis presented in §2.4 has been verified.

3.2 Highest level of abstraction: The most abstract form-meaning pairing for the word formation pattern "phrasal compounding"

In §3.1, pairings of form and meaning at different levels of specificity and abstractness have been presented. This section attempts one final, even bigger, step towards generalizations by investigating the following question: Through which combination of highly general form and meaning properties is the pattern "phrasal compounding" characterized?

Figure 9 subsumes all the properties which have been worked out within the bottom-up process. Therefore, it claims to represent the properties of all 1,576 PCs from the corpus and consequently – as I argue that the analyzed inventory is representative for the whole word formation pattern – the properties of phrasal compounding in general. It is important to note that I will focus on such aspects which have been carved out *empirically* in my study. Thus, the representation in Figure 9 is not complete. Cf. Hein (2015: Chapter II.2.2.2.) for a theoretic discussion of further aspects which are relevant for an abstract constructional representation of PCs.

The connection of form and meaning aspects in Figure 9 is an adequate, highly abstract representation for the properties of phrasal compounding. But that does not mean that the spectrum of PCs is completely homogeneous: I argue that the PC-spectrum can be divided into two types, i.e. there exist two different underlying constructions for the pattern at a more specific level. This assumption is a) based on the results of my empirical analyses and b) also justified by theoretical assumptions spelled out in Hein (2015: Chapter II.2.2).

The two specific PC-constructions can be distinguished from each other with the help of the syntactic properties of the first constituent: Compounds whose first constituent is formed by a sentence/a sentence-like structure or a phrase with the status of a CM are always linked to an explicative reading (Figure 10). In contrast, the meaning side of compounds with a different syntactic unit in non-head-position is much more open i.e. variable (cf. Figure 11): Only an explicative

---

[21]LE = linking element.

PC-Construction (empirically carved out aspects)		
Form	Structure	$[[\text{Syntagma}]_{+/\text{-lexicalized}}$ $[+/\text{-LE}^{21}]$ $[\text{Substantive}]_{\text{non-der./de-adj./de-subst./}}$ $_{\text{deverb.; }+/\text{-valent}}]_{\text{N; PC; }+/\text{- SynthC}}$
	Gender/Part of Speech	like second constituent
Meaning	Semantic	Specification of the second constituent through the first constituent: instantiation of subject-orientated, object-orientated, attribute-like and adverbial patterns Open relation between the two constituents (Relevant factors for interpretation: valence grammatical properties of the head; lexical properties of the head; conceptual knowledge about the constituents; discourse knowledge; encyclopedic knowledge)

Figure 9: PC-Construction (empirically carved out aspects)

reading is blocked here. As a consequence, the interpretation of the complex word is made accessible through basic semantic relations in the first case, while in the latter case basic semantic relations as well as valence grammatical properties of the head noun can form the starting point for the interpretation.

The two constructions differ also in the realization of linking elements (no linking elements are possible for Figure 10, while Figure 11 *potentially* allows for the realization of linking elements). Moreover, there is an important difference regarding their pragmatic properties: First, it has been theoretically argued in Hein (2015: Chapter II.2.2.2.4) that the adoption of specific communicative functions in

---

[19]The properties which are subsumed in Figure 9 hold for both sub-constructions and are not repeated in Figures 10 and 11.

[20]Cf. Lawrenz (2006: 213 ff.) for further remarks concerning the property of PCs to adopt specific communicative functions.

Explicative-Construction (Attribute-like-Construction)[19]

Form	Structure	[[Sentence / sentence-like structure / Phrase$_{+CM}$] – [Substantive]]$_{N; PC; - SynthC}$
Meaning	Pragmatic	+ specific communicative functions in the sense of Jakobson (1960)[20] {appellative/expressive/phatic/referential/ poetic/code} More expressive than prototypical determinative compounds: highly expressive

e.g. *Alles-oder-Nichts-Devise* ('all-or-nothing slogan')
"Im fremden-Bett-schlaf-ich-immer-schlecht-Sensibelchen"
Is-was?-Dreistigkeit

Figure 10: Explicative-Construction (Attribute-like-Construction)

the sense of Jakobson (1960) is limited to PCs with CMs in nonhead position (e.g. *Schmeiß-keine-Plastiktüte-in-den-Wald-Gerede* ('don't-throw-plastic bags-in-the-woods talk') – appellative function). Moreover, I assume that this type of PC (Figure 10) causes stronger effects of expressivity than PCs whose first constituent is not a CM (cf. Hein 2015: Chapter II.2.2.2.3).[24]

3.3 Modeling the relation between PC-constructions with different degrees of abstractness: "Constructicon"

Section 3.1 and 3.2 presented the most important constructions that I carved out in Hein (2015) for the pattern of phrasal compounding. One central question for a study that tries to model compound properties within a usage-based constructional approach is *how these constructions at different levels of specificity and abstractness are related to each other.*

Answering this question is equivalent to modeling a construction taxonomy or a so-called "Constructicon" (Ziem & Lasch 2013: 95).

The corresponding theoretical background can only be discussed briefly here

---

[24] Cf. Meibauer (2007) for a fruitful discussion of the expressivity of PCs and its sources.

**Attribute-like / Adverbial- / Subject-orientated- /
Object-orientated-Construction**

Form	Structure	[[Phrase$_{-CM}$/sentence-like structure$_{-CM}$/Sentence$_{+ProperName}$] [+/-LE] - [Substantive]]$_{PC;\ N;\ +/-\ SynthC}$
Meaning	Pragmatic	More expressive than prototypical determinative compounds; less expressive than PCs of the type Figure 10

e.g. *Wild-West-Sportler* ('wild-west athlete')
Take-That-Kollege
Zweite-Wahl-Obst
Ein-Mann-Zuständigkeit
Vater-Sohn-Freundschaft
Open-Air-Schläfer
Rote-Rosen-Verkäufer
"Don Quichotte"-Dichter

Figure 11: Attribute-like / Adverbial- / Subject-orientated- / Object-orientated-Construction

(cf. Hein 2015: Chapter II.2.1.3.6 for a detailed discussion): Crucial is the assumption that "constructions form a structured inventory of a speaker's knowledge of the conventions of their language" (Croft 2001: 25). This language knowledge is modeled in the form of a taxonomic network that consists of constructions which are related to each other (Ziem & Lasch 2013: 95).

Concerning the *kind* of the relations that are assumed within the constructicon, one can find divergent views within the different constructional approaches.

In line with the usage-based orientation of my study, I am using so-called "Inheritance hierarchies" (Goldberg 2003: 222) to model the relation between the stipulated constructions:

> Inheritance hierarchies have long been found useful for representing all types of knowledge, for example, our knowledge of concepts. The construction-based framework captures linguistic generalizations within a particu-

lar language via the same type of inheritance hierarchies [...]. Broad generalizations are captured by constructions that are inherited by many other
constructions; more limited patterns are captured by positing constructions
at various midpoints of the hierarchical network (Goldberg 2003: 222).

Using inheritance hierarchies offers the possibility to carve out a cognitive model
for the representation and processing of language knowledge without considering metaphorically the human brain as a computer (Ziem & Lasch 2013: 97).
Such hierarchies consist of different nodes and are a result of schematization,
understood as an inductive process which generalizes over different constructions (Deppermann 2006: 49). The superordinated node hands down properties
to the subordinated notes, and the degree of abstraction is minored from the top
to the bottom of the model (cf. Ziem & Lasch 2013: 98).

Before discussing the most important aspects of the model that I am proposing
for the explanation of phrasal compounding, two more aspects of the underlying theoretical assumptions have to be emphasized: I understand inheritance as
a partial process (e.g. Goldberg 1995; Lakoff 1987), which means that a more specific construction does not have to inherit *all* the properties of a subordinated,
i.e. more abstract construction. In other words, "inheritance can be blocked if it
conflicts with information in the more specific case" (Croft & Cruse 2004: 276).
Therefore, partial generalizations are also possible in my model. In addition, the
principle of "real copying" is adopted from the cognitive-linguistic approach that
is maintained by Lakoff and Goldberg. This means that I allow for the representation of *redundant* information in my network.

Based on Figure 12, an empirically gathered constructicon that explains the
functioning of the word formation pattern of phrasal compounding is proposed
for the first time.[25]

The level of abstraction decreases from top to bottom. On the top of level (2)
of the constructicon, I place the most general construction that was stipulated
to capture the properties of the complete pattern of phrasal compounding (cf.
§3.2). This form-meaning pairing is entitled "Phrasal-compound-construction"
in Figure 12 and inherits some central formal and semantic properties – but *not
all* the properties – from a general construction for prototypical determinative
compounds (1). Because of the acceptance of partial inheritance this is feasible.[26]

---

[25] Note that I can only describe the most important aspects in this paper. The complete constructicon with detailed explanations can be found in Hein 2015: Chapter III.3.1.4.

[26] In Hein 2015: Chapter II.2.2.2 I motivated elaborately why it is justified and important to stipulate a specific construction for PCs vis-à-vis a general construction for prototypical determinative compounds. Shortly summarized: PCs can be considered as determinative compounds

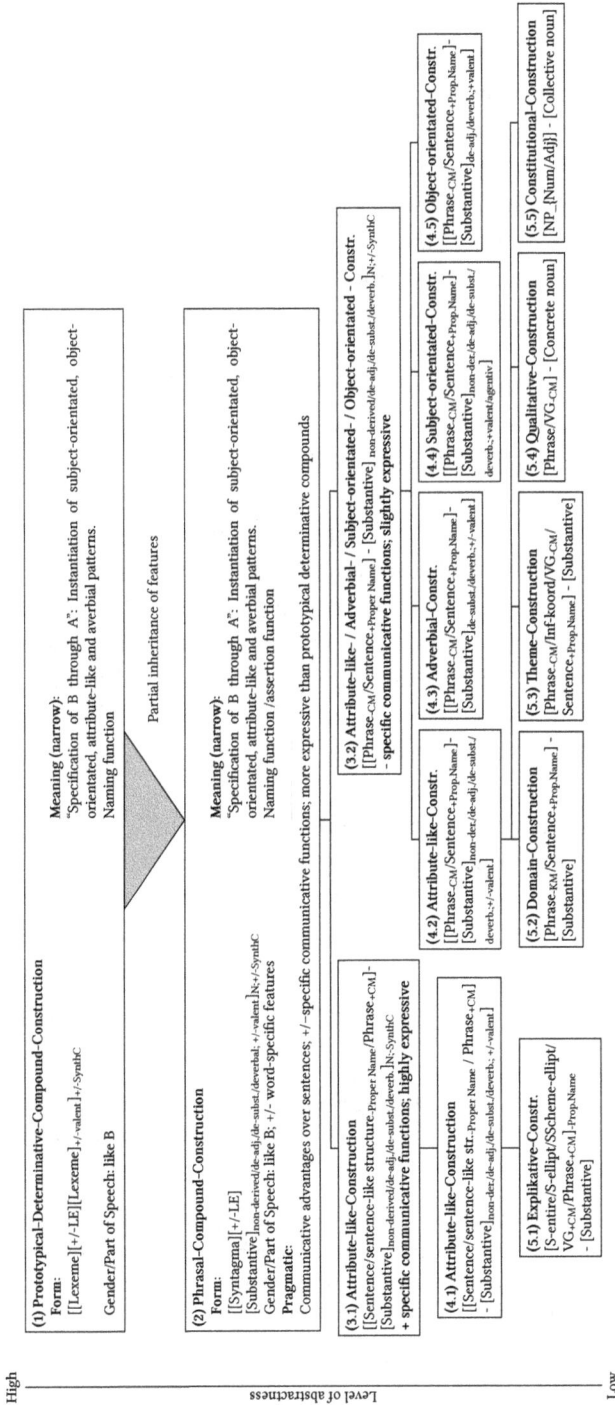

Figure 12: "PC-Constructicon"

At the next level (3), the empirical observation that phrasal compounding can be split into two more specific patterns is integrated[27]: I implemented that compounds with a sentence/a sentence-like structure or a phrase with the status of a CM as a first constituent (level 3.1) behave fundamentally different than compounds whose first constituent is built by a phrase without CM-status or a sentence which is a proper name (level 3.2). Both constructions at the third level inherit the central properties of the general PC-construction at level 2, but they are more concrete insofar as the syntax of the first constituent, the type of meaning and such pragmatic properties that are not likewise displayed in all PCs are concretized.

At level 4, the derivation type of the head noun and its valence grammatical properties are specified in addition. For example, at this level it is fixed that adverbial readings are blocked in PCs with a deadjectival or a non-derived nominal head (cf. Figure 6 in §3.1.2).

The constructions at level 5 ("explicative", "domain", "theme", "qualitative", "constitutional") correspond to those frequent, universal form-meaning correlations which – in part – have been discussed in §3.1.1. In contrast to the constructions at levels 2 to 4, they do not cover the complete formal and semantic potential of phrasal compounding. Instead, they represent only those correlations between form and meaning which are particularly well established.[28]

In the preceding paragraphs, I have provided an insight into the complex taxonomy that has been developed in Hein (2015) by presenting a shortened and simplified version of the constructions found in my data[29].

In conclusion, the "dynamic" of the constructicon has to be explained – even if I do not claim "psychological reality" in the sense of carving out a one-to-one reproduction of the mental representation of phrasal compounding.

Being confronted with a PC, the recipient initially tries to interpret it according to the most established form-meaning pairings of the constructicon. The recipi-

---

because of their basic grammatical properties, but there are some formal, semantic and especially pragmatic specifics (e.g. the producing of more expressive effects than with prototypical determinative compounds) that argue for the stipulation of a separate PC-constructicon.

[27] However, phrasal compounding is also representable through one mutual form-meaning pairing on a more abstract level (2).

[28] It is striking that all constructions at level 5 are instantiations of the rough pattern "attribute-like". For the other three rough patterns, no form-meaning pairings that are just as well-established can be stipulated. This corresponds to the observation stated in §3.1.2 that in PCs attribute-like readings are the most common.

[29] For example, I omitted the three most specific levels of the original taxonomy. Moreover, the important question how some 'singular cases' can be integrated into the constructicon is not discussed in this paper (cf. Hein 2015: Chapter III.3.1.4.2.

ent thus is aware that for a PC with a non-derived head noun, an attribute-like or a subject-orientated meaning is the most expectable (cf. level 4 of the constructicon). In case that the received PC is not in accordance with one of those well-established readings, the recipient falls back on a more abstract pattern of the constructicon (cf. level 3) and adjusts the received complex word with the interpretation potential offered at this level.

Similarly, the producer of a PC is aware which semantic goals are typically realizable through the use of a certain formal type of PC, e.g. through the use of a PC with a non-derived noun in head position. In case the intention of the speaker/writer cannot be brought in line with the quite specific, established form-meaning correlations at level 4, he falls back on a more abstract pattern that represents that basically each of the four "rough patterns" is instantiable in PCs.

4 Conclusion

All in all, the empirical practicality of the conducted bottom-up process, e.g. the possibility to structure the inventory of the 1,576 analyzed PCs with the help of pairings of form and meaning at varying degrees of abstraction, indicates that the properties of this word-formation type can be captured adequately through the mechanisms of construction grammar.

Looking at the frequency and the productivity of PCs, it is also justified and plausible in theoretical terms a) to ascribe them the theoretical status of a construction within a usage-based model and b) to assume their *mental* representation based on constructions.

While PCs have the status of a marginal phenomenon in traditional generative approaches (cf. Meibauer 2003, Hein 2011) and should not even exist according to some of these approaches, I carved out a usage-based model that can explain the functioning of the word formation pattern of phrasal compounding.

Finally, my paper highlights the degree to which a constructional perspective provides interesting and new insights into the properties of the word-formation type examined here: As the conducted bottom-up model takes the formal and semantic properties of the *second constituent* as its starting-point, I argue that the properties of the head are the key through which the inventory of PCs can be systematized on the first level – and not the abstract syntactic properties of the first constituent.

Last but not least, the approach presented here should be understood as an attempt to show "how the notion "construction" can be made fruitful for morphological analysis and theorizing" (Booij 2010: 1).

Katrin Hein

Acknowledgements

This paper is based on the findings of my doctoral thesis (Hein 2015). Special thanks go to Gerd, Anette and Max Horten for improving my English.

References

Baayen, Harald R. 1992. Quantitative aspects of morphological productivity. In Geert E. Booij & Jaap von Marle (eds.), *Yearbook of morphology 1991*, 109–149. Dordrecht: Kluwer Academic Publishers.

Booij, Geert E. 2010. *Construction morphology*. Oxford et al.: Oxford University Press.

Corpus Linguistics Programme Area. 2016. http://www1.ids-mannheim.de/fileadmin/kl/dokumente/flyer-en-dereko.pdf.

Croft, William. 2001. *Radical Construction Grammar: Syntactic theory in typological perspective.* Oxford: Oxford University Press.

Croft, William & David A. Cruse. 2004. *Cognitive linguistics.* Cambridge et al.: Cambridge University Press.

Deppermann, Arnulf. 2006. Construction grammar – eine Grammatik für die Interaktion? In Arnulf Deppermann, Reinhard Fiehler & Thomas Spranz-Fogasy (eds.), *Grammatik und Interaktion. Untersuchungen zum Zusammenhang von grammatischen Strukturen und Gesprächsprozessen*, 43–65. Radolfzell: Verlag für Gesprächsforschung.

Eichinger, Ludwig M. 2000. *Deutsche wortbildung. Eine Einführung.* Tübingen: Narr.

Fandrych, Christian & Maria Thurmair. 1994. Ein Interpretationsmodell für Nominalkomposita: Linguistische und didaktische Überlegungen. *Deutsch als Fremdsprache* 31. 34–45.

Goldberg, Adele E. 1995. *Constructions. A construction grammar approach to argument structure.* Chicago et al.: University of Chicago Press.

Goldberg, Adele E. 2003. Constructions: A new theoretical approach to language. *Trends in Cognitive Sciences* 7. 219–224.

Goldberg, Adele E. 2006. *Constructions at work: The nature of generalization in language.* Oxford: Oxford University Press.

Hein, Katrin. 2011. Phrasenkomposita – ein wortbildungsfremdes Randphänomen zwischen Morphologie und Syntax? *Deutsche Sprache* 39. 331–361.

Hein, Katrin. 2015. *Phrasenkomposita im Deutschen. Empirische Untersuchung und konstruktionsgrammatische Modellierung* (Studien zur Deutschen Sprache 67). Tübingen: Narr.

Hölzner, Matthias. 2007. *Substantivvalenz: Korpusgestützte U]ntersuchungen zu Argumentrealisierungen deutscher Substantive.* Tübingen: Niemeyer (= Reihe Germanistische Linguistik 274).

Institut für Deutsche Sprache. 2011. *Deutsches Referenzkorpus/Archiv der Korpora geschriebener Gegenwartssprache 2011-I.* Mannheim: Institut für Deutsche Sprache. www.ids-mannheim.de/DeReKo, accessed 2011-03-29.

Jakobson, Roman. 1960. Linguistics and poetics. In Thomas A. Sebeok (ed.), *Style in language*, 350–377. Cambridge et al.: Technology Press of MIT.

Kay, Paul. 1997. *Words and the grammar of context* (CSLI lecture notes 40). Stanford: Center for the Study of Language & Information.

Lakoff, George. 1987. *Women, fire, and dangerous things. What categories reveal about the mind. 4. Auflage, paperback ed.* Chicago et al.: University of Chicago Press.

Langacker, Ronald W. 1987. *Foundations of cognitive grammar.* Stanford: Stanford University Press.

Langacker, Ronald W. 1988. A Usage-Based model. In Brygida Rudzka-Ostyn (ed.), *Topics in cognitive linguistics* (Current issues in linguistic theory 50), 127–161. Amsterdam: Benjamins.

Langacker, Ronald W. 2000. A dynamic Usage-Based model. In Michael Barlow & Suzanne Kemmer (eds.), *Usage-based models of language*, 1–63. Stanford: Center for the Study of Language & Information.

Lawrenz, Birgit. 2006. *Moderne deutsche Wortbildung. Phrasale Wortbildung im Deutschen: Linguistische Untersuchung und sprachdidaktische Behandlung* (Philologia 91). Hamburg: Dr. Kovač.

Levinson, Stephen C. 2000. *Presumptive meanings. The theory of generalized conversational implicature.* Cambridge, MA: MIT Press.

Lieber, Rochelle. 1992. *Deconstructing morphology. Word formation in syntactic theory.* Chicago: University of Chicago Press.

Meibauer, Jörg. 2003. Phrasenkomposita zwischen Wortsyntax und Lexikon. *Zeitschrift für Sprachwissenschaft* 22. 153–188.

Meibauer, Jörg. 2007. How marginal are phrasal compounds? Generalized insertion, expressivity, and I/Q-interaction. *Morphology* 17. 233–259.

Schlücker, Barbara. 2012. Die deutsche Kompositionsfreudigkeit. Übersicht und Einführung. In Livio Gaeta & Barbara Schlücker (eds.), *Das deutsche als kompo-*

sitionsfreudige Sprache. Strukturelle Eigenschaften und systembezogene Aspekte (Linguistik – Impulse & Tendenzen 46), 1–25. Berlin et al.: de Gruyter.

Trips, Carola. 2012. Empirical and theoretical aspects of phrasal compounds: Against the 'syntax explains it all' attitude. In Angela Ralli, Geert Booij, Sergio Scalise & Athanasios Karasimos (eds.), *Online Proceedings of the eighth Mediterranean Morphology Meeting*, 322–346. Patras: University of Patras.

Trips, Carola. 2016. An analysis of phrasal compounds in the model of parallel architecture. In Pius ten Hacken (ed.), *The semantics of compounding*, 153–177. Cambridge: Cambridge University Press.

Tuldava, Juhan. 2005. Stylistics, author identification. In Reinhard Köhler (ed.), *Quantitative linguistik. Ein internationales handbuch* (Handbücher zur Sprach- und Kommunikationswissenschaft 27), 368–387. Berlin: de Gruyter.

Ziem, Alexander & Alexander. Lasch. 2013. *Konstruktionsgrammatik. Konzepte und grundlagen gebrauchsbasierter ansätze.* Berlin et al.: de Gruyter (= Germanistische Arbeitshefte 44).

Zifonun, Gisela, Ludger Hoffmann & Bruno. Strecker. 1997. *Grammatik der deutschen sprache.* Berlin: de Gruyter (= Schriften des Instituts für Deutsche Sprache 7).

Chapter 6

Phrasal compounds in Japanese

Kunio Nishiyama
Ibaraki University

Although Japanese does not have phrasal compounds analogous to English *an over the fence gossip* or *a who's the boss wink*, it does have phrasal compounds like *kireena mati-dukuri*, literally 'clean city-making,' meaning construction of a clean city. This example illustrates one of several types of phrasal compounds in Japanese. The criteria that classify phrasal compounds in Japanese are (i) whether the head of the compound is a predicate, (ii) if a predicate, whether the head is of Sino-Japanese or of native origin, (iii) if not a predicate, whether the compound involves coordination or cliticization.

One source of phrasal compounding is noun incorporation. When an argument incorporates into a Sino-Japanese verbal noun predicate, we get what Shibatani & Kageyama (1988) refer to as post-syntactic compounds, which have phrasal accent. In contrast, when an argument incorporates into a verbal noun predicate of native origin, we get a phrasal compound with word accent. The phrasal nature is evidenced by modifier stranding, and there are some conditions (e.g., pragmatic factors like cliché) on modifier stranding. There are three other sources of phrasal compounding which do not involve noun incorporation: natural coordination, enclitics, and proclitics. The first two have word accent and the last has phrasal accent. Whether a compound has word accent or phrasal accent is predicted by its structure: right branching compounds have phrasal accent (Kubozono 1995; 2005). Kageyama's (1993; 2001; 2009) notion of Word Plus is reconsidered and reclassified into three distinct classes: right-branching compounds, constructions involving proclitics, and phrases involving genitive deletion.

1 Introduction

The term "phrasal compound" refers to compounds containing a phrase, in apparent violation of Botha (1981) No Phrase Constraint, exemplified by the following English examples:

Kunio Nishiyama. Phrasal compounds in Japanese. In Carola Trips & Jaklin Kornfilt (eds.), *Further investigations into the nature of phrasal compounding*, 149–183. Berlin: Language Science Press. DOI:10.5281/zenodo.885125

(1) a. an over the fence gossip

    b. a who's the boss wink (Lieber 1992)

Apparently parallel examples in Japanese are as follows:

(2) a. Tokyo-kara-no   nimotu
      Tokyo-from-GEN package

    'a package from Tokyo'

    b. dare-ga   bosu-da-teki taido
      who-NOM boss-COP-like attitude

    'a who's the boss attitude'

In (2a), the genitive marker *no* emerges between PP and the head noun. Thus, the example is not a compound but a phrase like its English translation. In (2b), a morpheme *-teki* 'like' attaches to the sentence 'who's the boss.' The morpheme usually attaches to a word (e.g., *hankoo-teki* 'rebellion-like, rebellious'), but it has recently acquired the ability to attach to a phrase (the example in (2b) has an innovative or substandard flavor). The attachment of *-teki* is a case of encliticization, which is discussed in §4.2. *-teki* is also discussed in §5, but in the present context, it suffices to notice that (2b) as a whole is not a compound but a phrase like 'a "who's the boss"-like attitude,' consisting of a modifier and the head noun. In short, neither of the examples in (2) is a compound. This is evidenced by the fact that (2a) and (2b) have phrasal accent. Accent in Japanese is described in §2.

Although the examples in (2) are not phrasal compounds, Japanese does have phrasal compounds like the following:

(3) kireena mati-dukuri
    clean   town making

    'construction of a clean town' (Kageyama 2009: 518)

Here, *mati-dukuri* is a compound, and *kireena* modifies a part of the compound, resulting in a syntactic bracketing of [*kireena mati*]*-dukuri*. In other words, we have modifier stranding. This is a case of a bracketing paradox, for the bracketing in terms of phonological words is [*kireena*] *mati-dukuri*. It is reminiscent of *criminal lawyer*, with the meaning of a lawyer who practices criminal law (cf. Beard 1991). With this meaning, the syntactic bracketing is [*criminal* *law*]yer. The difference is that (3) does not involve bound derivational morphemes but compounding.

The purpose of this paper is to describe and analyze phrasal compounds in Japanese. Most of the examples discussed in this paper are reproduced from previous studies. However, in those previous studies, such examples of phrasal compounds are not discussed within an explicit perspective of phrasal compounds. This paper integrates several types of compounds within such a perspective. In addition to the type illustrated in (3), Japanese has a number of other types of phrasal compounds. The criteria used for classifying phrasal compounds in Japanese are as follows: (i) Whether the head of the compound is a predicate; (ii) if the head is a predicate, whether it is of Sino-Japanese origin (i.e. whether it is a vocabulary item in Japanese which is of Chinese origin), or whether it is of native origin; (iii) if the head of the compound is not a predicate, whether the compound involves coordination or cliticization.

This paper is organized as follows. §2 briefly introduces accent in Japanese, which is crucial in differentiating between words and phrases. In §3, phrasal compounds formed by noun incorporation are discussed. There are two subtypes: one type involving Sino-Japanese verbal nouns (3.1) and one type involving verbal nouns of native origin (§3.2). §4 discusses phrasal compounds without noun incorporation. There are three subtypes: one involving natural coordination (§4.1), one involving suffixes (enclitics) (§4.2), and one involving prefixes (proclitics) (§4.3). In §5, Kageyama's (1993; 2001; 2009) notion of Word Plus is reconsidered and reclassified into several existing notions.

2 Accent in words and phrases in Japanese

Just like English *green hóuse* versus *gréenhouse*, accent differentiates between words and phrases in Japanese. Key features of accent in Japanese are summarized as follows (see also Kawahara 2015) (H is for high and L for low):

(4) *Accent in Japanese*

   a. Accent is defined as falling pitch (HL).
   b. A word is either accented or unaccented.
   c. Where the accent falls is specified for each accented word.
   d. A word can have at most one accent.
   e. A word starts as either LH (rising pitch) or HL (falling pitch) (the latter of which instantiates accent on the first mora).

In this paper, the feature in (4d), i.e. that a word can have at most one accent, becomes crucial. The following examples illustrate accent in words:

(5) a. inu 'dog' LH (unaccented)

   b. nèko 'cat' HL (accent on the first mora)

   c. huransu 'France' LHHH (unaccented)

   d. dòitu 'Germany' HLL (accent on the first mora)

   e. yooròppa 'Europe' LHHLL (accent on the third mora, segmented yo.o.ro.p.pa)

When relevant, accent is represented with a grave diacritic on the accented vowel in this paper.

Given that a compound is a word, there should be at most one accent in a compound, according to (4d). The accentuation rules of compounds are complicated (cf. Kubozono 2008; Nishiyama 2010), but typically accent falls on the first mora of the right-hand element, regardless of how each element in the compound is accented independently.[1] This is illustrated in the following examples:

(6) a. dòitu + bùngaku → doitu-bùngaku, *dòitu-bùngaku

   'German literature'

   b. LHHH LHH   LHHH HLL   LHHH LHH
       booeki + kaisya → booeki- gàisya *booeki- gaisya

   'a trading company'

(6a) is a case of compounding of *dòitu* 'Germany' and *bùngaku* 'literature', both of which are accented on the first mora. **dòitu-bùngaku*, which has two accent positions, is ruled out by (4d). The correct form *doitu-bùngaku* bears accent on the first mora of the right-hand element. Thus, the right-hand element seems to retain the position of its accent in the compound. But this is not the case in (6b), where both of the elements *booeki* and *kaisya* are unaccented originally. Here, the resulting compound *booeki-gàisya* is likewise accented on the first mora of the right-hand element, and thus has the pitch contour LHHH-HLL. The alternative **booeki-gaisya* (LHHH-LHH) is ruled out, because there cannot be an instance of rising pitch after falling pitch in a word. On the assumption that a compound is a word that obeys the word accent rules, the pitch contour LHHH-LHH is ruled out, for the H-LH part instantiates rising pitch after falling pitch.

In this paper, when there is at most one accent in a word, I refer to it as *word accent*. In contrast, *phrasal accent* refers to independent accent for each word in a phrase. This typically happens when a phrase includes the genitive *no*:

---

[1] The rationale behind this accentuation is to mark the root boundary (cf. Kubozono 2008).

(7) dòitu-no   bùngaku
Germany-GEN literature

'literature of Germany' (cf. (6a))

Here, the accent of each element, *dòitu* and *bùngaku*, is retained. This is because (7) is a phrase. (7) is to be compared to the compound *doitu-bùngaku* in (6a), where there is only one accent. Given that words are either accented or unaccented, *phrasal accent* refers to not only multiple accent but also to instances of falling pitch followed by rising pitch, which is prohibited in a word.

Another feature of accent in Japanese crucial in this paper is its sensitivity to the internal structure of compounds. Concretely, when three elements are involved, while left-branching compounds obey the compound accentuation rule (having at most one accent), right-branching compounds violate it, resulting in multiple accent. This is illustrated in the following examples (cf. Kubozono 2005: 13):

(8)   *Left-branching vs. right-branching*

   a. [dòitu   + bùngaku] + kyookai   → doitu-bungaku-kyòokai
       Germany   literature   association

       'Association of German Literature'

   b. dòitu   + [bùngaku + kyookai]   → dòitu : bungaku-kyòokai
       Germany   literature   association

       'German Association of Literature'

(8a) is a compound consisting of [*dòitu* + *bùngaku*] and (inherently unaccented) *kyookai*. This means that the compound has the left-branching structure, and the resulting *doitu-bungaku-kyòokai* 'Association of German Literature' has only one accent, namely word accent. In contrast, (8b) is a compound consisting of *dòitu* and [*bùngaku* + *kyookai*] (i.e., right-branching), and the resulting *dòitu : bungaku-kyòokai* 'German Association of Literature' has multiple accent, namely phrasal accent, which is reflected by the colon (:).

The distinction between word accent and phrasal accent is crucial throughout this paper. Basically, we can identify the word/phrasal status of word strings by the accent pattern. Thus, when the string [A B] has word accent, A and B are taken to form a compound, and are cited as "A-B".

In the present context, the behavior of right-branching compounds is exceptional: they have phrasal accent, but are *not* phrases syntactically. That they are not syntactic phrases is shown by the following example:

(9) *doitu   to   huransu : bungaku-kyookai
     Germany and France   literature association

'associations of literature in Germany and France'

Here, the left-hand element is a coordination of proper nouns, and thus is a phrase. The ungrammaticality of (9) shows that right-branching compounds are not phrasal compounds, despite having phrasal accent. (We return to coordination in §4.1.) This is a case where a phonological notion and a syntactic notion do not match: phrasal accent is a phonological notion, and does not always reflect the syntactic status of a phrase.[2] In this sense, phrasal accent in itself is not helpful in deciding whether a compound is a phrasal compound or not. Note, however, that whether the accent is word-like or phrasal is crucial in determining whether compounding is involved or not, as mentioned above.

Some notes on notations and terminology in this paper are in order. "A-B" represents compounds with word accent, which are called *real compounds*. In contrast, "A : B" represents compounds with phrasal accent (like 8b), which are called *pseudo compounds*.[3]

To recap, the following premise is crucial in the following sections:

(10) Right-branching compounds have phrasal accent.

Before concluding this section, let us see why right-branching compounds are exceptional. Kubozono (1995: 107) notes that right-branching A+[B+C] is harder to process than left-branching [A+B]+C (see also Hawkins 1990 and Sugioka 2008). To remedy the processing difficulty, right-branching compounds are exceptionally multiple-accented (phrasal-accented), making constituency easy to identify.

3 Noun-incorporated phrasal compounds

This section discusses phrasal compounds formed by noun incorporation. Unlike noun incorporation familiar from polysynthetic languages, noun incorporation

---

[2] The term "phrasal compounds" is used in Ito & Mester (2007) to refer to compounds with phrasal accent. Their term is based on the *phonological* notion of "phrase" that comes between "intonational group" and "word" in the prosodic hierarchy. Crucially, "phrasal compounds" in Ito & Mester (2007) are *not* phrasal compounds as defined in this paper (and in this volume as well) as XP-X, namely utilizing the *syntactic* notion of "phrase".

[3] Kageyama (1993; 2001; 2009) uses the colon : for what he terms post-syntactic compounds (discussed in §3) and | for what he terms Word Plus (including (8b), discussed in §s 4 and 5). As far as accent is concerned, they all have phrasal accent. Moreover, I argue in §5 that there is no need to postulate Word Plus as a novel concept. Therefore, I use only the colon notation.

in Japanese is limited to verbal noun predicates (or nominalized verbs).[4] Depending on whether the predicate is of Sino-Japanese or of native origin, the resulting phrasal compounds behave differently with respect to accent, and this led previous studies to treat them separately. I claim that this dichotomy is theoretically unmotivated. Phrasal compounds involving Sino-Japanese predicates are discussed in §3.1, and those involving predicates of native origin are discussed in §3.2.

3.1 Noun incorporation resulting in phrasal accent: Sino-Japanese verbal nouns

This section discusses "post-syntactic compounds" in the sense of Shibatani & Kageyama (1988) (henceforth S&K). The analysis in S&K is extended in Kageyama & Shibatani (1989) (K&S) and Kageyama (1993) and is also mentioned in Kageyama (2009). The following summarizes the key features of the compounds analyzed in S&K:

(11)   *Features of noun-incorporated pseudo compounds*

    a.   They have phrasal-accent.

    b.   The right-hand element is a Sino-Japanese verbal noun predicate.[5]

    c.   The left-hand element is the complement of the right-hand predicate.

    d.   The complement is in a case-marked position before incorporation.

Due to the feature in (11a), the examples discussed in this section are called pseudo compounds.

Consider first the following three examples:

(12)   a.   yooroppa-ryòkoo
          Europe-traveling

          'Europe-traveling'
          (real compound, with word accent)

    b.   yooròppa-o ryokoo-tyùu
          Europe-ACC traveling-while

          'while traveling in Europe'
          (the temporal suffix -*tyuu* 'while' attached to a VP)

---

[4] With the exception of several (lexicalized) verbs like *tabi-datu* 'trip-set.out,' where the verb remains non-nominalized, noun incorporation resulting in a verb is quite limited and unproductive, unlike noun incorporation involving verbal nouns as discussed in this section.

[5] Kageyama (1993: 240f) notes that an adjectival noun can also be the right-hand element of a noun-incorporated pseudo compound. We will return to adjectival nouns in note 13.

    c. yooròppa : ryokoo-tyùu
        Europe   traveling-while

      'while traveling in Europe'
      (pseudo compound, with phrasal accent)

(12a) is a case of a real compound; it has word accent, i.e., only one accent position on the first mora of the right-hand element. (12b) is obtained by attaching a temporal suffix *-tyuu* 'while' to the VP 'travel Europe.' Note that the object is Accusative-marked. (12c) is a case of noun-incorporated pseudo compound. It is a pseudo compound because it is phrasal-accented (i.e. multiple-accented).

As noted by S&K (p. 462), a manner adverb can intervene between the object and the predicate in (12b), but not in (12c):

(13)   a. yooròppa-o nonbiri ryokoo-tyùu
           Europe-ACC leisurely traveling-while

           'while traveling in Europe leisurely'

    b. *yooròppa : nonbiri ryokoo-tyùu
          Europe   leisurely traveling-while

          'while traveling in Europe leisurely'

This shows that (12c) is not simply derived from (12b) by case deletion. More specifically, (12c) is not a phrase but a word (compound).

One phenomenon that points to the involvement of noun incorporation is modifier stranding (cf. Baker 1988). Modifier stranding also indicates that a phrase is involved in the compounding. As demonstrated by S&K, the compounds in question allow modifier stranding:[6]

---

[6] Kageyama (2009: 525) says that noun-incorporated pseudo compounds (post-syntactic compounds in his terminology) do not tolerate modifier stranding, but this refers to a different type of modifier stranding. Kageyama's example is as follows:

(i)   a. hidari-asi-o kos-setu
        left-leg-ACC bone-break

      'to break the bone of the left leg'.

Here, *hidari-asi* is supposed to be modifying *kos*, but this is not literally the case. *Kos* is a Sino-Japanese lexical item for 'bone' and can be used only in Sino-Japanese compounds. When modified by *hidaro-asi* independently, the correct word for 'bone' is a native word *hone*, as:

(ii)   a. hidaro-asi-no hone
         left-leg-GEN bone

       'the bone of the left leg'

(14)   a.   kono zikken   : syuuryoo-go
            this   experiment   finish-after

            'After this experiment finishes,' (S&K: 471)

       b.   [watasi-ga ima yatteiru] zikken: syuuryoo-go
            I-NOM   now doing   experiment finish-after

            'After the experiment that I am now doing finishes,' (S&K: 472, adapted)

Note that a modifier (a demonstrative in (14a) and a relative clause in (14b)) of *zikken* 'experiment' is stranded.[7]

As in (13), an adverb can intervene between *zikken* and *syuuryoo* in a clause as in (15a), but not in a compound as shown in (15b):

(15)   a.   kono zikken-ga   yooyaku syuuryoo-go
            this   experiment-NOM finally   finish-after

            'After this experiment finally finishes'

       b.   *kono zikken   : yooyaku syuuryoo-go
            this   experiment   finally   finish-after

            'After this experiment finally finishes,'

Compare (15b) with (14a). This shows that there is no phrasal boundary between *zikken* and *syuuryoo* in (14); they form a compound, as S&K argue.

In addition to an accusative NP (12) and a nominative NP (14), a genitive NP can also incorporate:[8,9]

---

[7] In this paper, I use the term "modifier" loosely as "being a part of the argument DP." Thus, it is immaterial whether the modifier is an adjunct or a specifier in the phrase structure.

[8] A dative NP can also incorporate:

   (i)   butyoo-e-no   syoosin
         department.head-DAT-GEN promotion

         'promotion to the department head'

   (ii) butyoo : syoosin (K&S: 154)

   no here is more like a linker, as we saw in (2a).

[9] I leave open the exact theoretical mechanism of noun incorporation. It is generally assumed (cf. Baker 1988) that noun incorporation is restricted to internal arguments. Therefore, one might think that (16)) as well as (14)) involve incorporation of an unaccusative subject, which is underlyingly an object. However, Kageyama (2009: 517f, 2013) shows that an agentive noun can also incorporate:

Kunio Nishiyama

(16) a. zyukensee-no zooka(-no   riyuu)
          applicant-GEN increase(-GEN reason)
          '(the reason of) increase of applicants'

      b. zyukensee : zooka(-no   riyuu)
          applicant   increase(-GEN reason)
          '(the reason of) increase of applicants'

(16a) is an ordinary noun phrase involving a genitive-marked argument. (16b) is a case of a pseudo compound formed by incorporation of the (originally genitive-marked) argument.

In fact, S&K (1988) are not explicit about the relevance of noun incorporation in the formation of the compounds in question, and suggest (p. 480, n. 15) that the genitive is deleted in examples like (16b). It is in K& S (1989: 155) and Kageyama (1993: 236) that the noun incorporation analysis is entertained. Concretely, they say that (16a) and (16b) have the common caseless, non-incorporated structure:

(17) a. [zyukensee zooka] $_{\text{VNP}}$ b. [zyukensee zooka] $_{\text{VNP}}$
         ↓ case realization   ↓ compounding (noun incorporation)
         [zyukensee-no zooka]   [zyukensee : zooka]

With case realization, we get (17a) (=16a), and with noun incorporation, we get (17b) (=16b).

(i) Spielberg : seesaku-no   eega
     S.   production-GEN movie
     'a movie that Spielberg produced'

Although Kageyama argues that the 'internal argument constraint' is still valid, for the agent compounds in question must be used adjectivally as above, this raises the question of whether the Baker-style incorporation is involved in the compounds in question. To complicate the issue, there are counterexamples to the internal argument constraint itself (cf. Mithun 2010 and Lieber 2010, among others). Due to such considerations, one might opt for merger under adjacency (cf. Marantz 1988 and Halle & Marantz 1993) or the First Sister Principle of Roeper & Siegel (1978) as the mechanism of the compounding in question, but I leave further discussion on the issue for future research. Incidentally, Kageyama (2009: 525) notes that the incorporation in question is not a case of Pseudo Noun Incorporation in the sense of Massam (2001), a phrase structure in which an NP directly merges with a V, because the incorporated elements in Japanese are not phrases. Specifically, although a phrasal argument can be in the original structure before incorporation, only the head can participate in compounding, with the modifier stranded, as we saw in (14).

3.2 Noun incorporation resulting in word accent: verbal nouns of native origin

Japanese abounds in compounds with a nominalized verb of native origin as the right hand element and its argument as the left hand element:

(18)   gomi-atume 'garbage collecting'
       yuki-kaki 'snow plowing'

   Unlike the compounds discussed in the previous section, the compounds in (18) have word accent, which will be illustrated in §3.2.1. This section discusses such compounds. §3.2.1 discusses compounds with a phrasal complement as evidence for phrasal compounding, and seeks an account for why they have word accent, in contrast to the phrasal-accented compounds discussed in the previous section. §3.2.2 offers conditions on modifier stranding. §3.2.3 compares noun-incorporated compounds discussed in this paper and the so-called synthetic compounds (in English) like *mountain climbing*.

3.2.1 Compounds with a phrasal complement and compound accentuation

Sugioka (2002: 496) argues that compounds of the type illustrated in (18) are formed by noun incorporation—a proposal which I basically follow here. (But I leave the exact mechanism of noun incorporation open (cf. note 9), and argue in §3.2.3 that the compounds in (18) are structurally ambiguous.) In (18), the left-hand element of the compound is a word, so it is not clear whether a phrase is involved. To make sure that phrasal compounding is involved, a modifier is called for, and indeed, with this type of compounds, sometimes (but not always, see §3.2.2) modifier stranding is possible.

(19)   a. [titi-no   haka]-mairi   (cf. Kageyama 2009: 521)
          father-GEN grave-visiting

          'visiting father's grave' (lit. [father's grave]-visiting)

       b. [asagao-no   tane]-maki   (Kageyama 1993: 334)
          morning.glory-GEN seed-sowing

          'sowing seeds of morning glory' (lit. seed-sowing of morning glory)

   This shows that the compounds above are formed in the phrasal syntax. Since a predicate participates in this type of compounding, noun incorporation is likely to be involved, as suggested by Sugioka (2002). I return to evidence for this in §3.2.3.

That compounding is really involved in (19) is confirmed by accent. (20a) illustrates accent of a VP in a sentence, while (20b) illustrates accent of the corresponding verbal noun:

(20) a. LHLLL   HL(L)   HL
          asagao-no   tane(-o)   mak-u
          morning.glory-GEN seed(-ACC) sow-PRES
          'to sow seeds of morning glory'
      b. LHLLL   LHLL
          asagao-no   tane-maki
          morning.glory-GEN seed-sowing
          'sowing seeds of morning glory'

As shown in (20a), *asàgao*, *tàne*, and *màk* are all accented, containing falling pitch (HL). (The presence of the accusative marker does not affect accent). But in (20b), *tane-maki* has word accent in that it contains only one accent position. Crucially, the accents of the original words *tàne* and *màk* are fused into one. This shows that *tane-maki* behaves as a word, confirming the presence of compounding.

Another piece of evidence for compounding comes from *rendaku* (sequential voicing), as observed in (3) (repeated below):

(21) kireena mati-dukuri
      clean   town making
      'construction of a clean town'

Here, the verb for 'make' is originally *tukur-*, and the sound change in *dukuri* above is due to *rendaku* voicing, a hallmark of compounding (cf. Tsujimura 2007: 50ff; Ito & Mester 2003; Kubozono 2005, among others).

As a mechanism for the compounding in (3) and (22), Kageyama (1993: 335) does not endorse his own incorporation analysis that he entertains for (16b). The main reason seems to be accent: (12c), (14), and (16b) have phrasal accent but (19a) and (19b) have word accent, and Kageyama seems to be assuming that a syntactic derivation should always result in phrasal accent and cannot result in word accent. However, a syntactic derivation like incorporation *can* result in word accent. Consider the following example of a verb-verb compound:

(22) [doa-o   osi]-tuzuke(ru)
      door-ACC push-continue
      'to keep on [pushing the door]'
      (cf. Kageyama 1989; 1993; Nishiyama 2008; Fukuda 2012)

There is a consensus in the literature that the compound in (22) is formed syntactically (by verb incorporation).[10] Crucially for the current context, *osi-tuzuke(ru)* has word accent.[11] It might be that verb incorporation and noun incorporation (if Japanese has both) have different mechanisms. But to the extent that (19) and (22) share common features (i.e., a word-accented compound containing a phrase), there is no reason for analyzing them separately, i.e., forming the compound in (19) in the lexicon and forming the compound in (22) in the syntax, as Kageyama does.[12]

But a question remains: why do (12c), (14), and (16b) have phrasal accent, while (19a) and (19b) have word accent, if they are all formed by incorporation? One prominent difference between phrasal-accented phrasal compounds as in (12c), (14), and (16b) and word-accented phrasal compounds as in (3), (18), (19) is that while the verbal noun in the former is a Sino-Japanese word, the verbal noun in the latter is of native origin. But there are a few cases of phrasal-accented noun-incorporated compounds with a native verbal noun:

(23) a. tosyo : kasi-dasi
          book   lend-let.out

          'checking out books'

      b. bentoo   : moti-komi
          lunch.box   hold-let.in

          'bringing lunch box in' (Kageyama 1993: 229)

The obvious difference between (3), (18), (19) and (23) is that the latter involve a nominalized compounded verb-verb predicate. Thus, one suspects that what's

---

[10] See Kageyama (1989) and Nishiyama (2008) for details. One piece of evidence for the syntactic derivation is that the complement can be passivized:

(i) doa-ga   os-are-tuzuke-ta
     door-NOM push-Pass-continue-Past

     'The door kept being pushed.'

Given that passivization happens in the syntax, the compound *os-are-tuzuke* is formed in the syntax as well.

[11] Specifically, while *os* and *tuzuke* are inherently unaccented, the compound *osi-tuzukè(ru)* has accent in the right-hand element. The accentuation rule of verb-verb compounds in Japanese is to place accent in the right-hand element, regardless of the accent pattern of the original words. *(ru)* is added at the end to derive the present/citation form of the compound, and [i] after *os* is a linking element. See Nishiyama (2016) for details.

[12] Remarkably, the observation that (19) and (22) are parallel goes back to Sakakura (1952: 114).

going on is right-branching compounding accentuation. Recall from (10) that right-branching compounds have phrasal accent.

Let us suppose, therefore, the following:

(24)   When a complement incorporates into a Sino-Japanese predicate, the predicate is reanalyzed as right-branching, resulting in phrasal accent.

Intuitively, both right-branching and Sino-Japanese words are 'heavy' in a sense. Recall from §2 that right-branching compounds have phrasal accent *for ease of processing*. A similar situation might hold in Sino-Japanese verbal nouns. For our purpose it suffices to capture the "reanalysis" above as resegmentation; while *ryokoo* 'trip' is usually taken as monomorphemic, it is analyzed as bimorphemic *ryo-koo* after incorporation.

In fact, Sino-Japanese words in general consist of bound roots (like *philosophy*), but this is not the only basis for (24); recall that with Sino-Japanese nouns, we have a word-accented compound as *doitu-bùngaku* 'German literature'. Probably the predicate-argument relation is important, so that, when noun incorporation happens, phrasal accent is required to make the morpheme boundary (or *phrasal boundary*) explicit. This requirement is removed when the predicate is of native origin, for it is easier to recognize. It is well known that phonological rules in Japanese apply differently in native words and Sino-Japanese words (e.g., *rendaku* sequential voicing; cf. Tsujimura 2007: 50ff; Ito & Mester 2003;Kubozono 2005, among others). What is special about (24) is that it is limited to predicates.[13]

3.2.2 Conditions on modifier stranding

In the last subsection, we discussed compounds with a stranded modifier. But modifier stranding is not always possible, and this subsection offers conditions on modifier stranding.

---

[13] As mentioned in note 5, an adjectival noun can also be the right-hand element of a noun-incorporated pseudo compound. The majority of adjectival nouns are Sino-Japanese, but there are also certain instances of adjectival nouns of native origin. As Kageyama (1993: 241) notices, whether Sino-Japanese or of native origin, an adjectival noun can be the right-hand element of a noun-incorporated pseudo compound (with phrasal accent) One example of an adjectival noun of native origin is the following:

(i)   hyoozyoo : yutaka-na hito
      expression rich-MOD person

      'a person with diverse facial expressions' (*na* is a modifier marker)

In Nishiyama (1999), I argued that adjectival nouns (nominal adjectives in the terminology of Nishiyama (1999)) are bimorphemic (like compounds), and this might be the reason why (i) has phrasal accent, though the incorporation host (i.e., *yutaka*) is of native origin.

Consider first the following examples:

(25) a. uma-nori
          horse-riding
          'horseback riding'

     b. *[ookina uma]-nori
          big   horse-riding (S&K: 471)

     c. *[titi-no   uma]-nori
          father-GEN horse-riding
          'riding on father's horse'

Why is modifier stranding impossible here, in contrast to the compounds in
(19)? Kageyama (1993: 334) notes that the incorporated noun in (19) (with a
stranded modifier) is a *relational noun* and needs further specification. One typical case of relational nouns is a parent, i.e. a noun whose meaning is defined
only in relation to a child. In the same way, a grave is so-named only when it is
known that somebody is buried there, and every seed is a seed of some kind of
plant. A horse, in contrast, is not such a relational noun.

There is another condition. Consider (3), repeated below:

(26) [kireena mati]-dukuri
      clean   town making
      'construction of a clean town'

Here the noun *mati* 'town' is not a relational noun, but modifier stranding
is possible. One thing to notice here is that the modifier has a limited semantic range: instead of *kireena* 'clean', one can also use *sumiyoi* 'comfortable' or
zizokukanoona 'sustainable', but not *kyodaina* 'giant,' in this kind of compound.

Thus, we are dealing here with a construction based on a template, i.e., [*Xish
town*]-*construction*, where X has a positive (or ecological) meaning. This is reminiscent of the contrast between [*American history*]*teacher* versus *[*recent history*]*teacher* (Bresnan & Mchombo 1995: 193f). Carstairs-McCarthy (2002: 81f)
cites similar examples like [*open door*]*policy* versus *[*wooden door*]*policy*, and
says that the left-hand element must be a *cliché* for a left-branching compound
like [*open door*]*policy* to be possible.

How an expression is recognized as a cliché is purely a matter of pragmatics
and beyond the scope of this paper.[14] Bresnan & Mchombo (1995) argue that

---

[14] For example, [*small car*]*driver* is possible while *[*green car*]*driver* is not, because *small car* is
a cliché but *green car* is not. However, as Sproat (1993: 251) notes, in an imaginary world in

what looks like a phrase in phrasal compounding is lexicalized, but this 'lexical-ization' can be instant or impromptu, for it accommodates "context-dependent innovation".

I take the two conditions mentioned above (one semantic, the other pragmatic) as the output conditions on the construction [$_{XP}$ Mod X]-X; when a construction with this schema does not meet these conditions, it is filtered out. In this sense, instantiations of this construction are independent of the mechanism for com-pounding. Whether the mechanism is syntactic incorporation or morphological merger, it produces the construction, obeying ordinary principles imposed on it. It is only after the construction [$_{XP}$ Mod X]-X is produced when the semantic and pragmatic conditions become relevant.

When there is no predicate involved in compounding, there can be no noun incorporation. Therefore, phrasal compounding should be impossible in such a case. This prediction is generally confirmed:

(27) *[doitu-no   bungaku]-kyookai
      Germany-GEN literature-association

      'Association of German Literature'

(27) is a compound of *doitu-no bungaku* 'literature of Germany' and *kyookai* 'association,' and it cannot mean 'Association of German Literature.' It has a meaning of 'German Association of Literature,' but it is derived from a different structure *doitu-no [bungaku-kyookai]*.

However, when a cliché is involved, phrasal compounding becomes possible even without noun incorporation:

(28)   a. [tiisana sinsetu]-undoo
           small   kindness campaign

           'campaign for doing small kindnesses'

       b. [midorino hane]-bokin
           green   feather fund.raising

           'fund raising for restoration of plants' (cf. Kubozono 1995: 129)

This is reminiscent of examples like *[open door] policy* vs. *[wooden door] policy* we saw above, and strongly suggests the relevance of cliché.[15]

---

which a gasoline rationing scheme is based on the color of one's vehicle, [*green car*] *driver* will be acceptable. This is a typical characteristic of pragmatics, namely how language is used in the actual world.

[15] Although this cliché account captures modifier stranding as in (28), it cannot be extended to the case with a relational noun as in (19), because relational nouns are defined semantically,

Returning to noun-incorporated compounds resulting in phrasal accent as in (12c), (14), and (16b), modifier stranding in such examples is less constrained than in the ones resulting in word accent discussed in this section. Thus, as we saw in (14), a demonstrative and a relative clause can be stranded. It is true, as S&K (p. 471) note, that the following example with an adjective is ungrammatical:

(29) ?*[utukusii yooròppa] : ryokoo-tyùu   (cf. 12c)
       beautiful Europe   traveling-while

'while traveling in beautiful Europe'

However, with a cliché complement, adjective stranding seems possible. The following example is constructed from (3) by replacing the native words by Sino-Japanese words with a similar meaning:

(30) [kireena tosi] : kensetu
       clean   town   construction]]

'construction of a clean town'

In contrast to (29), (30) is acceptable. So when a cliché is involved, an adjective can be stranded in the formation of noun-incorporated compounds resulting in phrasal accent. But if S&K's observations are correct, a demonstrative and a relative clause cannot be stranded, and this contrasts with the formation of noun-incorporated compounds resulting in word accent, which requires a relational noun or a cliché for modifier stranding, as we saw in the last subsection. Why the difference?

I hypothesize that the phrasal accent that results in the formation of noun-incorporated compounds involving a Sino-Japanese predicate makes the compounding less tight, as attested by a pause that can intervene between the left-hand and right-hand elements, and this renders the syntactic constituency easy to recognize. This might make modifier stranding in this case less constrained. In the last subsection I stated that noun-incorporated compounds involving a Sino-Japanese predicate are harder to process than those involving a predicate

---

while cliché is defined pragmatically. Jaklin Kornfilt (p.c.) suggests that, if phrasal compounding is possible even if the right-hand element is not a predicate, we can dispense with noun incorporation altogether as a mechanism to derive phrasal compounds. But it is not clear whether the two types of phrasal compounds—ones whose right-hand element is a predicate and ones whose right-hand element is not a predicate—are derived by the same mechanism. First, the former is more productive. Second and relatedly, although the pragmatic condition (being a cliché) can be relevant in both types of phrasal compounds, the former involves another condition not observed in the latter: the relational noun condition as in (19).

of native origin, and that this results in phrasal accent on the former. The conjecture in this subsection implies that the resulting phrasal accent "promotes" noun-incorporated compounds involving a Sino-Japanese predicate to an advantageous position for processing, and makes modifier stranding easier for them.

3.2.3 Noun-incorporated compounds vs. synthetic compounds

At this point, one might wonder how the noun-incorporated compounds discussed so far are related to the so-called synthetic compounds (in English) like *mountain climbing* or *truck driver*. Synthetic compounds are conventionally defined as compounds in which there seems to be a thematic relation between the two parts. As is well known, there is a long debate over whether *truck driver* has the structure/derivation of *[truck] [driver]* or *[[truck driv]er]* (cf. Roeper & Siegel 1978;Lieber 1983;Spencer 1992: 324ff;Ackema & Neeleman 2004, and Harley 2009, among others). I remain neutral regarding the situation in English, but in this subsection I argue that in Japanese, there is another type of compounds that look like synthetic compounds but are *not* formed by noun incorporation.

First, recall from (12) (adapted):

(31)   a. yooroppa-ryòkoo
           Europe-traveling

           (real compound, with word accent)

      b. yooròppa : ryokoo
           Europe   traveling

           (pseudo compound, with phrasal accent)

Both (31a) and (31b) are formed by compounding *yooroppa* 'Europe' and *ryokoo* 'traveling.' The former results in word accent, and the latter in phrasal accent. In the terminology of this paper, the former is a real compound and the latter a pseudo compound.

Although (12a) and (12c) are synonymous, there is a case where there is a semantic difference between a real compound and a pseudo compound consisting of the same elements. Consider:

(32)   a. katee-hòomon (real compound)
           home-visiting

           'a teacher's visit to a pupil's home' (specialized meaning)

b. katee : hoomon (pseudo compound)
   home   visiting
   'a home visit (compositional) (S&K: 478)

As noted by S&K, (32a) with word accent has a specialized meaning of 'a teacher's visit to a pupil's home,' but (32b) with phrasal accent has a compositional meaning.

To capture the above differences, I propose that real compounds and noun-incorporated compounds have the following structure and derivation:

(33)   a. real compounds, (12a) and (32a)

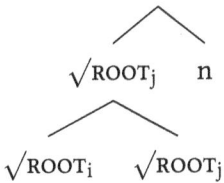

$$\sqrt{\text{ROOT}_j} \quad n$$

$$\sqrt{\text{ROOT}_i} \quad \sqrt{\text{ROOT}_j}$$

b. noun-incorporated compounds, (12c) and (32b)

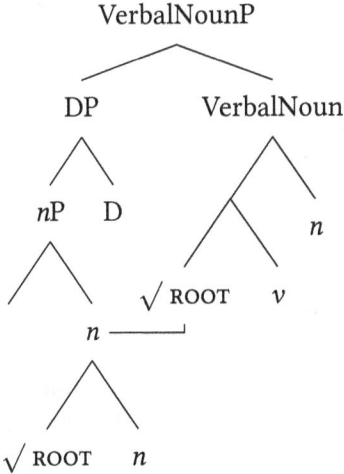

VerbalNounP

DP   VerbalNoun

*n*P D   *n*

          $\sqrt{\text{ROOT}}$ *v*

n ⌐

$\sqrt{\text{ROOT}}$ *n*

I assume that roots are categorially neutral and a functional head like *n* or *v* categorizes the root (cf. Marantz 1997). *n* and *v* form phases, in whose complement the semantics is fixed (cf. Embick 2010). Therefore, (33a), the structure for (32a), can have a specialized meaning.[16] In contrast, in (33b), the structure for (32b),

---

[16] Strictly speaking, (33a) is a structure for a dvandva like *oya-ko* 'parent-child,' and the com-

the meaning of *katee* is fixed by *n* before incorporation. Therefore, subsequent incorporation has no semantic effect and (32b) has a compositional meaning. In (33b), only the categorized root is incorporated. Therefore, any other parts of the DP (if there are any) are stranded. This is what we observed in (3), (14), (19), and (30).

One implication of the above analysis is that real compounds like *yooroppa-ryokoo* 'Europe-traveling' (12a) and *katee-hoomon* 'home-visiting' (32a), although they look like synthetic compounds like *mountain climbing*, do *not* involve noun incorporation. In other words, despite appearances, there is no thematic relation between the right-hand element (apparent predicate) and the left-hand element (apparent argument) in (12a) and (32a). In this sense, there is no structural difference between *yooroppa-ryokoo* 'Europe-traveling' and *yooroppa-rengoo* 'the European Union,' and referring to the former as a synthetic compound is in fact a misnomer. Any relationship in these compounds is established based on our world knowledge after the structure in (33a) is constructed.

Unlike (12c) and (32b), when noun-incorporation involves a verbal noun of native origin, the resulting compound has word accent. Therefore, one cannot tell whether the structure is (33a) or (33b). The only way to tell is whether there is modifier stranding. Thus, when there is modifier stranding, we can safely say that the structure is (33b), involving noun incorporation. However, without modifier stranding (like (18)), a compound with a verbal noun of native origin is simply ambiguous between (33a) and (33b). Wiese (2008) takes a similar position regarding synthetic compounds in German. What is important from a cross-linguistic point of view is that, when a Sino-Japanese verbal noun is involved, we can differentiate the two kinds of compounds, namely word-accented compounds and phrasal-accented compounds. Given that all the phrasal-accented compounds discussed in §3.1—compounds with a Sino-Japanese verbal noun with a temporal suffix attached—have a thematic relation, while many of the word-accented compounds (like *doitu-bungaku* LHH-HLLL 'German literature') do not, accentuation can be a diagnostic when the analysis can be ambivalent (as in the case involving *yooroppa* 'Europe' and *ryokoo* 'traveling' in (12) that tells us whether there is a thematic relation within a compound (as (12c)) with the structure of (33b)) or not (as (12a) with the structure of (33a)).

Although I remain agnostic about whether the Baker-style incorporation is involved for the compounding in question (cf. note 9), there is one piece of evidence for this approach. Consider the following example:

---

pounds in (12a) and (32a) have a more articulated structure as proposed by Ito & Mester (2003: 83f). But I abstract away from this issue and (over)simplify the structure.

(34) [(*osanai) te]-dukuri
         childish hand-making
      '(*children's) hand-made' (Sugioka 2005: 220)

te-dukuri 'hand-made' itself is well-formed, but it cannot have a stranded modifier. This is a case where an adjunct (the instrumental) constitutes the left-hand
element of a compound. Given that only arguments can undergo (the Baker-
style) noun incorporation, it is expected that a compound containing an instrument cannot have the structure in (33b); it must have the structure in (33a). Since
only the structure in (33b) allows modifier stranding, it is expected that *te-dukuri*
'hand-made' does not allow modifier stranding, which is the case, as in (34).[17]

Admittedly, there is a pragmatic condition (i.e., being a cliché) for modifier
stranding as discussed in the previous subsection, and (34) might be ruled out
by that condition. But modifier stranding is systematically not observed with instrumental compounds. For example, another case of an instrumental compound
is *enpitu-gaki* 'pencil-written, written with a pencil', but this also does not allow
modifier stranding. This is expected if the Baker-style incorporation is involved.

Phases are assumed to be where not only semantics but also phonology is fixed.
However, the structure in (33b) results in either word accent or phrasal accent,
depending on whether the right-hand element is 'heavy' (i.e., right-branching or
Sino-Japanese) or not. Besides, consider:

(35) a. tàne 'seed' (accent on the first mora)
      b. [asàgao-no   tanè]-maki
          morning.glory-GEN seed sowing

          'sowing seeds of morning glory'
          (accent on the second mora of *tane*) = (19b)

tàne 'seed' has accent on the first mora by itself (35a). But when incorporated,
accent is on the second mora (35b). This suggests that accentuation and incorporation go hand in hand, both applying after syntax at PF. Specifically, if we
assume that accent in Japanese is not inherently specified for each word, but that
accentuation applies to the structure obtained after all the morphological derivations are complete (cf. Kubozono 2008;Nishiyama 2010),[18] there is no accent shift

---

[17] For this kind of argument, it is immaterial whether the modifier *osanai* 'childish' is structurally
   an adjunct or a specifier. It is the adjunct (instrumental) status of *te* 'hand' that is crucial.
[18] In (4c), I introduced the traditional view that the position of accent is specified for each noun
   in Japanese for expository purposes. In Kubozono's 2008 alternative view, nouns in Japanese
   are accentuated by the default antepenultimate accent rule, and nouns whose accent is not

from (35a) to (35b). In (35b), *tane* receives accent on the second mora after compounding. In this sense, S&K's terminology '*post*-syntactic compounds' seems really appropriate (although their original analysis is restricted to cases involving a Sino-Japanese verbal noun). Also, this analysis lends support to Chomsky's (2001) 2001 conjecture that head movement is not part of narrow syntax.

4 Phrasal compounds without noun incorporation

As we saw in (28), there are examples of phrasal compounds whose right-hand element is not a predicate, i.e., phrasal compounding without noun incorporation. This section presents three other types of phrasal compounding without noun incorporation, namely natural coordination (§4.1), suffixes/enclitics (§4.2), and prefixes/proclitics (§4.3).

4.1 Natural coordination

The following examples contain coordination as the "phrasal" part of phrasal compounds:

(36) a. LHHHH LHH-HLLL
     [karaoke to   geemu]-taikai
     [karaoke and   game]
      'contest for taikai' (Kageyama 2009: 518)

    b. HL   L   LHH-HHHLLL
       [bizyo to yazyuu]-syookoogun
       [beauty and beast]-syndrome
       (used in a blog as synonymous to the Stockholm Syndrome)

Specifically, the examples in (36) involve 'co-compounds' or 'natural coordination' forming a conceptual unit (e.g., *father-mother* denoting parents, cf. Wälchli 2005), again a kind of cliché. This usage of co-compound extends the original terminology (a.k.a. dvandva), which does not contain an overt conjunction.

By considering contrasts in accentuation, we can confirm that in (36a), *[karaoke to geemu]* is a phrase and *geemu-taikai* is a compound. The contour of *[karaoke to geemu]* is LHHHH LHH, with two rising pitch accents, which is typical for

---

antepenultimate (including unaccented nouns) are lexically specified as such. Such specifications and the default rule are realized after all the morphological derivations are complete. For accent in verbs in Japanese, see Nishiyama (2010).

phrases. The word *taikai* 'content' is inherently unaccented (LHHH), but *geemu-taikai* has the contour LHH-HLLL, showing that the accent falls on the first mora of *taikai*. As we saw in §2, this behavior is typical of compound accentuation.

As we saw in (9) (repeated below), right-branching compounds, which have phrasal accent, do not allow a coordinate phrase as the left-hand element:

(37)   *doitu   to   huransu : bungaku-kyookai
      Germany and France   literature association
      'associations of literature in Germany and France'

(9) was cited in §2 to show that right-branching compounds, despite having phrasal accent, are not phrases but words. Since the coordinated phrase in (9) is not a natural coordination, (9) cannot be ruled in as a phrasal compound.

4.2 Suffixes (enclitics)

In the following examples, a bound morpheme attaches to a phrase:

(38)   a.   LHH-HH
         [dai-kigyoo-no   syatyoo]-**kyuu**
         big-company-GEN president equivalent
         'equivalent to the president of a big company' (Kageyama 1993: 327)
   b.   LH-HLL
         [sakunen-no ziko]-**irai**
         last.year-GEN accident
         'since last year's accident' (cf. Kubozono 1995: 131)
   c.   LH-HH
         [atama-ga ookii hito]-**yoo**
         head-NOM big   people
         'for the use by big-headed people'

Accent is specified in the last part to show that the sequence consisting of the host + -*kyuu*/-*irai*/-*yoo* has word accent, and therefore that the latter morphemes are integrated as part of the word. One can say that -*kyuu*, -*irai*, and -*yoo* are suffixes, but they may better be analyzed as clitics, which are often characterized as phrasal affixes. If so, (38) involve cliticization rather than compounding. The choice of terminology is immaterial here.

The enclitics in question are originally Sino-Japanese bound roots which have turned into clitics. As expected, there are also proclitics which originate from Sino-Japanese bound roots; those are discussed in the next section.

4.3 Prefixes (proclitics)

Previous studies of the morphemes discussed in this subsection (Poser 1990; Kageyama 2001; 2009) have referred to them as prefixes. However, based on the criterion mentioned in the previous subsection, namely that these morphemes attach to an entire phrase, it is preferable to call them proclitics. They are illustrated by the following examples:

(39)   a. HL LHH-HLLL
           zen : gaimu daizin
           ex   foreign minister

      b. HL LHHH
           han : taisei
           anti establishment

Note that the examples have phrasal accent. Other proclitics with this property include *hòn-* 'this,' *mòto-* 'former,' *gèn-* 'current,' *kàku-* 'each,' *bòo-* 'a certain,' *dòo-* 'above-mentioned,' *ryòo-* 'both,' *ko-* 'deceased,' *hi-* 'non.'

The proclitics can attach to coordinate structures, revealing their phrasal nature:

(40)   a.   LHHHLL   LHLLL   late Hasegawa-mr and Uemura-mr
            ko : [Hasegawa-si to Uemura-si]
            'the late Mr. Hasegawa and Mr. Uemura' (adapted from Kageyama 2001: 265)

      b.   LHH   H LHHH
           gen   : [syusyoo   to   gaisyoo]
           current prime.minister and foreign.minister
           'current prime minister and foreign minister'

As in (36), accent reveals the phrasal nature of the coordinate structure.

In addition, the inherently anaphoric proclitic *dòo-* 'above-mentioned' violates the anaphoric island constraint, again strongly suggesting its phrasal status:

(41)   daitooryoo-wa asu   yuukoo-zyooyaku-ni tyooinsuru doo:
       president-TOP tomorrow amenity-treaty-DAT sign   said
       zyooyaku: saisyuu-an   niyoruto
       treaty   final-version according.to
       'The President is going to sign the amenity treaty tomorrow. According to the final version of the said treaty,...' (Kageyama 2001: 258)

Here, *doo-* in the second sentence refers to *yuukoo* 'amenity' of *yuukoo-zyoo-yaku* 'amenity treaty'. *doo-* itself is also a part of the compound *[doo: zyooyaku: saisyuu-an]*. In other words, both the anaphor and the antecedent are a part of a word, violating the anaphoric island constraint, which says that anaphoric relations cannot be established within a word.

While natural coordination in (36) and enclitics in (38) result in word accent, proclitics in (39) and (40) result in phrasal accent. Again this may be related to the fact that proclitics tend to yield a right-branching structure (cf. (10)). Even with a binary structure as in (39b), the clitic status of the left-hand element makes the right-hand element relatively heavy, and this might induce the reanalysis of the right-hand element as bimorphemic, as with the case of noun-incorporated compounds with Sino-Japanese predicates discussed in (24).

5 Reconsidering "Word Plus"

Kageyama (1993; 2001; 2009) proposes the new term Word Plus, which covers all the phrasal-accented compounds minus what he and S&K term post-syntactic compounds as discussed in §3.1. The level of Word Plus comes between a word and a phrase, and this is meant to capture the dual (i.e., word and phrasal) nature of the examples in question.

In my view, the notion Word Plus subsumes heterogeneous examples. First of all, many instances of Kageyama's Word Plus are right-branching compounds of the type in (8b), which cannot be analyzed as involving a phrase, as we saw in (9). This leaves us with prefixes (discussed in §4.3) and non-right-branching pseudo compounds. Let us discuss them in turn.

We saw in §4.3 that the proclitics in question have phrasal nature, in that they can attach to a phrase. But Kageyama argues that they have a word-like nature as well. The evidence comes from ellipsis:

(42) *A-wa gen   : kaityoo-to   suruai-de,   B-wa zen :
      A-TOP current   president-with acquainted-COP B-TOP ex
      kaityoo-to   siriai-da
      president-with acquainted-COP

      'A is acquainted with the current president, and B is acquainted with the ex-president.' (Kageyama 2001: 251)

The strikethrough indicates (cataphoric) ellipsis under identity. If *gen* is replaced with *genzai-no* 'current-GEN' and *zen* is replaced with *mae-no* 'former-

GEN', the sentence becomes grammatical. On the assumption that ellipsis is possible with phrases, Kageyama argues that (42) is evidence for the word-like nature of the proclitics in question.

However, (42) is independently ruled out, because a clitic *gen=- –* a bound morpheme – does not have a host after ellipsis. Alternatively, (42) is accounted for by assuming that the presence of the genitive is required for recovering the elided part. This is analogous to the following contrast in English:

(43)   a.   John's dog is bigger than Bill's ~~dog~~.

     b.   * John's dog is bigger than Bill~~'s dog~~.

Lobeck (1990) proposes an analysis of ellipsis based on Spec-Head agreement, but regardless of the validity of this analysis, whatever account captures the contrast in (43) would also account for (42).

Another piece of evidence that Kageyama cites for his observation that the proclitics in question are word-level (as opposed to phrasal level) entities is the following:

(44)   a.   yuumee-na haiyuu
          famous-MOD actor

     b.   ??yuumee-hàiyuu
          famous-actor

     c.   tihòo-no   tòsi
          province-GEN city

     d.   tihoo-tòsi
          province-city

(45)   a.   bòo   : [yuumee (*na) haiyuu]
          certain famous   MOD actor
          'a certain famous actor'

     b.   kàku : [tihoo   (*no) tòsi]
          each   province GEN   city
          'each provincial city' (Kageyama 2001: 249f)

yuumee-na haiyuu 'famous actor' (44a) and *tihòo-no tòsi* 'provincial city' (44c) are phrases, and the former cannot be a compound (44b), but the latter can (44d). The examples in (45) illustrate cases with proclitics, and the modifier marker *na* and the genitive marker *no* cannot appear here. This means that the prolicitcs cannot attach to a phrase (with *na* or *no*) but must attach to a word (i.e. here, to a compound). The contrast between (44b) and (45a) is telling: the compound *??yuumee-hàiyuu* does not exist by itself, but with the proclitic *bòo-*, the compound must be used. If *bòo-* and *kàku-* are clitics, they should be able to attach to a full phrase, and (45) should be possible with *na/no*, contrary to fact. This, according to Kageyama, is evidence for the word-like nature of the proclitics in question.

The above point is well taken, but cross-linguistically, the distinction between clitics and affixes is often not categorial but a matter of degree. For example, Romance clitics are often analyzed as being on a grammaticalization path towards agreement markers (namely suffixes) (cf. Suñer 1988, among others). Thus, the hybrid nature of the morphemes in question might simply reflect the hybrid nature of clitics in general, and this alone is not sufficient as a motivation for postulating a novel level of Word Plus.

Non-right-branching pseudo compounds are of two types: binary compounds with phrasal accent and left-branching compounds with phrasal accent. The former is illustrated by the following example:

(46)   kyùusyuu : nànbu
      Kyuusyuu   southern.part
      'Southern Kyusuyu' (Kubozono 1995: 70, also cited in Kageyama 2001: 261)

We have been assuming that (exceptional) phrasal accent in compounds is due to a right-branching structure. So why does (46) have phrasal accent, unlike ordinary compounds (with word accent), although it is not right-branching?

One important point is that (46) optionally can have the genitive between the two parts of the construction, and when this happens, we have phrasal accent, as expected:[19]

(47)   kyùusyuu-no   nànbu
      Kyuusyuu-GEN southern.part
      'southern part of Kyuusuyuu'

It is reasonable to analyze (46) as involving genitive deletion. Therefore, (46) is not a compound in a strict sense, but is better called a phrase in disguise.

Since the genitive usually cannot be left out, I conjecture that it is the *cliché* nature of (46) that makes genitive deletion possible. Thus, Kyuusyuu is an island

---

[19] Kubozono (1995: 70) notes that person names also have phrasal accent. Here as well, the genitive marker used to appear between the family name and the given name; however, this usage of the genitive marker has become obsolete.

stretching from north to south, and is usually referred to as having a northern and a southern part.[20]

A similar deletion process is involved with -*teki* (repeated):

(2)   dare-ga   bosu-da-teki tàido
      who-NOM boss-COP-like attitude
      'a who's the boss attitude'

teki- usually attaches to a root and derives an adjectival noun, which requires *na* as the modifying marker as in (48a):

(48)   a. hankoo-teki-na   tàido
           rebellion-like-MOD attitude
           'rebellious attitude'

      b. hankoo teki : tàido
           rebellion-like   attitude
           'rebellious attitude'

But as (48b) shows, the modifying marker *na* can be left out, resulting in what looks like a pseudo compound (with phrasal accent). In (2b) as well, *na* can emerge after -*teki*. The alternation between (48a) and (48b) is analogous to the presence and absence of *no* in (47) and (46).

Apparent left-branching pseudo compounds are illustrated as follows:

(49)   a. booeki-gàisya   : syatyoo
           trading-company   president

      b. siritu-dàigaku   : kyoozhu
           private-university   professor (Kageyama 2009: 518f)

The genitive deletion analysis proposed above for binary pseudo compounds can be extended to this case. These examples are also fixed expressions; they refer

---

[20] Kubozono's (1995: 71f) account is couched in terms of "semantic unity." Regarding this, Kageyama (2001: 261) states that "it is difficult to delimit the range of phrase-like [pseudo] compounds in term of their internal semantic relations." In the context of the current discussion, Kubozono's insight is reinterpreted as a pragmatic factor leading to cliché. It should also be noted that the examples in (46) and (47) are different from *haha no hi* 'Mother's Day' and *ama no zyaku* 'devil's advocate', which do not allow genitive deletion. Kageyama (2001: 268) cites them as Japanese equivalents of possessive compounds (e.g., *a girls' school*), and says that "those expressions are completely lexicalized." This is corroborated by the fact that they have word accent, as opposed to (46) and (47), which have phrasal accent.

to some distinguished titles, and *syatyoo* 'president' cannot be replaced by *sarari-iman* 'salaried worker' and *kyoozyu* 'professor' cannot be replaced by *syokuin* 'worker' in this kind of expression.

To summarize, Kageyama's notion of Word Plus is not a natural class and should be reclassified into three distinct classes: right-branching compounds, constructions involving proclitics, and phrases involving genitive deletion.

The genitive-deletion analysis is actually suggested by Kageyama & Shibatani (1989: 163, n. 7) for right-branching pseudo compounds as in (8b). However, as we saw in (9), the right-branching pseudo compounds of the type in (8b) cannot contain a phrase. Therefore, it is unlikely that they involve genitive deletion.

In fact, in later works Kageyama (1993: 342, 2001; 2009) does not endorse his own earlier suggestion of genitive deletion mentioned above and develops the Word Plus analysis instead. In particular, he notes (2001:250f, Kageyama (2009):519) notes that partial ellipsis is impossible with pseudo compounds, although it is possible when the genitive is present.

(50) A-wa siritu-daigaku *(no) ~~kyoozyu-de~~, B-wa kokuritu-daigaku
A-TOP private-university GEN professor COP B-TOP national-university
*(no) kyoozyu desu
GEN professor COP

'A ~~is a professor~~ (of) a private university, and B is a professor of a national university.' (adapted from Kageyama 2009: 519)

This might be taken as evidence against the genitive-deletion analysis. However, as mentioned after (42), the contrast in question is accounted for by assuming that the presence of the genitive is required for recovering the elided part. Thus, the ungrammaticality of (50) without *no* is not an obstacle for postulating genitive deletion for deriving left-branching pseudo compounds as in (49).

6 Conclusions

This paper has discussed phrasal compounds in Japanese, reanalyzing and reclassifying examples discussed in the previous studies in this area. One important mechanism for phrasal compounding is noun incorporation, although I leave open the exact mechanism of this process. I have extended Shibatani & Kageyama's (1988) and Kageyama & Shibatani's (1989) analysis of post-syntactic compounds (involving Sino-Japanese verbal noun) to verbal nouns of native origin. A noun-incorporation analysis for compounds involving verbal nouns of native origin has been proposed by Sugioka (2002), but I have refined the analysis. Specifically, compounds involving verbal nouns of native origin are structurally ambiguous, with one structure involving noun incorporation and the other without noun incorporation. Only when there is modifier stranding can we be certain that noun incorporation is involved.

Through the classification of phrasal compounds, I have claimed that Kageyama's (1993; 2001; 2009) notion of Word Plus should be reclassified into three existing types, namely right-branching compounds, constructions involving proclitics, and phrases involving genitive deletion.

Here is a table summarizing the proposed analyses and classes of phrasal compounds in Japanese:

Table 1: Summary and representative examples of types of phrasal compounds in Japanese

noun incorporation Sino- Japanese verbal noun	verbal noun of native origin	
yooròppa : ryokoo 'Europe traveling' (12c)	*asagao-no tane-maki* 'sowing seeds of morning glory' (19b) relational noun	*kireena mati-dukuri* 'construction of a clean town' (3) cliché

NO noun incorporation modifying structure	coordinate structure	prefix/ proclitic	suffix/ enclitic
tiisana sinsetu-undoo 'campaign for doing small kindness' (28a) cliché	*bizyo to yazyuu-syookoogun* 'beauty and beast-syndrome' (36b) cliché	*dai-kigyoo-no syatyoo-kyuu* 'equivalent to the president of a big company' (38a)	*zèn : gaimu-dàizin* 'ex-foreign minister' (39a)

Phrasal compounds are classified primarily by whether noun incorporation is involved or not. If it is, a further division is made according to whether the predicate is of Sino-Japanese or of native origin. With a Sino-Japanese verbal noun, the resulting compound has phrasal accent. In contrast, with a verbal noun of native origin, one cannot tell whether the compound is formed by noun incorporation or not without modifier stranding. This is why the above examples have modifier stranding, to make the case for the phrasal status of the complement of the verbal noun. There are two licensing conditions for modifier stranding: the complement of the predicate—the left-hand element of the compound—should be a relational noun or a part of a cliché.

If no noun incorporation is involved, there are four subclasses. With modifying structures and coordinate structures, the licensing condition is again cliché. Prefixes/proclitics and suffixes/enclitics originate in Sino-Japanese bound roots, but they have become clitics, so that they attach to a phrase. Given the ability of clitics to attach to entire phrases, they don't have to obey any conditions (such as cliché) in order to participate in the formation of phrasal compounds.

Lastly, I summarize and clarify my standpoint regarding the relationship between accent and syntax. As we saw in (8b), *dòitu : bungaku-kyòokai* 'German Association of Literature' has phrasal accent, but is not a phrasal compound. Conversely, there are cases of phrasal compounds with word accent. *kìreena mati-dùkuri* 'construction of a clean town' in (3) has word accent in the *mati-dùkuri* 'city-making' part, but it is a phrasal compound as a whole. Furthermore, *yooròppa : ryokoo-tyùu* 'while traveling in Europe' in (12c) has phrasal accent but is analyzed as a compound. These situations manifest a kind of syntax-phonology mismatch and might give an impression that accent is not a reliable diagnostic for determining whether a string is a word or a phrase.

However, I believe that the hypothesis that accent in Japanese reflects the syntactic status is basically correct. Specifically, whenever a string [A B] has word accent, it is always analyzed as a compound. In the case of *kìreena mati-dùkuri* 'construction of a clean town' in (3), the word status of the *mati-dùkuri* part is independently confirmed by *rendaku* sequential voicing, as we saw in §3.2.1. In this sense, the other two cases are exceptional, but not without a reason. *dòitu : bungaku-kyòokai* 'German Association of Literature' in (8b) has phrasal accent because it is a right-branching compound, which requires a special treatment for ease of processing, as we saw at the end of §2. For *yooròppa : ryokoo-tyùu* 'while traveling in Europe' in (12c), accent is really unhelpful, but the fact that an adverb cannot intervene between the two parts shows that it is not a phrase but a word, as we saw in (13). Its (exceptional) phrasal accent has been attributed to the Sino-Japanese nature of the verbal noun.

Acknowledgements

Earlier versions of this paper were presented in a meeting of the Lexicon Study Circle at Keio University and at the Workshop on Phrasal Compounds at University of Mannheim. I thank Carola Trips and Jaklin Kornfilt for inviting me to the workshop. For valuable comments and suggestions, I thank the audiences, Yoko Sugioka and Ichiro Yuhara. I also thank Jaklin Kornfilt for detailed and helpful comments on the earlier version of this paper. This study has been supported by grants from the Japan Society for the Promotion of Science (Grant # 23520454, 15K02470).

References

Ackema, Peter & Ad Neeleman. 2004. *Beyond morphology: Interface conditions on word-formation*. Oxford: Oxford University Press.

Baker, Mark. 1988. *Incorporation*. Chicago: University of Chicago Press.

Beard, Robert. 1991. Decompositional composition: The semantics of scope ambiguities and ʻbracketing paradoxes. *Natural Language and Linguistic Theory* 9. 195–229.

Botha, Rudolf P. 1981. A base rule theory of Afrikaans synthetic compounds. In Michael Moortgat, Harry van der Hulst & Teun Hoekstra (eds.), *The scope of lexical rules*, 1–77. Dordrecht: Foris.

Bresnan, Joan & Sam Mchombo. 1995. The lexical integrity principle: Evidence from Bantu. *Natural language and linguistic theory* 13. 181–254.

Carstairs-McCarthy, Andrew. 2002. *An introduction to English morphology*. Edinburgh: Edinburgh University Press.

Chomsky, Noam. 2001. Derivation by phase. In Michael Kenstowicz (ed.), *Ken Hale: A life in language*, 1–52. Cambridge, MA: MIT Press.

Embick, David. 2010. *Localism and globalism in morphology and phonology*. Cambridge: MIT Press.

Fukuda, Shin. 2012. Aspectual verbs as functional heads: Evidence from Japanese aspectual verbs. *Natural Language and Linguistic Theory* 30. 965–1026.

Halle, Morris & Alec Marantz. 1993. Distributed Morphology and the pieces of inflection. In Kenneth Hale & Samuel Jay Keyser (eds.), *The view from building 20: Essays in linguistics in honor of Sylvain Bromberger*, 111–176. Cambridge, MA: MIT Press.

Harley, Heidi. 2009. Compounding in distributed morphology. In Rochelle Lieber & Pavol Štekauer (eds.), *The Oxford handbook of compounding*, 129–144. Oxford: OUP.

Hawkins, John A. 1990. A parsing theory of word order universals. *Linguistic Inquiry* 21. 223–261.

Ito, Junko & Armin Mester. 2003. *Japanese morphophonemics: Markedness and word structure.* Cambridge: MIT Press.

Ito, Junko & Armin Mester. 2007. Prosodic adjunction in Japanese compounds. *MIT Working Papers in Linguistics 55: Formal Approaches to Japanese Linguistics* 4. 97–111.

Kageyama, Taro. 1989. The place of morphology in grammar: Verb-Verb compounds in Japanese. *Yearbook of Morphology* 2. 73–94.

Kageyama, Taro. 1993. *Bumpoo to gokeesee [Grammar and word formation].* Tokyo: Hituzi Syobo.

Kageyama, Taro. 2001. Word Plus: The intersection of words and phrases. In Jeroen van de Weijer & Tetsuo Nishihara (eds.), *Issues in Japanese phonology and morphology,* 245–276. Berlin: de Gruyter.

Kageyama, Taro. 2009. Isolate: Japanese. In Rochelle Lieber & Pavol Štekauer (eds.), *The Oxford handbook of compounding,* 512–526. Oxford: Oxford University Press.

Kageyama, Taro. 2013. Postsyntactic compounds and semantic head-marking in Japanese. *Japanese/Korean Linguistics* 20. 363–382.

Kageyama, Taro & Masayoshi Shibatani. 1989. Mozyuuru bunpoo no gokeeseeron: No meesiku kara no hukugoogo-keesee. [on word-formation in module grammar: Compounding out of genitive noun phrases]. In *Nihongogaku no sintenkai [New developments in Japanese linguistics],* 139–166. Tokyo: Kuroshio.

Kawahara, S. 2015. The phonology of Japanese accent. In H. Kubozono (ed.), *Handbook of Japanese phonetics and phonology,* 445–492. Berlin: Mouton de Gruyter.

Kubozono, Haruo. 1995. *Gokeesee to oninkoozoo* (Word formation and phonological structures). Tokyo: Kuroshio.

Kubozono, Haruo. 2005. Rendaku: Its domain and linguistic conditions. In Kensuke Nanjo Jeroen van de Weijer & Tetsuo Nishihara (eds.), *Voicing in Japanese,* 5–24. Berlin: Mouton de Gruyter.

Kubozono, Haruo. 2008. Japanese accent. In Shigeru Miyagawa & Mamoru Saito (eds.), *The Oxford handbook of japanese linguistics,* 165–191. Oxford & New York: Oxford University Press.

Lieber, Rochelle. 1983. Argument linking and compounds in English. *Linguistic Inquiry* 14. 251–285.

Lieber, Rochelle. 1992. *Deconstructing morphology. Word formation in syntactic theory.* Chicago: University of Chicago Press.

Lieber, Rochelle. 2010. On the lexical semantics of compounds: Non-affixal (de)verbal compounds. In Sergio Scalise & Irene Vogel (eds.), *Cross-disciplinary issues in compounding*, 127–144. Philadelphia: John Benjamins.

Lobeck, Ann. 1990. Functional heads as proper governors. *NELS* 20. 348–362.

Marantz, Alec. 1988. Clitics, morphological merger, and the mapping to phonological structure. In Michael Hammond & Michael Noonan (eds.), *Theoretical morphology*, 253–270. New York: Academic Press.

Marantz, Alec. 1997. No escape from syntax: Don't try morphological analysis in the privacy of your lexicon. In *Proceedings of the 21st Annual Penn Linguistic Colloquium: University of Pennsylvania Working Papers in Linguistics*, vol. 4.2, 201–225.

Massam, Diane. 2001. Pseudo noun incorporation in Niuean. *Natural Language and Linguistic Theory* 19. 153–197.

Mithun, Marianne. 2010. Constraints on compounds and incorporation. In Sergio Scalise & Irene Vogel (eds.), *Cross-disciplinary issues in compounding*, 37–56. Philadelphia: John Benjamins.

Nishiyama, Kunio. 1999. Adjectives and the copulas in japanese. *Journal of East Asian Linguistics* 8. 183–222.

Nishiyama, Kunio. 2008. V-V compounds. In Shigeru Miyagawa & Mamoru Saito (eds.), *The Oxford Handbook of Japanese linguistics*, 320–347. Oxford & New York: Oxford University Press.

Nishiyama, Kunio. 2010. Penultimate accent in Japanese predicates and the verb–noun distinction. *Lingua* 120. 2353–2366.

Nishiyama, Kunio. 2016. The theoretical status of ren'yoo (stem) in Japanese verbal morphology. *Morphology* 26. 65–90.

Poser, William. 1990. Word internal phrase boundary in Japanese. In Sharon Inkelas & Draga Zec (eds.), *The Phonology-Syntax Connection*, 279–288. Chicago: University of Chicago Press.

Roeper, Thomas & Muffy E. A. Siegel. 1978. A lexical transformation for verbal compounds. *Linguistic Inquiry* 9. 199–260.

Sakakura, Atsuyoshi. 1952. *Nihon-bunpoo-no hanasi [Lectures on Japanese grammar]*. Osaka: Sougensha. Revised (1974) by Tokyo: Kyouiku Shuppan.

Shibatani, Masayoshi & Taro Kageyama. 1988. Word formation in a modular theory of grammar: A case of postsyntactic compounds in Japanese. *Language* 64. 451–484.

Spencer, Andrew. 1992. *Morphological theory*. Malden: Blackwell.

Sproat, Richard. 1993. Morphological non-separation revisited: Review article: Deconstructing morphology, by rochelle lieber. *Yearbook of Morphology* 1992(1992). 235–258.

Sugioka, Yoko. 2002. Incorporation vs. Modification in deverbal compounds. *In Japanese/Korean Linguistics* 10. 495–508.

Sugioka, Yoko. 2005. Multiple mechanisms underlying morphological productivity. In Salikoko S. Mufwene, Elaine J. Francis & Rebecca S. Wheeler (eds.), *Polymorphous linguistics: Jim McCawley's legacy*, 203–223. Cambridge: MIT Press.

Sugioka, Yoko. 2008. Remarks on asymmetry and recursion in compound formation. In Tetsuya Sano, Mika Endo, Miwa Isobe, Koichi Otaki, Koji Sugisaki & Takeru Suzuki (eds.), *An enterprise in the cognitive science of language: A festschrift for Yukio Otsu*, 65–78. Tokyo: Hituzi Shobo.

Suñer, Margarita. 1988. The role of agreement in clitic doubled constructions. *Natural Language and Linguistic Theory* 6. 391–434.

Tsujimura, Natsuko. 2007. *An introduction to Japanese linguistics (second edition)*. Malden: Blackwell Publishing.

Wälchli, Bernard. 2005. *Co-compounds and natural coordination*. Oxford & New York: Oxford University Press.

Wiese, Richard. 2008. Two levels of morphological structure. *Journal of Germanic Linguistics* 20(3). 243–274.

Chapter 7

Copying compound structures: The case of Pharasiot Greek

Metin Bağrıaçık
Ghent University

Aslı Göksel
Boğaziçi University

Angela Ralli
University of Patras

Unlike other Modern Greek dialects in which compounds are one-word structures, in Pharasiot Greek – an Asia Minor Greek dialect heavily influenced by Turkish – compounds are formed by two fully inflected words, where the left-hand constituent is marked with compound markers whose shape is conditioned morphologically. Based on structural similarities between compound structures in Pharasiot Greek and in Turkish, we claim that Pharasiot Greek compounding is selectively copied from Turkish. The compound marker role in Pharasiot Greek is assumed by what are originally genitive suffixes by identification of the genitive with the Turkish compound marker, which is exapted from a possessive suffix, attaching to right-hand constituent. We correlate certain structural differences between the two languages to the nature and the locus of the compound marker. Among these differences is the occurrence of phrasal constituents in the non-head position in Turkish and lack thereof in Pharasiot Greek. We show that the compound marker in Pharasiot Greek attaches to stems. As such, no phrasal constituent can be hosted in the position to which the compound marker attaches. In Turkish, on the other hand, since the compound marker attaches to the head, the non-head can easily host phrasal constituents. We test this correlation against Khalkha Mongolian, another Altaic language, in which, unlike Turkish, the compound marker attaches to the non-head. We show that similar to Pharasiot Greek, but unlike Turkish,

Metin Bağrıaçık, Aslı Göksel & Angela Ralli. Copying compound structures: The case of Pharasiot Greek. In Carola Trips & Jaklin Kornfilt (eds.), *Further investigations into the nature of phrasal compounding*, 185–231. Berlin: Language Science Press. DOI:10.5281/zenodo.885129

phrasal constituents cannot be hosted in the non-head position in Khalkha, verifying the correlation we proposed between the locus of the compound marker and the availability of phrasal non-heads.

1 Introduction

Despite the recent plethora of research on copying of morphological items (e.g., Johanson 1992; Gardani 2008; Seifart 2015a,b; Gardani et al. 2015 among many others), and the growing interest on structural copying (Bowern 2008; Lepschy & Tosi 2006; Lucas 2012; Grimstad et al. 2014; Lohndal 2013; Aboh 2015; Thomason forthcoming), the question whether compounds are prone to borrowing or not is a topic which still awaits addressing, and copying of compounding has been noted only sporadically, and often as calques (cf. Ralli 2014). This seems legitimate as *a priori* it is not clear what can actually be copied as or in a compound since cross-linguistically compounds involve little or no overt functional material. More importantly, compounding cross-linguistically has an unclear status between syntax and morphology (Anderson 1992; Aronoff 1994; Di Sciullo 2005 among many others, see also Scalise & Vogel 2010: 4–5 for an overview). As such, it becomes a challenge to make general arguments on what aspects of a compound could be copied. Given the lack of an established cross-linguistic definition of compounds and a consensus on its locus of generation, rather than attempting to make general arguments about (constraints on) 'compound copying', a more fruitful approach would be to document cases of 'possible compound copying' between languages whose compound structures are relatively well-documented. This is exactly what the current paper aims at. We present a case study of a compound-structure in Pharasiot Greek (henceforth PhG), an Asia Minor Greek dialect which is on the verge of extinction. We show that compounds in PhG display properties of two typologically different language systems, i.e., Turkish (Altaic) and Greek (Indo-European).

As noted by Ralli (2013b), typical Hellenic[1] compounds involve two lexemes which are concatenated with a compound marker, -*o*-, occurring in between the two. These can be attributive, subordinative or coordinative compounds. Such compounds are usually inflected as single stems and are phonological words bearing single accent. Although some dialects of Modern Greek may not exhibit certain compound types that the others do, across all the modern dialects (1), as well as in older varieties (2), the fact that compounds are concatenations of two

---

[1] We refer to all diatopic and diachronic varieties of Modern Greek as Hellenic in this paper.

(or more) lexemes with the compound marker *-o-*, i.e., the [X-o-X] template, is
constant.[2]

(1) a. lemonóðendro   (Modern Greek)
        lemon-o-ðendro
        lemon-CM-tree

        'lemon tree'

    b. ampelopérvolon   (Cypriot Greek, Andreou 2014: 132)
        ampel-o-pervolon
        vine-CM-field

        'vineyard'

    c. čavdarópsomin   (Pontic Greek, Papadopoulos 1961: 327)
        čavdar-o-psomin
        rye-CM-bread

        'rye bread'

    d. ðimunóspurus   (Aivaliot Greek, Ralli 2016)
        ðimun-o-spurus
        demon-CM-seed

        'very smart person'

(2) hoplitódromos   (Ancient Greek, Ralli & Raftopoulou 1999: 398)
    hoplit-o-dromos
    hoplite-CM-race

    'Hoplitodromos, race of soldiers'

---

[2] If there is ever a structural head, it is on the right (cf. Ralli 2013b, see also Andreou 2014
for exocentric compounds and definition of head in these compounds). This, however, is not
exceptionless. In Ancient Greek (i.a) as well as in Modern Greek dialect of Bovese (i.b) left-
headed compounds are attested, albeit in a rather limited number in the latter (Andreou 2014):

    (i) a. hippopótamos   (Ancient Greek)
             hipp-o-potamos
             horse-CM-river

             'hippopotamus'

        b. ššulófuro   (Bovese Greek, Andreou 2014: 134)
             ššul-o-furo
             wood-CM-oven

             'wood for oven'

In PhG, however, this Hellenic compounding structure depicted above is absent.[3] Instead, PhG compounds are productively formed as concatenations of two lexemes as fully inflected words, whereby the left-hand constituent, the non-head, is marked with a compound marker, *-u* or *-s*, depending on the gender of the noun (3), whose shape, but not distribution, mirrors that of genitive suffixes in the language (4):

(3) a. jorganú   xarái
        jorgan-**u** xarai
        quilt.N-CM face.N.NOM.SG
        'quilt cover'

    b. matrákas práða
        matraka-**s** praða
        frog.F-CM leg.N.NOM.PL
        'frog legs'

(4) a. tu   čočuxú   ta   γíða
        tu   čočux-**u** ta   γiða
        the.N.GEN.SG child.N.GEN.SG the.N.NOM/ACC.PL goat.N.NOM/ACC.PL
        'the child's goats'

    b. s   γrǽs   ta   γíða
        s   γrǽ-**s**   ta   γiða
        the.F.GEN.SG beldam.F.GEN.SG the.N.NOM/ACC.PL goat.N.NOM/ACC.PL
        'the beldam's goats'

Such concatenations as those in (3) can form subordinate and attributive compounds, and unlike all other Hellenic varieties, coordinative compounds cannot be formed in this way. The constituents in these compounds retain their own accents, thus causing the compound to behave as a phonological phrase in this respect. Besides, such compounds allow limited access to syntactic operations exerted on them, such as external modification of the head or coordination of the constituents. On the other hand, by undergoing derivation as single lexical items, or not allowing certain syntactic operations, such as scrambling or outbound anaphora, they behave as lexical items, hence they constitute an example of compounds as borderline cases between phrase-formation and word-formation.

We interpret the two facts about compounding in PhG, i.e., the lack of Hellenic compound structure [X-o-X] and (the emergence of) the productive subordinate

---

[3] It should be stated at the outset that in Cappadocian Greek, a Modern Greek dialect closely related to PhG, Hellenic compounds are rather restricted. The findings and arguments in this paper may or may not be extended to Cappadocian Greek. Since we have not investigated compounding in this variety, we will not incorporate such discussion into the current paper.

or attributive compounds where the non-head is marked with the compound markers -*u* or -*s*, (indicated hereafter as N-GEN N, by referring to the similarity of the compound markers to genitive suffixes) as one of the many end-products of the heavy and long-lasting influence of Turkish on PhG. More specifically, we argue that the N-GEN N compound pattern is copied from Turkish and incorporated into PhG word formation by evoking native morphological elements. This is verified by a number of interesting common characteristics of Turkish N+N compounds which are marked at their right periphery by the compound marker -*sI*, which itself is *exapted* from a possessive marker. Since no overt possessive markers exist in PhG, the compound marker of Turkish is identified with the PhG genitive marker. In other words, the pattern borrowing has taken place only selectively.

This selective pattern-borrowing account leads to an interesting question: how much of a pattern can be borrowed between (the) two languages? Turkish is known to productively accommodate phrasal strings in the left-hand, i.e., the non-head position of a N+N-*sI* compound. If the compound pattern in PhG is indeed borrowed from Turkish, then should we also expect the PhG N-GEN N compound pattern to be able to accommodate phrasal non-heads? The expectation might be legitimate but it is not confirmed: we will show that nothing of a phrasal sort can be hosted in the non-head position of the PhG N-GEN N template, once again verifying that the pattern is only selectively-copied. What renders phrasal non-heads unavailable in this N-GEN N requires its own story: We will argue that the morphological affixes employed as compound markers in the N-GEN N template are exapted from native inflectional affixes. Affixes in PhG, as in all other Hellenic varieties, attach to bare stems. This is a native rule. Thus, no phrasal element, even when the head of the phrase left-aligns with the affix, is a good candidate for this affix-attachment. Hence, the tension between the borrowed pattern and native word-formation rules is resolved by favoring the latter. Thus we see that the pattern is borrowed from Turkish but is constrained with native word-formation rules. Then coordination or external modification facts pertinent to the compounds on the one hand and their peculiar atomic behavior on the other require invoking an analysis which can capture such 'hybrid' elements between syntax and morphology. Without following a strict adherence to any in this paper, we will review certain possible analyses that can capture the peculiarities of these N-GEN N compounds as well as their possible locus of generation.

In Section 2 we present a brief overview of Hellenic compounding. Section 3 is devoted to the discussion on compounding in PhG and its differences from Hellenic compounding. Presenting certain similarities between PhG and Turkish in terms of their compound structures, Section 4 argues that the PhG compounding pattern is selectively copied from Turkish; however, native functional material is employed in the pattern. Section 5 delves into phrasal compounds in Turkish and lack thereof in PhG and argues that the lack of phrasal non-heads is epiphenomenal on the native compound markers employed in PhG. Section 6 raises some residual questions about the locus of N-GEN N compounding in PhG and provides tentative answers to these questions. Section 7 concludes.

2 Hellenic compounding

In a prototypical Hellenic compound, two lexemes are juxtaposed with a compound marker -*o*- interpolating between the two (Ralli 2008). The output, i.e., the compound, is a phonological word with a single stress (Nespor & Ralli 1994; 1996). The compound marker originates from an ancient thematic vowel, but became a compound marker already in the Hellenistic period (ca 3rd c. BCE – 3rd c. CE) (Anastasiadi-Symeonidi 1983; Ralli & Raftopoulou 1999; Ralli 2007; 2013b). At different periods of the language, the lexemes involved in compounding have been realized as roots or stems, yet at least in Modern Greek there is no difference between the two (cf. Ralli 2005: 23, Ralli 2013b: 8) and therefore, we will simply use the term 'stem' in the rest of the paper. A stem is a lexeme that cannot stand in a syntactic position on its own but can do so only when it is a word, i.e., when it bears (inherent or structural) inflectional material which can be overt or covert. The stems are inflected for gender, case and number, and they are assigned to distinct inflectional classes (ICs) (Ralli 2000; 2005). Such ICs are based on the presence of systematic stem allomorphy (for stem allomorphy see below) and the form of the entire set of fusional inflectional endings that are combined with the stems. In such a system, gender is a feature inherent to the stems, and nouns of the same gender value may inflect according to different paradigms or conversely, nouns of different gender values may inflect according to the same paradigm. An example of a stem as the representative of IC1 is given in Table 1 below.[4]

As shown in Table 1, the stem *anθrop-* carries the encyclopedic information, 'meaning', 'gender' and 'IC'. In this case it is 'masculine' and it belongs to IC1. IC1 involves (masculine or feminine) nominals which decline according to the paradigm in Table 1. According to Ralli (2000), there are eight ICs (IC1–IC8) active

---

[4] Henceforth, stems will be glossed with small capitals and word forms will be written in minuscule.

Table 1: The declension of the stem 'anθrop-', 'HUMAN' (masculine) in IC1.

Singular	nominative		accusative		genitive	
	stem	inflection	stem	inflection	stem	inflection
	anθrop	-os	anθrop	-o	anθrop	-u
	HUMAN	-NOM.SG	HUMAN	-ACC.SG	HUMAN	-GEN.SG
	'human' (nom.)		'human' (acc.)		'human' (gen.)	

Plural	nominative		accusative		genitive	
	stem	inflection	stem	inflection	stem	inflection
	anθrop	-i	anθrop	-us	anθrop	-on
	HUMAN	-NOM.PL	HUMAN	-ACC.PL	HUMAN	-GEN.PL
	'humans' (nom.)		'humans' (acc.)		'humans' (gen.)	

in Modern Greek today. The number of ICs, the way they are structured and which nouns belong to which ICs vary vastly both diachronically and among different dialects; however, for all Modern Greek dialects, as far as we can tell, there are ICs and nouns are located in different ICs.

In a typical Hellenic compound, the non-head, i.e., the left hand constituent of a compound is obligatorily a stem (which is formulated as *Bare-Stem Constraint* by Ralli & Karasimos 2009). As for the head position, i.e., the right-hand position of the compound, it can either be occupied by another stem or a word. Hence, the structures in (5) are available in Modern Greek as compound structures:

(5) a. [word [stem [stem STEM] -CM- [stem STEM]] -INFLECTION]

  b. [word [stem STEM] -CM- [word STEM-INFLECTION]]

(Ralli 2013b: 79, ex. (9))

The structure in (5a) is exemplified as (6a) and the structure in (5b) is exemplified as (7a). The compound constituents in their word forms are presented in (6b–c) and (7b–c) respectively:[5]

---

[5] In the following Modern Greek examples from this point onwards, we do not provide information about the gender of the stems, which is tangential to the current paper.

(6) a. anθropómorfos
         anθrop-o-morf-os
         HUMAN-CM-SHAPE-NOM.SG
         'anthropomorphic'

     b. ánθropos   c. morfí
         anθrop-os   morfi-Ø
         HUMAN-NOM.SG   SHAPE-NOM.SG
         'human'   'shape'

(7) a. anθropoθeizmós
         anθrop-o-θeizmos
         HUMAN-CM-THEISM.NOM.SG
         'anthropotheism'

     b. ánθropos   c. θeizmós
         anθrop-os   θeizm-os
         HUMAN-NOM.SG   THEISM-NOM.SG
         'human'   'theism'

Notice that as a reflex of the *Bare-Stem Constraint*, in both (6a) and (7a), the non-head is a stem (cf. the word forms in (6b) and (7b) respectively). The compounds in (6a) and (7a) differ, however, as to the shape of the head: in (6a), the head of the compound is realized by a stem. This is witnessed by the fact that the inflectional ending of the overall compound in (6a), i.e., *-os*, is different than the inflectional ending which the stem in head position would get in isolation (i.e., *-Ø*, cf. (6c)). In other words, the compound stem in (6a) is assigned to a different IC than the head noun (i.e., *morf(i)* 'shape'). Moreover, the stress of the overall compound is realized on a different syllable than when it falls on its constituents (cf. (6a) with (6b) and (6c)). This is formalized as the *Compound Specific Stress Rule* by Nespor & Ralli (1996), which operates on compounds where both constituents are stems, by assigning the stress to the antepenultimate syllable. Hence, the compound in (6a) has the templatic structure shown in (5a). In the compound in (7a), on the other hand, the head position is realized by a word-form, i.e., a lexeme with its own inflection. This is so since the inflectional ending of the compound (7a) and of the head word in isolation (7c) coincide; in other words, the compound in (7a) inherits its IC from its head. Moreover, the stress of the compound and the stress of the head noun in isolation fall on the same syllable (cf. (7a) with (7c)). Hence the compound in (7a) is formed on the template in (5b).[6]

Another peculiar characteristic of Hellenic nouns, which is directly relevant to compound formation, is the phenomenon of stem allomorphy. In Hellenic varieties, while a certain allomorph of a stem undergoes certain affixation, another allomorph of the same lexeme can be employed in other affixation processes. To illustrate the case, the lexeme 'body' shows this allomorphy between *soma-* and *somat-*. While the former is employed in singular nominative and accusative forms, the latter is employed in singular genitive, as well as in all the plural forms (see Table 2). More relevant to our paper, the latter, i.e., *somat-* is also the one which undergoes derivation (8a), and can also be employed in certain compounds as a stem (8b, 8c):

Table 2: *soma-* ~ *somat-* (neuter) 'BODY' stem allomorphy in IC8

	singular		plural	
nominative	soma	-Ø	somat	-a
accusative	soma	-Ø	somat	-a
genitive	somat	-os	somat	-on

(8) a. somatíðio
        somat-iði-o
        BODY-DER-NOM.SG
        'particle; corpuscle'

  b. somatofílakas   c. kiknosómatos
      somat-o-filakas   kikn-o-somat-os
      BODY-CM-GUARD.NOM.SG   SWAN-CM-BODY-NOM.SG
      'bodyguard'   'swan-bodied'

Note that in a few cases, the other stem, i.e., *soma-*, can also be employed in a compound (see 8d below). In this case, at first glance it is not clear whether the lexeme employed in the head position is the stem or the word form of the lexeme

---

[6] The templates in (5) are not the only ones operative in Modern Greek, nor is the compound type depicted here, i.e., [X-o-X] the sole compound structure. The discussion of all the compound types in Modern Greek is well beyond the aims of the current paper. For these cases, the reader is referred to Ralli (2013b).

Metin Bağrıaçık, Aslı Göksel & Angela Ralli

since their overt forms coincide when the word is in nominative case (cf. Table 2). The difference in the position of stress between the compound and the head noun in isolation, however, suggests that the form employed is a stem (cf. the stress on the compound in (8d) and the stress on the head constituent in isolation 8e):[7]

(8)　d.　xromósoma
　　　　xrom-o-soma-Ø
　　　　COLOR-CM-BODY-NOM.SG
　　　　'chromosome'

　　　e.　sóma
　　　　soma-Ø
　　　　BODY-NOM.SG
　　　　'body'

The structures presented as templates in (5) are highly productive in standard Modern Greek and in most Modern Greek varieties, and the permutations allowed are the following: N+N, A+A, V+V, A+N, N+V, Adv+V which are exemplified in (9–14) respectively:

(9)　N+N (stem + word)

　　a.　anθropoθeizmós
　　　　anθrop-o-θeizmos
　　　　HUMAN-CM-THEISM.NOM.SG
　　　　'anthropotheism'

　　b.　ánθropos
　　　　anθrop-os
　　　　HUMAN-NOM.SG
　　　　'human'

　　c.　θeizmós
　　　　θeizm-os
　　　　THEISM-NOM.SG
　　　　'theism'

(10)　A+A (stem + stem)

　　a.　asprómavros
　　　　aspr-o-mavr-os
　　　　WHITE-CM-BLACK-NOM.SG
　　　　'black and white'

　　b.　áspros
　　　　aspr-os
　　　　WHITE-NOM.SG
　　　　'white'

　　c.　mávros
　　　　mavr-os
　　　　BLACK-NOM.SG
　　　　'black'

---

[7] If the compound head is a word, it always retains its own stress. See Ralli (1988), where the location of word stress in Modern Greek is morpho-phonologically accounted for.

(11)   V+V (stem + word)

    a.   anavosvíno
       anav-o-svin-o
       TURN.ON-CM-TURN.OFF-1SG
       'I turn on and off'

    b.   anávo   c.   svíno
       anav-o   svin-o
       TURN.ON-1SG   TURN.ON-1SG
       'I turn on'   'I turn off'

(12)   A+N (stem+word)

    a.   kalóɣeros
       kal-o-ɣer-os
       GOOD-CM-OLD.MAN-NOM.SG
       'monk'

    b.   kalós   c.   ɣéros
       kal-os   ɣer-os
       GOOD-NOM.SG   OLD.MAN-NOM.SG
       'good'   'old man'

(13)   N+V (stem + word)

    a.   laɣokimáme
       laɣ-o-kim-ame
       HARE-CM-SLEEP-1SG
       'I doze'

    b.   laɣós   c.   kimáme
       laɣ-os   kim-ame
       HARE-NOM.SG   SLEEP-1SG
       'hare'   'I sleep'

(14)   Adv+V (stem + word)

    a.   krifokitázo
       krif-o-kitaz-o
       SECRET-CM-LOOK-1SG
       'I peek'

b. krifá
krif-a
SECRET-ADV
'secretly'

c. kitázo
kitaz-o
LOOK-1SG
'I look'

The information we provided above concerning Hellenic compounding might be the tip of an iceberg to the interested reader. However, this information is sufficient for the purposes of the current paper. For a more detailed account of compounding in (Modern) Greek, we refer the reader to Ralli (2013b).

3 Compounding in Pharasiot Greek

The dialect of Pharasa, along with the dialects spoken in Cappadocia, Pontus and Silli, is an Asia Minor Greek dialect which was spoken in at least seven villages in the southeast Kayseri province and north of Adana province of modern-day Turkey, in the area known also as Pharasa (Dawkins 1916) until 1923. In the years following 1923, the PhG speaking population was relocated to a few villages in Northern Greece according to the population exchange that was enacted as a supplementary protocol to the Treaty of Lausanne signed in 1923. The exact number of speakers before the population exchange is difficult to state as the accounts pertinent to the population of Pharasa also include the Turkish-speaking Orthodox population of the region. Based on earlier accounts (Xenofanis 1896, 1905–1910; Sarantidis 1899; Kyrillos 1815; Dawkins 1916), Bağrıaçık (in preparation) estimates that the number of PhG speakers before the population exchange was around 2000. Today, the dialect is spoken by about 25 second generation refugees in a few villages of Northern Greece. The dialect has long been assigned an unclear status, such as being a sub-dialect of Pontic (cf. Dawkins 1916, Dawkins 1937: 27), which nevertheless has curious connections with the dialect of Cyprus (Dawkins 1940: 22). It is also often treated as a variant of Cappadocian (Anastasiadis 1976), justified mostly by its geographical proximity to Cappadocia. The growing interest in micro-comparative work on Greek dialects and work especially on PhG, however, reveals that PhG must have diverged at a much earlier time-period than Cappadocian and Pontic (Karatsareas 2011, Bağrıaçık in preparation). Similar to other Asia Minor Greek dialects, PhG has been isolated from the rest of the Greek speaking world possibly in the early Medieval Greek period, and it had been heavily influenced by (Old) Anatolian Turkish at all levels of grammar. The dialect was also influenced by the neighboring Armenian dialects, though mostly at the lexical level. Beside retentions or innovations common to all Asia Minor Greek dialects, the dialect also exhibits remarkable differences from the rest of the Asia Minor Greek dialects at all levels of its grammar. Since the speakers of PhG have been living in Greece for the last 90 years, and are thus bilinguals in Standard Greek and PhG, the influence of Modern Greek is also observed in certain domains (see Bağrıaçık in preparation).

Of the numerous peculiar properties of PhG, one is the lack of prototypical Hellenic compounding depicted in section 2. The collections in the dialect both prior to the population exchange (e.g., de Lagarde 1886; Levidis 1892; Grégoire 1909; Dawkins 1916) or texts written in and on the dialect after the population exchange (e.g., Theodoridis 1960; 1964; 1966) contain no tokens of Hellenic-style compounding [X-o-X]. A recent dictionary of the dialect (Papastefanou & Karakelidou 2012) contains only a few instances of [X-o-X] compounds, which, however, seem to be borrowed from Modern Greek since they belong to medical or scientific jargons:

(15) emoréja
      em-o-reja
      BLOOD-CM-BURST.F.NOM.SG

      'hemorrhaging'   (cf. Modern Greek, *emoréja*)

This, however, does not mean that compounding is missing altogether in the dialect. There is a productive N+N compound structure in which both the head, i.e., the right hand constituent, and the non-head, i.e., the left-hand constituent, are word forms.[8,9]

---

[8] Such examples abound in the dictionary by Papastefanou & Karakelidou (2012). However, the indication of stress in these compounds is arbitrary; sometimes it is shown only once, sometimes both are indicated and sometimes they are omitted altogether. We assume that this is either because PhG does not have a uniform orthographic convention, or the stress pattern was unknown to the authors.

[9] There are also certain attributive A+N combinations (i), or N+N combinations (ii) as coordinate structures that are possible candidates for compounding. These structures, however, do not involve a compound marker and both constituents bear their own inflection and stress (see Bağrıaçık in preparation and Bağrıaçık et al. forthcoming for further details.):

   (i)   traxariéris   nomáts
         hairy.M.NOM.SG man.M.NOM.SG
         'ogre'

   (ii) ma   tatá
         mother.F.NOM/ACC.SG father.M.NOM/ACC.SG
         'mother-father'

We will not discuss the structures in (i–ii) in the current paper.

However, the inflection of the non-head constituent varies according to the gender of the base that it attaches to. Similar to Modern Greek, PhG nouns, simplex or complex (i.e., compounds or derived words), are assigned to different ICs. While masculine and neutral nouns of various ICs are affixed with -*ú* (16a), feminine nouns of various ICs are affixed with -*s* (17a). These suffixes are also employed for expressing the genitive in masculine/neuter and feminine nouns respectively (cf. (18a) and (18b)):

(16) a. zejtinú   álima
      zejtin-u   alima-Ø
      OLIVE.N-CM OIL.N-NOM.SG
      'olive oil'

    b. zejtín   c. álima
      zejtin-Ø   alima-Ø
      OLIVE.N-NOM.SG   OIL.N-NOM.SG
      'olive'   'oil'

(17) a. matrákas práði
      matraka-s práði-Ø
      FROG.F-CM LEG.N-NOM.SG
      'frog leg'

    b. matráka   c. práði
      matraka-Ø   praði-Ø
      FROG.F-NOM.SG   LEG.N-NOM.SG
      'frog'   'leg'

(18) a. tu   zejtinú   o   fajdás
      tu   zejtin-u   o   fajda-s
      the.N.GEN.SG OLIVE.N-GEN.SG the.NOM.SG BENEFIT.M-NOM.SG
      'the benefit of the olive'

    b. s   matrákas   ta   ftálmæ
      s   matraka-s   ta   ftalm-æ
      the.F.GEN.SG FROG.F-GEN.SG the.N.NOM/ACC.PL EYE.N-NOM/ACC.PL
      'the frog's eyes'

Therefore, at first glance it might be stated that -*u* or -*s* are genitive markers in (16)–(17) similar to the case in (18), and the structures in (16)–(17) are thus not compounds but indefinite/non-specific genitives. Below, we will provide detailed evidence for the fact that the structures in (16)–(17) are indeed compounds, behaving differently than the phrases in (18); however, for the time being, let us show that this view is in error by stating that the structure exemplified in (16)–(17) can also generate compounds where the constituents are not in a possession relation (19a). Moreover, attributive compounds (in the sense of Scalise & Bisetto 2009) can also be formed based on the same template (19b):

(19)   a. pejgirú   mamútsi
          pejgir-u   mamutsi-Ø
          HORSE.N-CM FLY.N-NOM.SG

          'horse fly'

        b. θalú   tupéki
           θal-u   tupeki-Ø
           STONE.N-CM MORTAR.N-NOM.SG

           'stone mortar'

Note that the genitive phrasal counterpart of (19a) in (20) does not show the semantic integrity that (19a) does; rather it refers to a discourse-salient entity:

(20)   tu   pejgirú   to   mamútsi
       tu   pejgir-u   to   mamutsi-Ø
       the.N.GEN.SG HORSE.N-CM the.N.NOM/ACC.SG FLY.N-NOM.SG

       'the fly of the horse'

Moreover, PhG genitive phrases in (18) and (20) clearly differ from the N-GEN N compound structures (16)–(17) by the fact that in a genitive phrase the genitive article is obligatory:

(21)   *(tu)   zejtinú   o/an   fajdás
       *(tu)   zejtin-u   o/an   fajda-s
       the.N.GEN.SG OLIVE.N-GEN.SG the.NOM.SG/a BENEFIT.M-NOM.SG

       'the/a benefit of the olive'

By not involving this genitive article, the structures in (16)–(17) and (19) diverge from genitive phrases.

     More important evidence for the fact that structures built on the N-GEN N template are not genitive phrases comes from a group of masculine nouns which receive the −u suffix only when they are in the non-head position of a compound (22). When they are in a genitive phrase, the suffix marking the genitive is zero (Ø) (23):

(22) ɣɯjmaðú   koftéða
     ɣɯjmað-u   kofteð-a
     GROUND.MEAT.M-CM MEATBALL.M-NOM.PL

'(a type of) meatballs'

(23) tu   ɣɯjmá   i   muruðía
     tu   ɣɯjma-Ø   i   muruðia-Ø
     the.M.GEN.SG GROUND.MEAT.M-GEN.SG the.F.NOM.SG SMELL.F-NOM.SG

'the smell of the ground meat'

The difference in the stem choice in (22) and (23) is an instance of stem allomorphy in PhG as *ɣɯjma- ~ ɣɯjmað-*, identical to stem allomorphy in Modern Greek (cf. Section 2). It is the stem *ɣɯjmað-* which is employed in compounding. The same stem is also employed in plural inflection, while *ɣɯjma-* receives singular inflectional suffixes. This latter point is exemplified by another lexeme of the same IC, *zopa- ~ zopað-* 'STOVE' in Table 3 below:

Table 3: *zopa- ~ zopað-* (neuter) 'STOVE' stem allomorphy in PhG (corresponding to IC2 of Modern Greek)

	singular		plural	
nominative	zopa	-s	zopað	-i
accusative	zopa	-Ø	zopað	-i
genitive	zopa	-Ø	zopað	-i/iun

If genuine genitive suffixes were employed when (masculine) nouns of IC2 are in the non-head position of a compound, then in (22) we would expect the zero genitive marker (Ø), and not *-u*, contrary to fact.[10] Therefore, we argue that the compound structure N-GEN N is not a genitive phrase (see also below for more

---

[10] There is another possible account for the *-u* attaching to IC2 stems in PhG, which ultimately cannot be maintained:

Such IC2 stems can occur in the non-head position of a compound, not only in PhG but in Modern Greek or in other dialects as well. Consider (i) and (ii) which are from Modern Greek and Lesbian/Aivaliot respectively:

(i) kimaðomixaní   (ii) kimaðumixaní
     kimað-o-mixani   kimað-u-mixani
     GROUND.MEAT-CM-machine   GROUND.MEAT-CM-machine
     'meat grinder'   'meat grinder'

structural differences between the two). Concomitantly, the -*u* and -*s* suffixes are not genuine genitive suffixes in the template N-GEN N. This means that they are in fact compound markers marking the process of compounding in PhG, which are exapted from the genitive suffixes, where *exaptation* should be defined as an unpredictable and leap-like shift of the function of a specific morpheme (Norde & Van de Velde 2016: 8). This is another difference between Hellenic compounding and PhG compounding: while in the former the compound marker is exapted from an ancient thematic vowel (see Section 2), PhG compounds are marked by compound markers exapted from the genitive and are sensitive to the gender of the base they attach to.

Another salient difference between Hellenic compounding and PhG compounding lies in the stress. As was discussed in Section 2, Hellenic compounds are phonological words. The stress falls on the stressed syllable of the head if the lexeme occupying the head position is a word. Otherwise, the *Compound Specific Stress Rule* positions the stress on the antepenultimate syllable. In either case, though, the whole juxtaposition has single stress. In PhG compounds, on the other hand, both constituents retain their own stress, hence the whole concatenation acts as a phonological phrase. While the primary accent falls on the stressable syllable of the non-head, the head carries a secondary stress. Hence the stress pattern of PhG compounds resembles that of respective genitive phrases (if there is a corresponding genitive phrase). The figures in (24b) and (25b) show the resemblance of the stress patterns of compounds and genitive phrases respectively (where the leftmost constituent receives main stress):[11]

(24) a. ((matrákas)$_\omega$ (práða)$_\omega$)$_\phi$
          matraka-s   praða
          FROG-CM   legs
          'frog legs'

The only difference between (i) and (ii) is the fact that in (ii), which is from Lesbian/Aivaliot, the compound marker is realized not as -*o*-, but as -*u*-. This, however, is only due to a phonological process in Northern Greek dialects, namely the raising of unstressed [o] to [u], cf. Chatzidakis (1905). In fact, such raising of unstressed [o] to [u] occurs in some villages of Pharasa, albeit not systematically, contrary to the case in Northern Greek dialects where the raising takes place across the board. Still, the -*u* attaching to IC2 stems in PhG (or to stems of any IC for that matter) might be argued not to be a genuine suffix exapted from the genitive, but to be underlyingly the compound marker [o], raised to [u]. This, however, cannot be maintained, since -*u* is always stressed (cf. (22)) and for [o] > [u] raising to take place -*u*, which, according to the scenario, is the hypothetical compound marker -*o*-, should have been unstressed.

[11] Hereafter, in order to avoid redundant morphemic glossing, we will not provide gender, case or number information in the examples when they do not directly affect the discussion.

b.

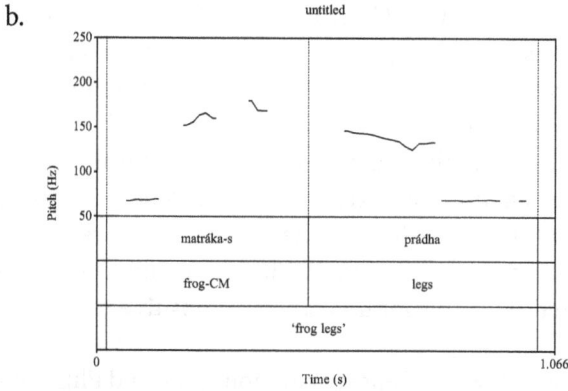

(25) a. ((s   matrákas)$_\omega$ (ta práða)$_\omega$)$_\phi$
          s   matraka-s ta praða
          the.GEN frog-GEN   the legs
      'the frog's legs'

b.

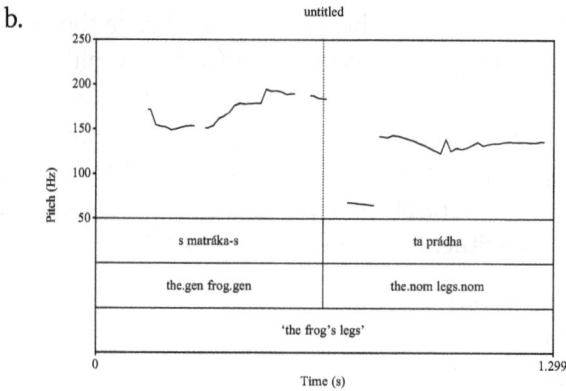

The affinity of compounds in PhG to genitive phrases is not only witnessed by the origin and the gender-sensitivity of the compound markers, and the phonological phrasehood of the compound. N-GEN N compounds also behave similar to genitive phrases in certain syntactic constructions. Such behavior again clearly sets them apart from Hellenic compounds which show no affinity with phrases.

Hellenic compounds are known not to allow any syntactic operation on their structure (Ralli 2007; 2013b); for example, the constituents in a Hellenic compound cannot be coordinated. Compare the ungrammatical coordinate structure in (26) to grammatical compounds in (27):

(26) * vamvakkekapnoxórafo   (Modern Greek)
      vamvak-ke-kapn-o-xoraf-o
      COTTON-and-TOBACCO-CM-FIELD-NOM.SG

      int.: 'cotton and tobacco field'

(27) a. vamvakoxórafo   b. kapnoxórafo
         vamvak-o-xoraf-o   kapn-o-xoraf-o
         COTTON-CM-FIELD-NOM.SG   TOBACCO-CM-FIELD-NOM.SG

         'cotton field'   'tobacco field'

PhG compounds, on the other hand, allow for the coordination of compound non-heads. In (28), the non-head is coordinated, and the whole structure has a unique denotation; a field where both barley and alfalfa are planted (biennially due to the toxicity of the latter):

(28) kočú   če rovú   tópus
      koč-u   če rov-u   topus
      BARLEY-CM and ALFALFA-CM field

      'a field where barley and alfalfa are planted'

However, the possibility for the non-head to host a coordinate structure correlates with the degree of semantic compositionality of the compound. In (29a), for example, the coordination of the non-head results in an ungrammatical structure:

(29) a. * širiðú če nékas   čarúxa
           širið-u če neka-s   čaruxa
           PIG-CM and WOMAN-CM shoes

         int.: 'shoes made from pigskin and women's shoes'

      b. širiðú čarúxa   c. nékas   čarúxa
         širið-u čaruxa   neka-s   čaruxa
         PIG-CM shoes   WOMAN-CM shoes

         'shoes made from pigskin'   'women's shoes'

The ungrammaticality is arguably due to the fact that the same thematic role could not be mapped onto both non-heads in (29a). The same results obtain in coordination of the head. In (30a), where the same thematic relationship occurs between the non-head and the heads, coordination of the head is acceptable. In (31a), however, coordination is ungrammatical:

(30) a. ɣuvalú   čeratú če petsí
          ɣuval-u   čeratu če petsi
          WATER.BUFFALO-CM horn   and skin
          'water buffalo horn and skin'

    b. ɣuvalú   čeratú   c. ɣuvalú   petsí
        ɣuval-u   čeratu   ɣuval-u   petsi
        WATER.BUFFALO-CM horn   WATER.BUFFALO-CM skin
        'water buffalo horn'   'water buffalo skin'

(31) a. * ɣaiðurú   gafás če melísi
          ɣaiður-u   gafas če melisi
          DONKEY-CM head and bee
          int.: 'yackety-yak and wasp'

    b. ɣaiðurú   gafás   c. ɣaiðurú   melísi
        ɣaiður-u   gafas   ɣaiður-u   melisi
        DONKEY-CM head   DONKEY-CM bee
        'yackety-yak'   'wasp'

As far as we can tell, *ke* 'and' in Hellenic varieties is a phrasal coordinator (see Ingria 2005 for Modern Greek). *Če* 'and' in PhG, which is ultimately the Hellenic *ke*, is, similarly, a phrasal coordinator. In (32) below, two genitive phrases are coordinated with *če*:

(32) tu   Andriá   če s   Nerkízas   to fšaxókko
      tu   Andria-Ø   če s   Nerkiza-s   to fšaxokko
      the.GEN Andreas-GEN and the.GEN Nerkiza-GEN the son
      'the son of Andreas and Nerkiza'

Hence, coordination facts on the one hand differentiate PhG compounds from Hellenic compounds and on the other hand underline the similarities between the PhG compounds and genitive phrases. Note, however, that unlike genitive phrases, coordination in compounds is not limitless and is constrained by the availability for the recovery of the semantic compositionality from the coordinated constituents.

Another difference between PhG and Hellenic compounding surfaces in external modification of the constituents. Although neither Hellenic nor PhG compounds allow the external modification of the non-heads, there is some evidence that PhG, but not Hellenic, compounds allow for the external modification of the head. In (33a), the ungrammaticality of the structure stems from the attempt to modify the non-head to the exclusion of the head of the Modern Greek compound. The PhG structure, similarly to (33a), is also ungrammatical (34a):

(33) Modern Greek

    a. * kaloaɣrotóspito
        kal-o-aɣrot-o-spit-o
        GOOD-CM-FARMER-CM-HOUSE-NOM.SG

        int.: '[good farmer]'s house'

    b. aɣrotóspito
        aɣrot-o-spit-o
        FARMER-CM-HOUSE-NOM.SG

        'farmer's house'

(34) PhG

    a. * méɣa ɣiðú   tirí
        meɣa ɣid-u   tiri
        big   GOAT-CM cheese

        'int.: [big goat] cheese'

    b. ɣiðú   tirí
        ɣid-u   tiri
        GOAT-CM cheese

        'goat cheese'

Such constraints do not operate on phrases (cf. 33a with 35 and 34a with 36):

(35) poli meɣálo spíti   (Modern Greek)
      very big   house

      'very big house'

(36) to méɣa tu   ɣiðú   ta čérata (PhG)
      to meɣa tu   ɣið-u   ta čerata
      the big   the.GEN goat-GEN the horns

      ''the horns of the big goat'

Although the facts pertinent to external modification of the non-head are the same between PhG and Modern Greek, the two systems show differences in external modification of the head of a compound. Modern Greek does not allow this either, however in PhG, such modification is acceptable (37 vs. 38a):

(37)   * aɣrotomeɣalóspito   (Modern Greek)
       aɣrot-o-meɣal-o-spit-o
       FARMER-CM-BIG-CM-HOUSE-NOM.SG
       int.: 'big [farmer's house]/ farmer's [big house]'

(38)   PhG

   a. ɣuvalú   tazó álima
       ɣuval-u   tazo alima
       WATER.BUFFALO-CM fresh butter
       'fresh buffalo butter'

   b. ɣuvalú   álima
       ɣuval-u   alima
       WATER.BUFFALO-CM butter
       'buffalo butter'

Similarly to the case in (36), the head of a genitive phrase can also be externally modified, as in (39):

(39)   tu   ɣiðú   ta méɣa ta čérata   (PhG)
       tu   ɣið-u   ta meɣa ta čerata
       the.GEN goat-GEN the big   the horns
       "the big horns of the goat'

The discussion so far has shown that N-GEN N compounds are structurally not on par with Hellenic compounds. Moreover, it has become clear that there is a striking parallelism between genitive phrases and N-GEN N compounds in PhG, albeit not an absolute one. Modern Greek compounds have long been discussed as morphological objects on which syntax cannot operate (cf. Ralli 2013b, for some dialects see also Andreou 2014). This is also shown partially in Section 2, and above with respect to the external modification and coordination facts. On the other hand, the phonological phrasehood of the compounds in PhG, the use of (originally) syntactic material to mark compounding, their visibility to syntactic coordination or modification – albeit to limited extent – imply their structural affinity to syntactic phrases. However, the differences between compounds and genitive phrases in terms of external modification of the non-head cast doubt on identification of phrases with compounds in PhG. There are in fact other peculiarities of these compounds that distinguish them from syntactic phrases. Although PhG DP is head final, as in other Asia Minor Greek dialects, fronting the head over the non-head is possible in genitive phrases (Bağrıaçık in preparation):

(40) ta čarúxa s   nékas
      [ta čaruxa]$_i$ s   neka-s e_i
      the shoes   the.GEN woman-GEN
      'THE SHOES of the woman'

N-GEN N compounds behave similar to Hellenic morphological compounds in disallowing such scrambling (see Bağrıaçık & Ralli 2015):

(41) a. * čarúxa nékas   b. nékas   čarúxa
          [čaruxa]$_i$ neka-s e_i neka-s   čaruxa
          shoes   woman-CM   woman-CM shoes
          int.: 'women's SHOES'   'women's shoes'

In a similar fashion, due to the non-referential character of the compound constituents, these constituents cannot be antecedents in outbound anaphora (Postal 1969; Sproat 1988) under normal circumstances, as shown in (42):[12]

(42) Čas íðini ta   yaiðurú   melísa ðóčin da.
      čas iðini ta [$_{CMPND}$ yaiður-u$_i$ melisa] ðočin da$_{*i}$
      when saw.3SG the   DONKEY-CM bees   hit.3SG 3OBJ.CL
      'When he saw the wasps, he hit it.'   (it ≠ donkey, cf. (31c))

Finally, similar to Hellenic compounds, PhG compounds can also undergo derivation by suffixation. There are two points, however, concerning this derivation. First, similar to the case across all Hellenic varieties, in PhG as well, derivational affixes attach to stems, i.e., to lexemes stripped of their inflection. This is shown with the non-derived noun in (43a), and denominal verbalizer, *-lat*, attaching to the bare stem of (43a) in the example in (43b):

(43) a. talɣás   b. talɣalátízi
          talɣa-s   talɣa-lat-iz-i
          WAVE-NOM.SG   WAVE-VBLZ-IPFV-3SG
          'wave'   'it waves/undulates'

Concerning N-GEN N compounds, similarly to simplex nouns, a derivational suffix attaches to a compound only when the head noun is stripped of its inflection. Hence the compound in (44a) acts as a stem (without the inflection on

---

[12] Such anaphoric reference to word constituents, however, can become grammatical by pragmatically evoking a suitable referent corresponding to a noun in the compound/complex word (Ward et al. 1991).

the head noun) in (44b), where the derivational suffix, in this case the relational suffix,[13] is attached to it:

(44) a. širiðú   γavurmás
           širið-u   γavurmas
           PORK-CM kavurma

           'pork kavurma'

    b. širiðú   γavurmalús
          širið-u   γavurma-lu-s
          PORK-CM KAVURMA-REL-NOM.SG

          'with pork kavurma'

The derivational suffixes that can attach to these N-GEN N are virtually limited to two suffixes that are also borrowed from Turkish. One is the relational suffix, exemplified in (44b), and the other is the privative suffix *-súz(i)* exemplified in (45b):[14]

(45) a. zejtinú   álima
           zejtin-u   alima
           OLIVE-CM oil

           'olive oil'

    b. ? zejtinú   alimasúzi
           zejtin-u   alima-suz-i
           OLIVE-CM OIL-PRV-NOM.SG

           'without olive oil'

No phrase in PhG, or in Hellenic in general, admits derivation of any sort. This is shown with the following PhG example. (46a) is a head-final relative clause. In (46b), the relational suffix is attached to the head of the relative clause which is stripped of its inflection; nevertheless the result is ungrammatical. That the ungrammaticality of (46b) does not stem from the head noun per se is witnessed by the grammatical (46c) in which the relational suffix attaches to the head noun of (46b) in isolation and the result is grammatical:

---

[13] The relational suffix *-lú(s)* (< Turkish *-lI*) is attached to nouns to form nouns and adjectives where the entity described possesses, is characterized by, or is provided with the object or quality expressed by the base (definition after Göksel & Kerslake 2005: 60–61, see also Kornfilt 1997: 445–446, Lewis 1967: 60–62).

[14] It should be noted that not all simplex or compound bases that admit the relational suffix also admit the privative suffix in PhG (cf. Bağrıaçık et al. forthcoming). We leave the investigation of the reasons for this discrepancy for future research.

(46) a.   tu   xeč   čo pnóni   to šexéri
          [RelC tu   xeč   čo pnoni   to šexeri]
            that never not sleep.3sG the city

       'the city that never sleeps'

    b. *   tu   xeč   čo pnóni   to šexerlús
        [RelC tu   xeč   čo pnoni   to šexer]-lu-s
           that never not sleep.3sG the CITY-REL-NOM.SG

       int.: 'native/inhabitant of the city that never sleeps'

    c.   šexerlús
       šexer-lu-s
       CITY-REL-NOM.SG
       'urban'

The discussion so far reveals that PhG N-GEN N compounds are of a 'hybrid' status between phrases and lexical items. Due to the fact that (i) they exhibit phrasal accent, (ii) their constituents are inflected lexemes, i.e, words, rather than bare lexemes, i.e., stems, and (iii) their constituents can be coordinated, and (iv) at least the head can be modified externally, they align with genitive phrases. However, they also diverge from genitive phrases at various points: they do not involve overt genitive articles (although they involve suffixes exapted from the genitive suffixes) and they do not allow focus extraction or outbound anaphora. More strikingly, unlike genitive phrases (or phrases in general) they undergo derivation – albeit with a limited number of affixes – as long as the head of the compound is stripped of its inflection. In section 6, we will present some possible solutions for their status between morphology and syntax, but before doing so, we will present a brief discussion on their origin and provide some further constraints on their structure in the next two sections.

4 On the origin of N-GEN N compounds

The loss of the Hellenic compounding template is probably an epiphenomenon of the emergence of the new type of N-GEN N compounds and the structure has possibly disappeared gradually. Such cyclical changes abound in languages (van Gelderen 2011), the most notable one being the negative cycle (Jaspersen's cycle). As such, in PhG, we may tentatively postulate a 'compound cycle', the (possibly gradual) replacement of a purely morphological compound structure [X-o-X], by the N-GEN N compound structure, which as we have seen in Section 3, has a hybrid status showing both phrasal and lexical idiosyncrasies. These idiosyncrasies, according to us, stem from another ongoing cycle in the current compound structure, namely that of the compound markers. Current markers in the compound, as we have seen in Section 3, are form-wise identical to genitive markers, but they are not identical to those markers semantically, functionally or distributionally. They do not always mark a head-dependent relationship as their genitive counterparts do, nor do they have the same distribution as their genitive counterparts. We have seen this last point in Section 3, where it was shown that stem allomorphy requires one stem of the same lexeme to host the genitive but another stem of the same lexeme to host the compound marker exapted from the genitive.

However, the distribution of the compound markers -*s* and -*u* are still somehow regular. They both attach to nominal bases.[15] Feminine nouns always receive -*s*, and -*u* is the elsewhere compound marker. Such regularities are usually identified with functional heads, morphological items being prone to idiosyncrasies. The ambiguous status of these markers between morphology and syntax has strong ramifications for the overall structure of the compound. We have seen some points in Section 3 that might be related to this assumption and we will elaborate on this point in more detail in section 5, but we should first answer how this new cycle has been initiated in the language in the first place.

It has been stated in the beginning of Section 3 that PhG exhibits a considerable number of differences from various other Modern Greek dialects, and a large number of these discrepancies have been explained in the literature as changes or innovations induced by contact with Turkish (Dawkins 1916; Andriotis 1948; Karatsareas 2011; 2014; Bağrıaçık in preparation). As Turkish influence on PhG is observed at all levels of the grammar, a reasonable attempt to account for the origin of the compound structure in PhG would be to look at compounding in Turkish. As it is stated in Thomason (forthcoming) any internal linguistic change can be regarded as an end-product of a chain of innovations initiated by some change in the remote past, and this change may to a great extent be a contact-induced one.

Turkish has various types of compounding (see Göksel 2009; Göksel & Haznedar 2007 for an overview), giving a survey of which is well beyond the aim of the

---

[15] Observe here the Dutch compound marker -*s*, which was exapted from the genitive suffix (Booij 1992) and which has an unpredictable distribution currently. Today it can attach even to verbal bases:

    (i)   voorbehoed-s-middel   < voorbehoed-en 'to save', (Dutch)
           SAVE-CM-agent
           'preservative'

current paper. Here, we will discuss a certain type of compounding in which two (or more) noun words[16] are juxtaposed with a compound marker (a.o. Kornfilt 1997: 474, Göksel 1988; van Schaaik 2002), namely *-(s)I(n)*[17] at the right periphery (this compound structure will henceforth be referred as N-N-*sI*):

(47)   yemek oda-sı   (Turkish)
       food   room-CM
       'dining room'

The compound marker at the right periphery is form-wise identical to the third person singular possessive suffix (48) (cf.Göksel 2009):

(48)   Çağla-nın   oda-sı
       Çağla-GEN.3SG room-POSS.3SG
       'Çağla's room'

-*sI* in N-N-*sI* compounds does not mark possession; nevertheless it retains some structural affinity with the possessive marker as the compound marker and the possessive marker (all members of the paradigm) are in complementary distribution (49), and both the possessive marker and the compound marker are closing suffixes (Göksel 2009), i.e., they both have to follow the plural marking (50) (Lewis 1967; Dede 1978; Kornfilt 1986; Göksel 1988; 1993; Schroeder 1999; van Schaaik 2002):

(49)   Çağla-nın   yemek oda-sı   / *oda-sı-sı
       Çağla-GEN.3SG food   room-POSS.3SG / room-CM-POSS.3SG
       'Çağla's dining room'

(50)   yemek oda-lar-ı   / *oda-sı-lar
       food   room-PL-CM / room-CM-PL
       'dining rooms'

In (49), the N-N-*sI* compound, *yemek odası* 'dining room' is embedded under a genitive-possessive construction, and is restricted by the genitive possessor. In such embedding, it is the possessive agreement marker, in this case the third

---

[16] We will refer to these constituents as words to separate them from the usage of the term 'stem' in Hellenic, remaining loyal to the convention adopted for Hellenic lexemes in sections 2 and 3. Nouns in Turkish do not differentiate between stems and words the way Hellenic does and nouns which are constituents in a compound are also word forms (i.e. they can stand alone).

[17] [s] in parentheses is deleted if the base ends in a consonant. [n] in parentheses surfaces only when case suffixes follow.

singular agreement marker, rather than the compound marker that is attached to the head noun (Dede 1978; Göksel 1988; Kornfilt 1986; van Schaaik 2002). In (50), it is shown that the plural marker has to attach directly to the head and the compound marker follows the plural marker, similar to the case in genitive-possessive constructions (cf. (51)):

(51) Çağla-nın   oda-lar-ı
      Çağla-GEN.3SG room-PL-POSS.3SG
      'Çağla's rooms'

It is partly due to this parallelism that N-N-*sI* compounds are often referred to as 'possessive compounds' (van Schaaik 1992; Hayashi 1996; Yükseker 1998). There are in fact some other structural similarities between possessive constructions and N-N-*sI* compounds, such as suspended affixation of -*sI*, i.e., the optional elision of -*sI* in all conjuncts but the last one in a coordination structure (cf. Kornfilt 2012 for suspended affixation, for compounds Bağrıaçık & Ralli 2015) as in (52), or ability of these compounds to host coordinate structures in both head and the non-head positions as in (53a)–(53b) respectively, or *wh*-extraction from the non-head position (54) (Uygun 2009; Göksel 2009; Bağrıaçık & Ralli 2013; 2015). Moreover, as it has been argued by Kamali & Ikizoğlu (2015), the stress pattern of N-N-*sI* compounds is the expected stress pattern of a phrase; the primary accent falls on the stressable syllable of the non-head and the head is somewhat deaccentuated (55):

(52) otomobil akü(-sü),   şanzıman(-ı) ve karoser*(-i)
      car   battery-(CM), gearbox(-CM) and body-CM
      'car battery, car gearbox and car body'

(53) a. ülke   birliğ-i   ve/ile beraberliğ-i
         country unity-CM and   solidarity-CM
         'national unity and solidarity'

      b. kedi ve köpek mama-sı
         cat and dog   food-CM
         'cat and dog food'

(54) a. portakal ne-si?
         orange   what-CM
         'the what (made) of orange?'

b. portakal çekirdeğ-i
   orange   pit-CM

   'orange pit'

(55) ((gemí)$_\omega$ (halat-i)$_\omega$)$_\phi$
      ship   rope-CM

      'warp'

However, the two constructions, N-N-*sI* compounds and genitive-possessive constructions, are not identical across the board. Scrambling of the constituents is strictly ungrammatical in N-N-*sI* compounds (Bağrıaçık & Ralli 2015) (56a), whereas in genitive-possessive constructions such scrambling is allowed (56b):[18]

(56) a. * oda-sı   yemek e_i (cf. (47))
         room-CM food

         'dining room/ROOM'

      b. oda-sı   Çağla-nın e_i (cf. (48))
          room-POSS.3SG Çağla-GEN.3SG

          'Çağla's room/ROOM '

Similarly, the head of the compound cannot be modified by head-adjacent functional elements such as the indefinite article or quantifiers; these constraints are illustrated in (57b) (Göksel 2009):[19]

(57) a. bir/her dükkan vitrin-i
          a/every shop   window-CM

          'the window of a/every shop'

      b. * dükkan bir/her vitrin-i
          shop   a/every window-CM

          int.: 'one/every shop window'

---

[18] Such scrambling can be the result of focusing of the possessee or backgrounding of the possessor.

[19] But adjectival modification of the head is allowed, albeit rather limitedly, with constructions denoting official positions or organizations (Hayashi 1996; Özsoy 2004):

(i) maliye eski   bakan-ı
     finance former miniter-CM

     'former minister of finance'

The occurrence of such striking similarities and differences between possessive constructions and N-N-*sI* compounds triggers differing views on the internal structure of the latter. Various scholars argue for the morphological status of Turkish compounds (Schroeder 1999; van Schaaik 2002; Aslan & Altan 2006; Kunduracı 2013). According to another view, the internal structure of N-N-*sI* compounds, which is formally identical to that of possessive constructions, belongs to the morphological module (Göksel 2009). Yet for other researchers, (Yükseker 1998; Bozşahin 2002; Uygun 2009; Gürer 2010; Bağrıaçık & Ralli 2015; Trips & Kornfilt 2015), N-N-*sI* compounds are generated syntactically and the differences between the possessive constructions and N-N-*sI* compounds are results of different syntactic structures. Tat (2013), on the other hand, argues that a post-syntactic morphology component must be responsible for the derivation of N-N-*sI* compounds. Reviewing all these accounts is beyond the aim of the current paper; directly relevant to our paper is the striking similarities between PhG N-GEN N compounds (Section 3) and Turkish N-N-*sI* compounds as depicted above. Such similarities underline their ambiguous status between lexical elements and phrases.

Both PhG and Turkish compounds involve compound markers exapted from nominal inflectional markers despite the difference between the exact source for the compound marker in the two languages: in PhG the source is the genitive, but in Turkish it is the possessive marker. As an extension of this, the Turkish compound marker is located at the head of the compound whereas the PhG compound marker attaches to the non-head. Another striking fact of similarity between the two compound structures comes from their stress patterns; in terms of their phonological structures both PhG compounds and Turkish compounds align with phonological phrases in the respective languages. Similarities also exist in how they react under syntactic operations: both languages allow hosting coordinate structures in the head or the non-head positions (or both), as long as, of course, the compounds are semantically transparent. External modification of the constituents is also possible to a certain degree. PhG compounds allow for the modification of the head by adjectives (38a); in Turkish, on the other hand, although functional elements cannot modify the head, adjectives can – albeit in a rather limited fashion (cf. fn. 19). Moreover, the non-head in Turkish can be modified externally, even by a relative clause:

(58) lise-ye   yeni başla-yan   ergen   tavr-ı
     high.school-DAT new start-SBJREL adolescent attitude-CM

'[adolescent who has just started high school] attitude'

(Kamali & Ikizoğlu 2015)

Hence both languages allow for external modification of certain constituents, but the availability of such modification seems to roughly correlate with the position of the compound marker; the lexeme hosting the compound marker cannot undergo external modification (except for the limited cases mentioned above). Such similarities between PhG and Turkish compounds and their differences from Hellenic compounding underline the close affinity of compounding in both languages to genitive constructions. Note once more that such modification is strictly ungrammatical for Hellenic compounds which have elsewhere been discussed as morphological compounds (cf. Ralli 2013b) and this morphological nature of Hellenic compounds is also presented briefly in Section 2.

However, such similarities should not identify these compounds with genuine phrases. There are also some similarities between PhG and Turkish compounds that indicate that their structure diverges from genuine phrases. We have seen in Section 3 that outbound anaphora in PhG compounds is allowed only when the referent can be pragmatically evoked. This is also valid for Turkish N-N-*sI* compounds. In both languages, compounds undergo derivation as long as native word formation rules are observed: In PhG, this requires the compound to be stripped of its inflection (44b, 45b) and in Turkish, the derivational suffix should precede the compound marker, since the latter is a closing suffix (59b):[20]

(59)   a.   şıllık tatlı-sı
           hussy dessert-CM

           'a type of baklava-like dessert'

      b.   şıllık tatlı-cı-sı
           hussy dessert-DER-CM

           'someone who makes/sells the dessert in (59a)'

Based on such similarities between PhG N-GEN N compounds and Turkish N-N-*sI* compounds, we assume that PhG productive N-GEN N compounds are built on a pattern copied from Turkish. However, it is obvious that this pattern copying is not global (Johanson 1992, Johanson 1993: 201–202), i.e., not all struc-

---

[20] Moreover, in neither of the languages is scrambling (from) within the compound allowed (see (41a) for PhG and (56a) for Turkish). Even though this similarity between compound structures in two languages and the contrast these compounds show with genitive phrases in the respective languages which allow scrambling of constituents are remarkable, we avoid making a strong statement with respect to availability of scrambling in compounds as a clear diagnosis for differentiating between morphological versus syntactic constructions. For a variety of reasons, in various languages, syntactic configurations exist where constituents are "frozen" so to speak, and thus cannot undergo any kind of movement. We thank Jaklin Kornfilt for pointing out this issue to us.

tural properties of compounding in Turkish are copied into PhG. As there are no overt possessive markers in Hellenic, the Turkish compound marker which retains strong affinity with the possessive agreement marker in its distribution and origin is identified with the native genitive markers in PhG. Some structural differences between the compound structures in the two languages seem to depend on the position and type of compound markers. One overt reflex of this became obvious in the degree of acceptability of externally modified constituents above. In both languages, the modifiability of a certain constituent correlates with whether the constituent is the one hosting the compound marker or not. Another such difference is the availability of suspended affixation, i.e., elision of affixation under coordination. In Turkish, functional heads allow for elision, and so does the compound marker which still retains its affinity to the possessive agreement marker (52). In PhG, or generally in Hellenic, such elision does not exist since affixes attach to stems which cannot stand alone in argument positions. As such, the compound marker in PhG cannot be elided in coordination:

(60)   * koč-   če rovú   tópus
       koč-*(u)   če rov-u   topus
       BARLEY-*(CM) and ALFALFA-CM field

       'a field where barley and alfalfa are planted'   (cf. (28))

Such minor differences between N-GEN N compounds and N-N-*sI* compounds reveal that the borrowed pattern is actually integrated into the native system of the recipient language by employing material already at its disposal (hence the selective copying of the pattern, Johanson 1992). The idiosyncrasies of this native material bring along certain structural constraints on the borrowed pattern. Since the native material employed is an affix, it exhibits the peculiarities of being an affix in PhG: Since affixes in PhG attach to stems, and because there are no word-level or phrase-level affixes in PhG, modification of their base becomes unavailable or these affixes can not be elided leaving behind stems. In the next section, we will present another difference between Turkish and PhG that once again stems from the nature of the compound markers involved.[21]

---

[21] Phrasal compound formation with the employment of genitive markers is also observed in Modern Greek, where the order of the non-head and the head follows the order of the genitive phrases. Ralli (2013b) argues for two types of a NN-GEN template. The first one, constructs (i.a), behaves similar to ordinary phrases in that they tolerate insertion of parentheticals and allows scrambling. The second type, dubbed as phrasal compounds by Ralli (2013b), emerged only in the last two centuries as calques from French (i.b). The order of their constituents cannot be scrambled nor can their structural integrity be interrupted by independent modification or by parenthetical insertion.

5 Phrasal compounds

Turkish N-N-*sI* compounds are notable for being able to host larger strings, phrases, in the non-head position (cf. van Schaaik 2002; Gürer 2010; Göksel 2015; Bağrıaçık & Ralli 2015; Trips & Kornfilt 2015 to name a few). An example of such compounds is already given in (58). Such phrases can also be full-blown finite clauses or nominalized clauses, and their status as bona fide phrases (as opposed to quotations) is discussed in Göksel (2015). The fact that these are compounds is witnessed by the occurrence of the compound marker on the head of the construction and by the strict adjacency between the clausal portions and the head:

(61) polis orantısız güç kullan-dı-Ø haber-i
police disproportionate force use-PST-3SG news-CM
'the news that the police used disproportionate force'

(62) polis-in orantısız güç kullan-dığ-ı haber-i
police-GEN.3SG disproportionate force use-FNOM-3SG news-CM
'the news that the police used disproportionate force'

(62) is the nominalized counterpart of (61) as the lack of tense marker and the occurrence of the factive nominalizer witness.[22] If we maintain that PhG com-

---

(i) Modern Greek

a. parayoyí kapnú
parayoy-i kapn-u
PRODUCTION-NOM.SG TOBACCO-GEN.SG
'tobacco production'

b. ayorá eryasías
ayora-Ø eryasia-s
MARKET-NOM.SG JOB-GEN.SG
'job market'

Concatenations such as (i.a) existed in Medieval Greek as well, yet as ordinary noun phrases which are not subject to constraints which PhG compounds show. Therefore we think that PhG compounding is a novel type of compound, as (i.b) is in Modern Greek.

[22] Bağrıaçık & Ralli (2015) relate the availability of phrasal non-heads to the assumption that N-N-*sI* compounds are syntactically generated in Turkish. Göksel (2015), on the other hand, analyzed them as being generated by morphology. Trips & Kornfilt (2015) argue that phrasal compounds with nominalized non-heads (62) bear tighter semantic and syntactic connections between the non-head and the head than those where the non-head is finite (61), and they are governed by stricter selectional requirements between the nominalized non-head and the head. Reviewing all the accounts for Turkish phrasal compounds is beyond the aims of the current paper, therefore we ignore the details about phrasal compounds and focus on the fact that

pounds are in fact formed on a pattern copied from Turkish, then we would le-
gitimately expect phrases in the non-head position of PhG N-GEN N compounds.
However, just as the non-head position in an N-GEN N compound cannot host a
noun externally modified by a simplex adjective (34a), neither can larger phrases
with a predicate, e.g., nouns modified by relatives, be accommodated in the same
position:

(63) *   tu   čo katéš   ɣwóses   o   nomatú xáli
      [RELC tu čo kateš   ɣwoses   o   nomat]-u xáli
           that not understand.3SG languages the.NOM.SG man-CM   situation

      int.: '[the man who does not listen to reason] situation'

      int.: 'the situation of someone who does not listen to reason'

In (63), the head noun stem *nomat-* 'man' is modified by a relative clause. The
structure is ungrammatical even when the head of the relative clause is stripped
of its inflection (cf. the word form in nominative *nomáts* with the stem *nomat-*
) as the compound marker requires. This is expected as the compound marker
attaches morphologically to a stem. It is not a phrasal affix which might attach
to a bar-level projection. Phrases, relative or adjectival, are syntactic objects and
thus are not eligible hosts for the compound marker, even though the head of the
phrase aligns with the compound marker and even though the base is stripped
of its inflection.

As can be expected, clauses without a head noun are not allowed in the non-
head position, either. In (64), a finite non-embedded clause occupies the non-
head position. In (65), the proposition is embedded under the factive complementizer tu (cf. Bağrıaçık in preparation. for complementation in PhG). In both
(64) and (65), the results are ungrammatical, even if the noun left-adjacent to the
compound marker is stripped of its inflection:

(64) *   kačevún ta pejgirú   meselés
      [kačevun ta pejgir-]-u meseles
          speak.3PL the HORSE-CM claim

      "the horse(s) speak(s)' claim'

(65) *   tu kačevún ta pejgirú   meselés
      [tu kačevun ta pejgir-]-u meseles
          that speak.3PL the HORSE-CM claim

      int.: '(the) claim that the horse(s) speak(s)'

Turkish N-N-*sI* compounds can host in the non-head position both phrases with a predicate,
i.e., clauses, and phrases without predicates (for an interesting argument about the existence
of predicate in the phrase, see Trips 2012 et seq).

The ungrammaticality of (64) and (65) can be reduced to the non-existence of a nominal head to which the genitive attaches. However, even in the existence of an noun, we saw that phrasal constituents are strictly barred from the non-head position (cf. 63) as the compound marker, being a morphological element, cannot take a phrase as its base.

Such an approach ties the non-availability of phrasal non-heads in PhG to the obligatory occurrence of the compound marker on the non-head and its selectional restrictions imposed on its base. As the compound marker is hosted on the head noun in Turkish, no such restriction occurs on the non-head. Note that a similar restriction occurs in Khalkha (Mongolian), which, although typologically related to Turkish, does not allow phrases with predicates in the non-head in their compound structure. The compound template in Khalkha is virtually identical to that in PhG, N-GEN N as in (66); the difference between the two is that while genitive is attached to a stem in PhG, in Khalkha it attaches to a word form. The compound structure is form-wise identical to genitive phrases in (67):

(66)   nom-yn san   (Khalkha, Svantesson 2003: 162)
       book-CM storage
       'library'

(67)   Baatar-yn   mal
       Baatar-GEN livestock
       'Baatar's livestock'

                                          (Khalkha, Gaunt et al. 2004: 16)

Now, although the non-head can host a coordinate structure in Khalkha, whereby ellipsis of affixation is observed (68), finite clauses cannot be hosted in the same position (69):

(68)   Soyol   Sport   Ayalal.žuulčlal-yn yam
       culture sports tourism-CM   ministry
       'The Ministry of Culture, Sports and Tourism'
                                          (Ágnes Birtalan, pers. comm.)

(69)   * [xen yavax be]-nii asuult
           who go.FUT Q-CM   question
       int.: "the 'who will go?' question'

In fact, propositions can be hosted in the non-head position, but only when the clause hosting the proposition is nominalized:

(70) ter ir-ž   čadax-güi   ge-dg-iin   učir
  he come-CVB can-MODNEG COMP-NMLZ-GEN reason
  'the reason that he cannot come' (Kullmann & Tserenpil 1996: 309)

(71) [Bold-ig   (ni) ire-x]-iin   medee
  Bold-ACC PRT come-NFUT-GEN news
  'the news that Bold comes' (Ágnes Birtalan, pers. comm.)

In (70) the nominalizing suffix -*d(V)g* is attached to the verbal complementizer, literally 'say so' (von Heusinger et al. 2011); hence the clause can be viewed as nominalized, and in (71) the future deverbal noun (*nomen futuri*) suffix -*x* is attached directly to the predicate of the clause turning the clause into a nominal. In these examples, (70)–(71), however, which correspond to noun-complement structures in English, it is not entirely clear whether we are facing compounds or genuine syntactic constructions, since the integrity, which can be observed in compounds such as in the Turkish example in (62) between the non-head and the head does not hold in these structures. For example in (72), which corresponds to (71), we see that the postposition *tuxai*, which assigns genitive case to its complement, can intervene in between the non-head and the head:

(72) [Bold-ig   (ni) ire-x]-iin   tuxai medee
  Bold-ACC PRT come-NFUT-GEN about news
  'the news that Bold comes' (Ágnes Birtalan, pers. comm.)

Hence, it is highly likely that the genitive in (71) is not inherent to the structure but is assigned by a covert postposition. If this analysis is on the right track, we see a discrepancy between Turkish and Khalkha in whether compounds allow phrases with predicates in their non-head positions. Turkish does, and Khalkha does not, the latter similar to PhG. We think that the reason for this is the position of the compound marker and its inability to take a phrase as its base. Hence, we assume tentatively that the availability of clauses in the non-head position of the compound correlates with whether it is the head or the non-head of the compound that hosts the compound marker.

 In summary, although PhG compound structure has been selectively copied from Turkish, it is still constrained by native word-formation strategies. Given that the compound marker in PhG is exapted from the genitive suffix by analogy to the Turkish compound marker exapted from the third person possessive suffix, and given that suffixes in PhG always attach to stems, phrases are not legitimate in the non-head position of a compound. In Turkish, on the other hand, since the compound marker attaches to the head-noun, phrasal constituents can be hosted in the non-head position. Extending the analysis to Khalkha reveals that, beside the formal properties of the compound marker, the locus of its attachment can also determine whether phrasal constituents can be hosted in the non-head or not.

6 Locus of compounding in PhG

We have stated in the previous section that PhG compounds cannot host phrase-level items in their non-head position. The non-availability of phrasal constituents has been argued to be due to the morphological character of the compound marker attaching to the non-head. Similarly to the rest of the inflectional and derivational suffixes, the compound marker also subcategorizes for a stem (and distinct compound markers subcategorize for stems of distinct genders). As such, phrase level items are banned from hosting the compound marker.

Although the compounds in PhG cannot host phrases in their non-head position, whether the compounds themselves are in fact phrasal or not is a remaining issue. In earlier work, Bağrıaçık & Ralli (2015) tied the availability of phrasal non-heads in a compound to the syntactic nature of the compounds. If this is on the right track, the non-availability of phrasal non-heads could serve as one diagnosis to reveal their non-syntactic character. However, in section 5, we have shown that the non-availability of phrases is an epiphenomenon of the selectional restrictions of the compound head.

Despite the lack of phrasal constituents in the non-head position, these compounds in fact show some characteristics, such as their phonological phrasehood or ability to host coordinate structures, which bring them close to phrases. On the other hand, by accepting certain derivational suffixes as stems and by not allowing constituents to act as antecedents or to scramble away, they behave as words. Hence they have an ambiguous status between word-structure and phrase structure, for both Lexicalist and Non-Lexicalist approaches to word formation, just as certain types of compounds in various other languages do (for Modern Greek, see Ralli 2013b, for Italian, Bisetto & Scalise 1999; Bisetto 2015, for Romance languages in general, see the papers in Scalise & Massini 2012). One way of accounting for this hybrid status is to posit that N-GEN N compounds are in fact outputs of a certain syntactic word formation process, and their structural tightness is analogous to syntactic incorporation of indefinite/generic complements to Vs (73). Notice that in (73), the complement does not bear an overt definite article and is marked as nominative instead of accusative. Furthermore,

it is strictly adjacent to the head. However, it can host a coordinate structure
(74):

(73) píčin   γámus
pičin   γam-us
made.3sg wedding-NOM.SG
's/he made (a) wedding'

(74) píčin   semáði   če γámus
pičin   semaði-Ø   če γam-us
made.3sg engagement-NOM.SG and wedding-NOM.SG
's/he made (an) engagement and (a) wedding'

Another way of accounting for the status of N-GEN N, again in a Lexicalist
framework, is to assume that N-GEN N compounds are in fact morphological,
(assuming that (inflectional) affixation is a lexical phenomenon, cf. Chomsky
1995) and what seems as the phrasal coordinator *če* 'and' is also a morphological
coordinator. This option, however, falls short of explaining why external modification of the head, even though limited, is available in N-GEN N compounds and
why these compounds have phrasal accent. These problems can be circumvented,
however, once we assume that these compounds are morphological but nevertheless belong to a 'transitional' category between morphology and syntax, (cf.
Kageyama 2001, see also Borer 1998), such as Word+ (Kageyama 2001), which
denotes units larger than words (assuming the hierarchical structure of words
in morphology, cf. Halle & Vaux 1998) but belong to the realm of morphology.
As such although component-wise they belong to morphology in terms of word
atomicity, they behave also like phrases, thereby showing differences from other
levels of morphological units, i.e., roots, stems and words. Another alternative,
without adhering to Lexicalist Hypothesis, N-GEN N compounds can be argued
to be formed post-syntactically, assuming that there is a morphology component
after syntax but before PF (cf. Halle & Marantz (1993)).

A final alternative account of these compounds would be to assume, following
Ralli (2013a), that compounding can have its own peculiar characteristics since
it often cuts across the two domains, morphology and syntax. Once not a radical
separation but a gradual transition is admitted between morphology and syntax, compounding can be located in between the two, exhibiting properties of
both core morphological elements and core syntactic structures. Phrasal compounds, in such a view, are most often not strictly syntactic and morphological
compounds are often not strictly morphological.

In this paper, we are not proposing a strict adherence to any of the options above. Suffice it to state here that N-GEN N compounds in PhG present a challenge for compounding as exclusively a morphological phenomenon or as exclusively as a syntactic phenomenon. This challenge is inherited as such by the borrowed compounding pattern into the dialect from Turkish.

7 Conclusions

In this paper, we presented an account of subordinative (and attributive) compounds in PhG, an endangered Asia Minor Greek variety heavily influenced by Turkish. As opposed to various other Hellenic varieties, compounds in PhG are exclusively composed of two fully inflected nouns, where the non-head, the left-hand constituent, is marked with one of the two compound markers, -*u* and -*s*, whose shape is conditioned morphologically. We proposed that these compound markers have been exapted from the genitive markers in the variety. Showing that Hellenic compound structure is built on at least one stem and involves a unique compound marker exapted from an Ancient Greek thematic vowel; we argued that PhG compound structure cannot be associated with Hellenic compounding. Certain structural similarities between the compound structures in PhG and in Turkish, however, enabled us to propose that PhG compounding is selectively copied from Turkish. The compound marker role in PhG is assumed by what are originally genitive suffixes, by possible identification of the genitive in PhG with the Turkish compound marker, which is exapted from the third person possessive suffix, attaching to the head noun, i.e., the right-hand constituent. We correlated certain structural differences between the two languages, PhG and Turkish, to the nature and the locus of the compound marker. Among these differences is the occurrence of phrasal constituents in the non-head position in Turkish and lack thereof in PhG. We have shown that the PhG compound marker, being a purely morphological affix, attaches to stems, similar to all affixes in the language (as well as in all Hellenic varieties). As such, no phrasal constituent can be hosted in the position to which the compound marker attaches. In Turkish, on the other hand, since the compound marker attaches to the head, the non-head can easily host phrasal constituents. We also tested this correlation against Khalkha Mongolian, another Altaic language, in which, however, the compound marker attaches to the non-head. We have shown that similar to PhG, but unlike Turkish, phrasal constituents cannot be hosted in the non-head position in Mongolian, verifying the correlation we proposed between the locus of the compound marker and the availability of phrasal non-heads. Apparent counterexamples in

Metin Bağrıaçık, Aslı Göksel & Angela Ralli

Khalkha, we argued, should involve a covert preposition which assigns genitive case, hence these are not compounds.

Acknowledgements

We are grateful to Jaklin Kornfilt, Carola Trips and one anonymous reviewer for their various comments and suggestions. Metin Bağrıaçık's contribution was supported by the FWO, Research Foundation – Flanders (FWO13/ASP/010). Aslı Göksel's contribution was supported by Boğaziçi University Research Fund Grant Number 11500 (16B12P1).

Abbreviations

ACC	accusative
ADV	adverbial suffix
CM	compound marker
CMPND	compound
COMP	complementizer
CVB	converbial
DAT	dative
DER	derivational suffix
F	feminine
FNOM	factive nominalizer
FUT	future
GEN	genitive
IPFV	imperfective
M	masculine
MODNEG	modal negation
N	neuter
NFUT	future nominal
NMLZ	nominalizer
NOM	nominative
OBJ.CL	object clitic
PL	plural
POSS	possessive
PRT	particle
PRV	privative
PST	past
Q	question marker
REL	relational
RelC	relative clause
SBJREL	subject relativizer
SG	singular
VBLZ	verbalizer

References

Aboh, Enoch Oladé. 2015. *The emergence of hybrid grammars: Language contact and change.* Cambridge, UK: Cambridge University Press.

Anastasiadis, Vasilis. 1976. *I sintaksi sto Pharasiotiko idioma tis Kappadokias [The syntax of the dialect of Pharasa in Cappadocia]*. Ioannina: University of Ioannina dissertation.

Anastasiadi-Symeonidi, Anna. 1983. La composition en grec moderne d'un point de vue diachronique. *Lalies* 2. 77–90.

Anderson, Stephen R. 1992. *A-Morphous morphology*. Cambridge: Cambridge University Press.

Andreou, Marios. 2014. *Headedness in word formation and Lexical Semantics: Evidence from Italiot and Cypriot*. Patras: University of Patras dissertation.

Andriotis, Nikolaos P. 1948. *To glossiko idioma ton Pharason [the dialect of Pharasa]*. Athens: Ikaros.

Aronoff, Mark. 1994. *Morphology by itself: Stems and inflectional classes*. Cambridge, MA: MIT Press.

Aslan, Erhan & Aslı Altan. 2006. The role of (-s)I in Turkish indefinite nominal compounds. *Dil Dergisi* 131. 57–75.

Bağrıaçık, Metin & Angela Ralli. 2013. NN-sI concatenations in Turkish: Construct-state nominals and phrasal compounds. In Umut Özge (ed.), *Proceedings of the 8th workshop on Altaic formal linguistics*, vol. 67 (MIT Working Papers in Linguistics), 13–24. Cambridge, MA: MIT Press.

Bağrıaçık, Metin & Angela Ralli. 2015. Morphological vs. Phrasal compounds: Evidence from Modern Greek and Turkish. *STUF–Language Typology and Universals* 68. 323–357.

Bağrıaçık, Metin. in preparation. *Complementation in Pharasiot Greek*. Belgium: Ghent University dissertation.

Bağrıaçık, Metin, Aslı Göksel & Angela Ralli. Forthcoming. Turkish phrasal suffixes in Pharasiot Greek. Unpublished Manuscript.

Bisetto, Antonietta. 2015. Do Romance languages have phrasal compounds? A look at Italian. *STUF–Language Typology and Universals* 68. 395–419.

Bisetto, Antonietta & Sergio Scalise. 1999. Compounding: Morphology and/or syntax? In Mereu Lunella (ed.), *Boundaries of morphology and syntax*, 31–48. Amsterdam/Philadelphia: John Benjamins.

Booij, Geert E. 1992. Compounding in Dutch. *Rivista di Grammatica Generativa* 4. 37–59.

Borer, Hagit. 1998. Morphology and syntax. In Arnold Spencer & Arnold Zwicky (eds.), *Handbook of morphology*, 151–190. Oxford: Basil Blackwell.

Bowern, Claire. 2008. Syntactic change and syntactic borrowing in Generative Grammar. In Gisella Ferraresi & Maria Goldbach (eds.), *Principles of syntactic reconstruction*, 187–216. Amsterdam/Philadelphia: John Benjamins.

Bozşahin, Cem. 2002. The Combinatory Morphemic Lexicon. *Computational Linguistics* 28. 145–186.

Chatzidakis, Georgios N. 1905. *Mesaionika kai Nea Ellinika.* Athinai: Pelekanos.

Chomsky, Noam. 1995. *The Minimalist Program.* Cambridge, MA: MIT Press.

Dawkins, Richard McGillivray. 1916. *Modern Greek in Asia Minor: A study of the dialects of Síli, Cappadocia and Phárasa, with grammar, texts, translation and glossary.* Cambridge, UK: Cambridge University Press.

Dawkins, Richard McGillivray. 1937. The Pontic dialect of Modern Greek in Asia Minor and Russia. *Transactions of the Philological Society* 36(1). 15–52.

Dawkins, Richard McGillivray. 1940. The dialects of Modern Greek. *Transactions of the Philological Society* 39(1). 1–38.

Dede, Müşerref Ağan. 1978. *A syntactic and semantic analysis of Turkish nominal compounds.* Ann Arbor, MI: University of Michigan dissertation.

Di Sciullo, Anna Maria. 2005. *Asymmetry in morphology.* Cambridge, MA: MIT.

Gardani, Francesco. 2008. *Borrowing of inflectional morphemes in language contact* (Eurpean University Studies, Series XXI Linguistics 320). Frankfurt am Main: Peter Lang.

Gardani, Francesco, Peter Arkadiev & Nino Amiridze (eds.). 2015. *Borrowed morphology* (Language Contact and Bilingualism 8). Berlin: Mouton de Gruyter.

Gaunt, John, G. Bayarmandakh & L. Chuluunbaatar. 2004. *Modern Mongolian: A course Book.* London & New York: Routledge.

van Gelderen, Elly. 2011. *The linguistic cycle. Language change and language faculty.* NY, USA: Oxford University Press.

Göksel, Aslı. 1988. Bracketing paradoxes in Turkish nominal compounds. In Sabri Koç (ed.), *Studies on Turkish linguistics,* 287–298. Ankara: METU Press.

Göksel, Aslı. 2009. Compounds in Turkish. *Lingua e Linguaggio* 8(2). 213–236.

Göksel, Aslı. 2015. Phrasal compounds in Turkish: Distinguishing citations from quotations. *STUF–Language Typology and Universals* 68. 359–394.

Göksel, Aslı & Celia Kerslake. 2005. *Turkish: A comprehensive grammar.* London & New York: Routledge.

Göksel, Aslı. 1993. *Levels of representation and argument structure in Turkish.* London: SOAS, University of London dissertation.

Göksel, Aslı & Belma Haznedar. 2007. Remarks on compounding in Turkish. MorboComp Project, University of Bologna.

Grégoire, Henri. 1909. Appendice: Notes sur le dialecte de Farasha. *Bulletin de Correspondance hellénique* 33. 148–159.

Grimstad, Maren B., Terje Lohndal & Tor A. Åfarli. 2014. Language mixing and Exoskeletal Theory: A case study of word-internal mixing in American Norwegian. *Nordlyd* 41. 213–237.

Gürer, Aslı. 2010. *EPP, subject positions and case checking in CNPCs in Turkish.* İstanbul: Boğaziçi University MA thesis.

Halle, Morris & Alec Marantz. 1993. Distributed Morphology and the pieces of inflection. In Kenneth Hale & Samuel Jay Keyser (eds.), *The view from building 20: Essays in linguistics in honor of Sylvain Bromberger*, 111–176. Cambridge, MA: MIT Press.

Halle, Morris & Bert Vaux. 1998. Theoretical aspects of Indo-European nominal morphology: The nominal declensions of Latin and Armenian. In Jay Jasanoff, Craig Melchert & Lisi Oliver (eds.), *Mír Curad: Studies in honor of Calvert Watkins*, 223–240. Innsruck: Institut für Sprachwissenschaft, University of Innsbruck.

Hayashi, Tooru. 1996. The dual status of possessive compounds in Modern Turkish. In Arpad Berta, Bert Brendemoen & Claus Schönig (eds.), *Symbolæ Turcologicæ: Studies in honor of Lars Johanson on the occasion of his sixtieth birthday*, vol. 6, 119–129. İstanbul: Swedish Research Institute in Istanbul.

von Heusinger, Klaus, Udo Klein & Dolgor Guntsetseg. 2011. The case of accusative embedded subjects in Mongolian. *Lingua* 121. 48–59.

Ingria, Robert J. 2005. Grammatical formatives in a generative lexical theory: The case of Modern Greek και. *Journal of Greek Linguistics* 6(1). 61–101.

Johanson, Lars. 1992. *Strukturelle Faktoren in türkischen Sprachkontakten.* Stuttgart: Steiner Verlag.

Johanson, Lars. 1993. Code-Copying in immigrant Turkish. In Guus Extra & Ludo Th. Verhoeven (eds.), *Immigrant languages of Europe*, 197–221. Clevedon, Philadelphia & Adelaide: Multilingual Matters.

Kageyama, Taro. 2001. Word Plus: The intersection of words and phrases. In Jeroen van de Weijer & Tetsuo Nishihara (eds.), *Issues in Japanese phonology and morphology*, 245–276. Berlin: de Gruyter.

Kamali, Beste & Didem Ikizoğlu. 2015. Compound stress in Turkish is phrase stress. In Deniz Zeyrek, Çiğdem Sağın-Şimşek, Ufuk Ataş & Jochen Rehbein (eds.), *Ankara papers in Turkish and Turkic linguistics*, 40–51. Wiesbaden: Harrassowitz Verlag.

Karatsareas, Petros. 2011. *A study of Cappadocian Greek nominal morphology from a diachronic and dialectological perspective.* Cambridge, UK: University of Cambridge dissertation.

Karatsareas, Petros. 2014. On the diachrony of gender in Asia Minor Greek: The development of semantic agreement in Pontic. *Language Sciences* 43. 77–101.

Kornfilt, Jaklin. 1986. The stuttering prohibition and morpheme deletion in Turkish. In Ayhan Aksu-Koç & Eser Erguvanlı-Taylan (eds.), *Proceedings of the second international conference in Turkish linguistics*, 59–83. Istanbul: Boğaziyi University Publications.

Kornfilt, Jaklin. 1997. *Turkish.* London & New York: Routledge.

Kornfilt, Jaklin. 2012. Revisiting 'suspended affixation' and other coordinate mysteries. In Laura Brugè, Anna Cardinaletti, Giuliana Giusti, Nicola Munaro & Cecilia Poletto (eds.), *Functional heads: The cartography of syntactic structures 7*, 181–196. Oxford & NY: Oxford University Press.

Kullmann, Rita & Dandii-Yadamyn Tserenpil. 1996. *Mongolian grammar.* Hong Kong: Jensco Ltd.

Kunduracı, Aysun. 2013. *Turkish N-N compounds: A process-based paradigmatic account.* AB, Canada: University of Calgary dissertation.

Kyrillos, Patriarch VI of Constantinople. 1815. *Istorikí perigrafí tou en Viénni proekdhothéntos chorografikoú pínakos tis megális Arxisatapías Ikoníou, nin próton típois ekdhotheísa [a historical account of the topographical table of the Greater Archisatrapia of Iconium, published formerly in Vienna, now formally published for the first time].* Constantinople: Patriarchikón Tipografeíon.

de Lagarde, Paul. 1886. *NeuGriechisches aus Klein Asien.* Göttingen: Eieterichsche Verlags-Buchhandlung.

Lepschy, Anna Laura & Arturo Tosi (eds.). 2006. *Rethinking languages in contact: The case of Italian.* Oxford: Legenda.

Levidis, Anastasios. 1892. Pragmateía perí tis en Kappadokía laluménis glóssis ipó Anastasíu M. Levídu metá ton dimodón asmáton, enigmáton, parimíon, efxón, katarón, orkón, kiríon onomáton, mithón, asmáton meseonikón, grammatikís, ke glossaríon októ, ke simióseon [A treatise by A.M Levidis on the language spoken in Cappadocia, with vernacular songs, riddles, wishes, curses, oaths, proper names, fables, medieval songs, grammar and glossary, and notes]. Manuscript deposited at Centre of Asia Minor Greek Studies (partly published).

Lewis, Geoffrey L. 1967. *Turkish grammar.* Oxford: OUP.

Lohndal, Terje. 2013. Generative grammar and language mixing. *Theoretical Linguistics* 39. 215–224.

Lucas, Christopher. 2012. Contact-induced grammatical change: Towards and explicit account. *Diachronica* 29. 275–300.

Nespor, Marina & Angela Ralli. 1994. Stress domains in Greek compounds: A case of morphology-phonology interaction. In Irene Philippaki-Warburton, Katerina Nicolaidis & Maria Sifianou (eds.), *Themes in Greek linguistics. Papers from the 1st international conference on Greek linguistics*, 201–208. Amsterdam/Philadelphia: John Benjamins.

Nespor, Marina & Angela Ralli. 1996. Morphology-Phonology interface: Phonological domains in Greek compounds. *The Linguistic Review* 13. 357–382.

Norde, Muriel & Freek Van de Velde. 2016. Exaptation: Taking stock of a controversial notion in linguistics. In Muriel Norde & Freek Van de Velde (eds.), *Exaptation and language change*, 1–35. Amsterdam/Philadelphia: John Benjamins.

Özsoy, Sumru. 2004. Dışişleri eski bakanı ve Türkçe'nin yeni yapısı. In *Kaf Dağı'nın ötesine varmak. Günay Kut armağanı*, vol. 3 (Journal of Turkish Studies/Türklük Bilgisi Araştırmaları (28)), 247–256. Harvard: Harvard University Press.

Papadopoulos, Anthimos A. 1961. *Istorikon leksikon tis ellinikis tis pontikis dialektou [historical dictionary of Pontic Greek], vol. 1–2*. Athens: Mirtidis.

Papastefanou, Georgios & Androniki Karakelidou. 2012. *I chameni ghlossa. Varasotiko-elliniko leksiko [The lost language. Pharasiot-Modern Greek dictionary]*. Geneva: no-info.

Postal, Paul. 1969. Anaphoric islands. In *Proceedings of the 5th Regional Meeting of the Chicago Linguistic Society*, 205–239. Chicago: CLS.

Ralli, Angela. 1988. *Eléments de la linguistique du grec modern: La structure du verbe*. Quebec: Université de Montréal dissertation.

Ralli, Angela. 2000. A feature-based analysis of Greek nominal inflection. *Glossologia* 11/12. 201–207.

Ralli, Angela. 2005. *Morfologia [morphology]*. Athens: Patakis.

Ralli, Angela. 2007. *I sinthesi lekseon: Diaglossiki morfologiki prosengisi [The composition of words: A cross-linguistic morphological approach]*. Athens: Patakis.

Ralli, Angela. 2008. Compound markers and parametric variation. *STUF–Language Typology and Universals* 61. 19–38.

Ralli, Angela. 2013a. Compounding and its locus of realization: Evidence from Greek and Turkish. *Word Structure* 6. 181–200.

Ralli, Angela. 2013b. *Compounding in Modern Greek* (Studies in Morphology 2). Dordrecht: Springer.

Ralli, Angela. 2014. Is is compound borrowing possible in language-contact settings? Paper presented at the 6th International Conference on Modern Greek Dialects and Linguistic Theory, 25–28 September 2014, Patras, Greece.

Ralli, Angela. 2016. *Leksiko dialektikis poikilias moschonision, kidoniaon ke voreioanatolikis lesvou [Dictionary of the dialectal varieties of moschonisi, kydonies ad northeastern lesbos].* Patras: University of Patras.

Ralli, Angela & Athanasios Karasimos. 2009. The bare-stem constraint in Greek compound formation. *Gengo Kenkyu* 135. 29–48.

Ralli, Angela & Maria Raftopoulou. 1999. I sinthesi os diachroniko fenomeno schimatizmu lekseon [Compounding as a diachronic word-formation process]. *Studies in Greek Linguistics* 19. 389–403.

Sarantidis, Archelaos I. 1899. *I Sinasos [Sinasos].* Athinai: Tipografeion Ioannou Nikolaïdou.

Scalise, Sergio & Antonietta Bisetto. 2009. The classification of compounds. In Rochelle Lieber & Pavol Štekauer (eds.), *The handbook of compounding*, 34–53. Oxford: Oxford University Press.

Scalise, Sergio & Francesca Massini (eds.). 2012. *Special issue on Romance compounds. Probus.* Vol. 24.

Scalise, Sergio & Irene Vogel. 2010. Why compounding? In Sergio Scalise & Irene Vogel (eds.), *Cross disciplinary issues in compounding*, 1–18. Amsterdam/Philadelphia: John Benjamins.

van Schaaik, Gerjan. 1992. The treatment of Turkish compounds in FG. In Michael Foretscue, Peter Harder & Lars Kristoffersen (eds.), *Layered structure and reference in a functional perspective*, 231–252. Amsterdam: John Benjamins.

van Schaaik, Gerjan. 2002. *The Noun in Turkish: Its argument structure and the compounding straitjacket.* Wiesbaden: Harrassowitz.

Schroeder, Christoph. 1999. *The Turkish nominal phrase in spoken discourse.* Wiesbaden: Harrassowitz Verlag.

Seifart, Frank. 2015a. Direct and indirect affix borrowing. *Language* 91(3). 92–113.

Seifart, Frank. 2015b. Does Structural-Typological similarity affect borrowability? *Language Dynamics and Change* 5(1). 99–113.

Sproat, Richard. 1988. On anaphoric islandhood. In Michael Hammond & Michael Noonan (eds.), *Theoretical morphology: Approaches in modern linguistics*, 291–301. San Diego: Academic Press.

Svantesson, Jan-Olof. 2003. Khalka. In Juha Janhunnen (ed.), *The Mongolic languages*, 154–176. London & New York: Routledge.

Tat, Deniz. 2013. *Word syntax of nominal compounds: Internal and aphasiological evidence from Turkish.* Tucson: University of Arizona dissertation.

Theodoridis, Theodoros. 1960. Pharasiotikes paradosis, mithi kai paramithia [Pharasiot customs, myths and stories]. *Laografia: Deltion tis Ellinikis Laografikis Etaireias* 19. 221–263.

Theodoridis, Theodoros. 1964. Pharasiotikes paradosis, mithi kai paramithia 2 [Pharasiot customs, myths and stories 2]. *Laografia: Deltion tis Ellinikis Laografikis Etaireias* 21. 209–336.

Theodoridis, Theodoros. 1966. Pharasiotikos istorikos dialogos [A historical dialogue in Pharasiot]. Unpublished Manuscript, deposited at the Center of Asia Minor Studies, Athens.

Thomason, Sarah. Forthcoming. Can rules be borrowed? In Roberto Zavala & Thomas Smith-Stark (eds.), *A festschrift for terry kaufman*.

Trips, Carola. 2012. Empirical and theoretical aspects of phrasal compounds: Against the 'syntax explains it all' attitude. In Angela Ralli, Geert Booij, Sergio Scalise & Athanasios Karasimos (eds.), *Online Proceedings of the eighth Mediterranean Morphology Meeting*, 322–346. Patras: University of Patras.

Trips, Carola & Jaklin Kornfilt. 2015. Typological aspects of phrasal compounds in English, German, Turkish and Turkic. *STUF – Language Typology and Universals* 68(3). 281–322.

Uygun, Dilek. 2009. *A Split-Model for category specification. Lexcial categories in Turkish*. Istanbul: Boğaziçi University dissertation.

Ward, Gregory, Richard Sproat & Gail McKoon. 1991. A pragmatic analysis of so-called anaphoric islands. *Language* 67. 439–472.

Xenofanis. 1896, 1905–1910. *Xenofanís, Síngramma periodhikón tu Sillógou Mikrasiatón, "Anatolís" [Xenophanes, Collection of the Magazine "Anatoli" of the Society of Asia Minor Greeks], vol I, II–VII*. Athens: Paraskeva Leoni.

Yükseker, Hitay. 1998. Possessive constructions in Turkish. In Lars Johanson, Éva Ágnes Ćsató, Vanessa Locke, Astrid Menz & Dorothea Winterling (eds.), *The Mainz meeting: Proceedings of the 7th international Conference of Turkish Linguistics*, 458–477. Wiesbaden: Harrassowitz Verlag.

Chapter 8

Phrasal compounds and the morphology-syntax relation

Jürgen Pafel

Universität Stuttgart

Phrasal compounds are not an entirely uniform domain: it is necessary to distinguish between four different types of phrasal compounds. I will discuss their characteristics and the distinct analytical challenges. Only one type – the ›genuine‹ phrasal compounds with the non-head corresponding to a non-quotative well-formed syntactic phrase – poses a special problem for the morphology-syntax relation. There are three options for generating ›genuine‹ phrasal compounds: Merge, Insertion, and Conversion. I will argue that Conversion is the most suitable option. The analysis of phrasal compounds will suggest a symmetrical relation between word and phrase formation (phrases can be built on the basis of words *and* words on the basis of phrases) and a ›parallel‹ view of morphological and syntactic structure as fully separate structures with distinct properties.

1 Introduction

At first glance, phrasal compounds seem to be a phenomenon which obviously demonstrates the intrusion of syntax into morphology: phrasal compounds seem to be words that contain syntactic phrases ([$_N$ XP - N]), i.e., phrasal compounds seem not to obey Lexical Integrity. A thorough analysis of this phenomenon, however, might suggest just the opposite: morphology and syntax are separate levels related by interface relations – so, at least, I will argue.

With respect to the relation between morphological and syntactic structure, we can currently distinguish at least three different theoretical positions: morphological structure is a proper part of syntactic structure (Distributed Morphology); morphological and syntactic structures differ to a significant degree, but do overlap to some degree or interact (Ackema & Neeleman 2004; Lieber & Scalise

Jürgen Pafel. Phrasal compounds and the morphology-syntax relation. In Carola Trips & Jaklin Kornfilt (eds.), *Further investigations into the nature of phrasal compounding*, 233–259. Berlin: Language Science Press. DOI:10.5281/zenodo.896369

2006); morphological and syntactic structures are fully separate structures with different properties (see, e.g., Bresnan 2001, Spencer 2010).

Related to these overall theoretical positions concerning the morphology-syntax relation, we have three options for generating phrasal compounds, i.e., three options for relating an XP to the non-head of a compound – Merge, Insertion, and Conversion: we can form a phrasal compound either by merging an XP with the N head of the compound (Lawrenz 2006; Lieber & Scalise 2006; Hein 2015), by inserting an XP in the non-head position of the compound (Ackema & Neeleman 2004; Sato 2010), or by converting an XP into an N which functions as the non-head of the compound (Harley 2009; Pafel 2015).

We will approach these theoretical questions on the basis of a distinction between four different types of phrasal compounds which we can find in Afrikaans, Dutch, English, German, Mandarin Chinese, the Romance languages, and Turkish. What we generally call phrasal compounds are, as we will see, not an entirely uniform domain. I will present the characteristics of these four different types and show that they pose different challenges for analysis. There is just one type – the ›genuine‹ phrasal compounds with the non-head corresponding to a non-quotative well-formed syntactic phrase – which poses a special problem for the morphology-syntax relation, a problem which an account of phrasal compounds has to tackle. I will discuss the question of which of the options for generating phrasal compounds is appropriate to cope with genuine phrasal compounds in such a way that the relation to the other types of phrasal compounds is respected. I will argue that Conversion is the most suitable option (an option which relies on a certain input-output rule), and I will argue that such an account of phrasal compounds presupposes a clear distinction between two aspects of the morphology-syntax relation: the relation between morphological and syntactic structure, on the one hand, and the relation between word formation and phrase formation, on the other. A thorough analysis of phrasal compounds suggests a symmetrical relation between word and phrase formation (phrases can be built on the basis of words *and* words on the basis of phrases) and a ›parallel‹ view of morphological and syntactic structures as fully separate structures with distinct properties.

2 Four types of phrasal compounds

At first sight, one is inclined to define phrasal compounds as compounds whose non-head is a syntactic phrase, as is frequently done in the literature.[1] But, at closer inspection, it becomes evident that the examples discussed – for instance in the literature on German phrasal compounds – are quite heterogeneous: not all of them strictly fit the initial definition. As for German, we can distinguish between four types of ›phrasal compounds‹ which differ with respect to (i) the non-head (not) corresponding to a well-formed syntactic phrase [±WELL-FORMED] and (ii) the non-head (not) being a quote [±QUOTATIVE].

Table 1: Types of phrasal compounds (WELL-FORMED=non-head being a well-formed syntactic phrase; QUOTATIVE=non-head being a quote)

	+WELL-FORMED	−WELL-FORMED
+QUOTATIVE	**Type I**	**Type IV**
−QUOTATIVE	**Type II**	**Type III**

Conceptually, the property of being a well-formed syntactic phrase is clear enough notwithstanding cases where it is difficult to decide whether a phrase is well-formed or not. The property of being quotative is more demanding. I use two criteria to distinguish quotative from non-quotative phrasal compounds. Firstly, paraphrase with pure quotes: in contrast to non-quotative phrasal compounds, the meaning of a quotative phrasal compound can most naturally be paraphrased using a pure quote (e.g. Prince-of-Thieves film = film with the title 'Prince of Thieves'). Secondly, interpretation of indexicals: in contrast to quotative phrasal compounds, indexicals in non-quotative phrasal compounds are interpreted like ordinary indexicals with respect to the relevant utterance situation (compare below § 2.3).

As we will see, it is compounds of **Type II** – which we will call ›genuine phrasal compounds‹ – which pose a special problem for the morphology-syntax relation, a problem which an account of phrasal compounds has to tackle. ›Quotative phrasal compounds‹ (i.e., **Type-I** and **Type-IV** compounds) do not pose a special problem for the morphology-syntax relation as they are N(oun)N(oun) compounds as a consequence of having a quote as non-head, and neither do **Type-III** compounds (›pseudo-phrasal compounds‹) whose non-head does not

---

[1] See, for instance, Meibauer (2003: 155), Lawrenz (2006: 7).

Jürgen Pafel

correspond to a phrase at all. It will become evident that the different types pose distinct analytical challenges.

The classification in Table 1 seems to be cross-linguistically relevant. Languages other than German seem to exhibit all four types (e.g., Afrikaans, Dutch, English, Turkish) or at least some of them (e.g., Mandarin Chinese, Romance languages), and there are languages with no phrasal compounds at all (e.g., Polish and other Slavic languages). As we will see, the classification is compatible with results of diverse researchers investigating phrasal compounds in different languages.[2]

2.1 Quotative phrasal compounds (Type I)

This type of phrasal compound ([+WELL-FORMED, +QUOTATIVE]) consists of a noun preceded by a quote:

(1)   a.   Afrikaans (Savini 1984: 50; 57)
           'hoe-gaan-dit-nog'-brief
           how-goes-it-well-letter

           'how-are-you letter'

      b.   Afrikaans (Savini 1984: 50; 57)
           ek-het-nog-n'-kaart-in-die-mou-waarskuwing
           I-have-still-a-card-in-the-sleeve-warning

           'warning by someone that he has still a card up his sleeve'

(2)   Dutch (Ackema & Neeleman 2004: 124, Booij 2002: 148)

      a.   'waarom-leven wij?' probleem
           'why-do-we-live? problem'

      b.   Doe-het-zelf-winkel
           'Do-it-yourself shop'

      c.   ver-van-mijn-bed-show
           'far-away-from-my-bed show'

(3)   English (Trips 2012: 324; 325; 326)

      a.   'wait and see' mentality

---

[2] What won't be dealt with here is to relate these types to the classification of semantic classes of heads, as we can find them in Meibauer (2003: §6.1.1), Trips & Kornfilt (2015: §2.2), Göksel (2015: §2.3) and Hein (2015: Kap. III.2.3).

    b. 'show the shirt' routine

    c. 'kick me please' type

    d. Prince-of-Thieves film

(4) German (Fleischer & Barz 1995: 45; Meibauer 2007: 250)

    a. Kaufe-Ihr-Auto-Kärtchen
       buy-your-car-card
       'I-buy-your-car card'

    b. Lauf-dich-gesund-Bewegung
       'run-yourself-fit movement'

    c. Trimm-dich-Pfad
       'keep-fit path'

(5) Mandarin Chinese (Wiese 1996: 185, Fuyuan Zhou (personal communication))

    a. 'yi-guo-liang-zhi'-zhengce
       one-country-two-system-politics
       'one-country-two-systems politics'

    b. 'Bai-hua-qi-fang'-yundong
       hundred-flower-simultaneously-blossom-campaign
       'Hundred Flowers Campaign'

(6) Turkish (Trips & Kornfilt 2015: 307; 308)

    a. "tavuk-mu-yumurta-mı" soru-su
       chicken-Q-egg-Q   question-CM
       'is-it-the-chicken-or-the-egg? question'

    b. "Bekle, gör-ür-üz" kafa-sı/tutum-u
       wait   see-AOR-1PL head-CM/attitude-CM
       'wait-and-(we shall) see-thinking/attitude'

The quote in these phrasal compounds is a ›pure quote‹, not a ›citation‹ (cf. Pafel 2011 for this contrast). A pure quote is part of a metalinguistic utterance as, e.g., in (7); a citation is part of a speech representation as, e.g., in (8). With respect to a citation, it makes sense to ask for the reference of indexicals and other referential expressions. Pure quotes differ: it makes no sense to ask for the reference of the indexical in (7) – in contrast to (8):

(7)   The sentence 'I buy your car' is a declarative sentence.

(8)   She said to me: »I buy your car.«

The quotes in phrasal compounds behave like the pure quote in (7): it makes no sense to ask for the reference of *me* in (3c), *Ihr* in (4a), *dich* in (4b), or the persons alluded to by the suffix *üz* in (6b).

Research on quotation came independently to the conclusion that pure quotes are nouns (cf. Jespersen 1924: 98 footnote 1; Klockow 1980: Kap. III.2.2.1; Ackema & Neeleman 2004: 153; Pafel 2007; 2011; Vries 2008: §5). Consequently, phrasal compounds of **Type I** are NN compounds and, semantically, they have the same structure as ordinary N_1N_2 compounds: »being an N_2 which stands in relation R to N_1« with R often being a pragmatically supplied relation of various kinds (as for the relation R in phrasal compounds compare Meibauer 2015). See (9a) for illustration. The compound contains the quote *'I buy your car'* and the head noun *card*, and it has the meaning: »being a card displaying the writing 'buy your car'« or, shorter, »card with the writing 'buy your car'«

(9)   a.   *Kaufe-Ihr-Auto-Kärtchen* = card with the writing 'buy your car'

    b.   *Lauf-dich-gesund-Bewegung* = movement with the slogan 'Run-yourself-fit'

    c.   *Prince-of-Thieves film* = film which has the title 'Prince of Thieves'

Multiple N recursion is possible with phrasal compounds. Phrasal compounds of Type I can be a proper part of compounds: they can be the head (see 10) or the non-head of a compound (see 11), and they even can be contained in a phrasal compound (in 12a a phrasal compound of Type I is part of a phrasal compound of the same type, in 12b it is part of a phrasal compound of Type III – cf. 18a, and in 12c it is part of a phrasal compound of Type II – cf. 29a):

(10)   German (personal knowledge)

    a.   Pseudo-Trimm-dich-Pfad
       pseudo-keep-fit-path

    b.   Hartz-IV-Trimm-dich-Pfad
       Hartz-IV-keep-fit-path

    c.   Hochglanz-'Kaufe Ihr Auto'-Kärtchen
       high-gloss-'buy your car'-card

(11) German (personal knowledge)

    a. Trimm-dich-Pfad-Gestaltung
       keep-fit-path-construction

    b. Trimm-dich-Pfad-Bewegung
       keep-fit-path-movement

    c. 'Kaufe Ihr Auto'-Kärtchen-Inflation
       'buy your car'-card-inflation

(12) German (personal knowledge)

    a. 'Du schaffst es!'-Trimm-dich-Pfad
       'You succeed!'-keep-fit-path

    b. Vor-Trimm-dich-Pfad-Zeit
       before-keep-fit-path-time

    c. Zwischen-den-Zeilen 'Ihr könnt mich mal'-Attitüde
       between-the-lines-'Up yours!'-attitude

Thus, phrasal compounds of **Type I** are regular NN compounds morphologically and semantically. Further they obey the principle »Words do not contain syntactic phrases«, i.e., they obey one version of Lexical Integrity (cf. Pafel 2015).

The fact that pure quotes are nouns has an interesting consequence. There must be some ›conversion‹ of phrases into words, as far as phrasal compounds of **Type I** are concerned. See the example in (13) and its analysis in (14) for illustration: the sentence *I think so* is quoted, and is located at the position of the noun in a noun phrase, and it is inflected as a noun.

(13) English (cf. Jespersen 1924: 96 footnote 1)
    His speech abounded in many I think so's.

(14) a. [sentence I think so]

    b. [noun phrase many [noun I think so's]]

    c. [word[N] [stem[N] I think so] -s]

Thus, quotation and its analysis is a relevant topic, if we are interested in phrasal compounds. Note that possibly every language which exhibits phrasal compounds has phrasal compounds of **Type I**. Quotation is interesting as we find the same puzzling and challenging phenomenon: something which is a syntactic phrase gets a new life as a word or morpheme if it is quoted. Therefore, the question should be relevant to our topic of which options we have in dealing with generating pure quotes (see § 3).

Phrasal compounds of **Type I** are distinguished as a special class of phrasal compounds by several researchers partly independent of one another (see Göksel 2015, Pafel 2015, Trips & Kornfilt 2015).

As phrasal compounds of **Type I** are NN compounds, we could create a category of ›quotative compounds‹ as a special type of NN compounds: they either have a quote as non-head constituent (cf. 15 and the examples already presented of phrasal compounds of **Type I**), or they have a quote as the head of the compound (cf. 16):

(15)   a. English
           for phrases

       b. German
           für-Phrasen
           '*for* phrases'

       c. Turkish (Göksel 2015: 375)
           yavasca sözcü-gü
           slowly   word-CM
           '(the) word *slowly*'

       d. Mandarin Chinese (Fuyuan Zhou (personal communication))
           ba-zi-duanyu
           ba-sign-phrase
           '*ba*-phrase'

(16)   German
       Höflichkeits-*Sie*
       'politeness *you*'

Thus, in the end, what we called phrasal compounds of **Type I** can be subsumed under a subtype of NN compounds (cf. Göksel 2015).

We can also deal with **Type IV** in the same vain. These phrasal compounds have a quote as non-head which is not a well-formed syntactic phrase, but a sequence of sentences or sentence-fragments. Compare the following examples (I made up examples (17b) and (17c) myself):

(17)   a. German (Schmidt 2000: 142)
           'Versuche-mir-zu-verzeihen', 'Ich werde-dich-ewig-lieben'-Briefchen
           try-me-to-forgive, I-will-you-forever-love-letter
           'Try-to-forgive me', 'I-will-love-you-forever letter'

b. German (personal knowledge)
'Nein-vielleicht-doch-ja-vielleicht-aber-eigentlich-doch-nicht'-
Gestammel
no-perhaps-after-all-yes-perhaps-but-rather-after-all-not-
stammering
'no-perhaps-after-all-yes-perhaps-but-rather-after-all-not
stammering'

c. English (personal knowledge)
'Hi-Hi-See-You' conversation

2.2 Pseudo-phrasal compounds (Type III)

The non-head of these phrasal compounds ([–WELL-FORMED, –QUOTATIVE]) neither corresponds to a well-formed syntactic phrase, nor is it quotative, compare
Lawrenz (2006: 139) and Pafel (2015) for German:

(18)   German (Ortner et al. 1991: 44; Fleischer & Barz 1995: 45; Schmidt 2000:
146; Meibauer 2003: 155)

a. Vor-Nobelpreis-Ära
'before-Nobel prize era'

b. Vor-Ort-Bericht
'on-site report'

c. Zweibettzimmer
'double bedroom'

d. Vater-Sohn-Konflikt
'father-son conflict'

e. Vorher-Nachher-Bilanz
'before-and-after account'

f. Jeder-gegen-jeden-Krieg
'everyone-against-everyone war'

The non-head constituent in (18a), i.e., *Vor-Nobelpreis*, does not correspond to
a well-formed syntactic phrase, but has a well-formed morphological structure
which mimics a syntactic phrase in the sense that it is built by the same lexical
material in the same order, exhibits a similar prosodic structure and is related
to a phrasal semantics having the meaning »before the time when Nobel prizes
were awarded«.

Jürgen Pafel

(19) Vor-Nobelpreis-Ära
      Morphological structure: $[[P+N]_P +N]_N$
      Meaning: era before the time when Nobel prizes were awarded

Therefore, it is not unreasonable to take them to be phrasal compounds, as the non-head exhibits properties of phrases, even if it does not correspond to a well-formed *syntactic* phrase. The same holds for the non-heads in the other examples.

Phrasal compounds of **Type III** obey Lexical Integrity: the non-head constituent of a pseudo-phrasal compound is not a well-formed syntactic phrase.

It seems that there are similar compounds in other languages, too – but it is at times difficult to judge whether or not the non-head corresponds to a well-formed syntactic phrase.

(20) English (Trips 2012: 323; 324)

    a. 'famous for fifteen minutes' type
    b. 'first in last out' policy
    c. 'two for the price of one' sales
    d. 'always on the top' option

(21) Afrikaans (Savini 1984: 44; 65; 67; 71)

    a. tafel-en-bank-eenheid
       table-and-bench-unit
       'unit consisting of a table and (a) bench'
    b. been-rek-ruimte
       leg-stretch-space
       'space in which to stretch one's legs'
    c. slaap-wakkerbly-patroon
       sleep-awake-stay-pattern
       'pattern of sleeping and staying awake alternately'
    d. vaal-haar-nooi
       dull-hair-girl
       'girl with dull hair'
    e. nege-oog-reus
       nine-eye-gaint
       'giant with nine eyes'

(22) Dutch (Booij 2002: 148; 150)

    a. breed band antenne
       'broadband aerial'

    b. twee persons bed
       'double bed'

    c. aardappel schrap machine
       'potato scraper'

    d. gooi-en-smijt-film
       throw-and-smash-film
       'slapstick film'

(23) Turkish (Göksel 2015: 362)

    a. yan-ar   dön-er   meyva
       burn-PTCP turn-PTCP fruit
       Lit. 'burning-turning fruit'

    b. ana   baba gün-ü
       mother father day-CM
       '(a) crowded (place)'

The so-called *polirematiche* 'multiword expressions' in Romance languages like the ones in (24) and (25) are sometimes called phrasal compounds. They consist of a noun followed by a preposition and a noun (N+P+N):

(24) Italian (Bisetto 2015: 397)

    a. carta di credito
       'credit card'

    b. unità di misura
       'unit of measurement'

(25) French (Bisetto 2015: 397)

    a. verre à vin
       'wine glass'

    b. fil de fer
       'wire'

According to Bisetto (2015: 397f.), the preposition and the following noun differ in their properties from PPs, and therefore it seems wrong to analyze the P+N part as a PP. This means they look like compounds of **Type III**.

2.3 Genuine phrasal compounds (Type II)

The non-head of these phrasal compounds ([+WELL-FORMED, –QUOTATIVE]) corresponds to a well-formed syntactic phrase, but it is not quotative.

(26)   Afrikaans (Savini 1984: 39; Botha 2015: 141; 142; 143)

    a. laat-in-die-aand   drankie
        late-in-the-evening drink

        'drink taken late in the evening'

    b. uit-die-bottel-drink   alkoholis
        from-the-bottle-drink alcoholic

        'alcoholic who drinks straight from the bottle'

    c. van-die-rak-pak
        from-the-shelf-suit

        'suit bought off the peg'

    d. maklik-om-te-maak-poeding
        easy-for-to-make-pudding

        'pudding which is easy to make'

(27)   Dutch (Ackema & Neeleman 2004: 124; Booij 2002: 146)

    a. hoestend publick syndroom
        'coughing-audience syndrome'

    b. ijs met slagroom fobie
        'ice-cream with whipped-cream phobia'

    c. vier-kleuren druk
        'four-color printing'

    d. hete-lucht ballon
        'hot-air ballon'

(28)   English (Lieber 1992: 11; Trips 2012: 323)

    a. over-the-fence gossip

    b. slept-all-day look

    c. sex-in-shiny-packets literature

(29) German (Brogyanyi 1979: 161; Lawrenz 2006: 7)

    a. Zwischen-den-Zeilen-Widerstand
       'between-the-lines resistance'

    b. In-Kontakt-bleiben-Geschenke
       'keep-in-touch presents'

    c. Neid-auf-Reichtum-ohne-Leistung-Steuer
       'envy-of-wealth-without-effort tax'

    d. Schwerer-als-Luft-Flugobjekte
       'heavier-than-air flying objects'

    e. Liebe-auf-den-ersten-Blick-Paar
       'love-at-first-sight pair'

(30) Turkish (Trips & Kornfilt 2015: 307; 308)

    a. baba-lar ve ogul-lar toplanti-si
       father-PL and son-PL   meeting-CM
       'fathers-and-sons meeting'

    b. tabiat-a   dön-üs   politika-si
       nature-DAT return-NOM policy-CM
       'return-to-nature-policy'

    c. [Ne paha-sin-a   olur-sa ol-sun tabiat-i   kurtar-ma]
       what cost-3SG-DAT be-COND be-OPT nature-ACC save-NFNOM
       politika-si
       policy-CM
       'Saving nature whatever the cost policy'

(31) Mandarin Chinese (Fuyuan Zhou (personal communication))

    a. fan-fu-zhengce
       against-corruption-policy

    b. dusheng-zinü-zhengce
       single-child-policy
       'one-child policy'

The non-head constituent – for example *over the fence* in (28a) – exhibits all characteristics of a well-formed phrase in form and meaning. The phrasal compound itself, however, has the canonical semantic structure of an N_1N_2 compound: »being an N_2 which stands in relation R to N_1« (being gossip which is transmitted over the fence). Or, see (29a): *zwischen-den-Zeilen* 'between the lines' is a well-formed PP and the compound has the meaning: »being a resistance which hides (or, is located) between the lines«

The exocentric VN compounds in Romance languages like the ones in (32) marginally have a subtype where the verb combines with a phrase, an NP, as in (33).[3]

(32) Italian (Bisetto 2015: 399f.)

    a. cambiavalute

        'money changer'

    b. portavalori

        'amored car' (lit. 'carry valuables')

(33) Italian (Bisetto 2015: 399f.)

    a. ammazza [libertà digitali]

        'digital freedom killing'

    b. ammazza [gente che non c'entra niente]

        'killing people that have nothing to do with it'

These compounds seem to belong to **Type II**. See Bisetto (2015) for further candidates of phrasal compounds in Italian (which we might classify as belonging to **Type II**).

Type-II compounds differ from quotative phrasal compounds (i.e., **Type-I** and **Type-IV** compounds) in the interpretation of indexicals (cf. Pafel 2015: 277). We have seen in § 2.1 that it does not make sense to ask, with respect to **Type-I** compounds, for the reference of indexicals in the non-head. However, indexicals in the non-head of **Type-II** compounds differ. We can transform the attributive interrogative clause in (34a) into the non-head of a compound (34b) with no noticeable change of meaning (admittedly, (34b) is a quite uncommon way to say what the perfectly normal (34a) says – but it is a possible sentence):

(34) German (personal knowledge)

    a. Ich habe die Frage,   ob   ich glücklich bin, beantwortet.

        I   have the question whether I   happy   am answered

        'I have answered the question of whether I am happy.'

---

[3] Note that the compounds in (33) appear as the second noun in a superordinate compound in the corpus data of Bisetto (2015).

b. Ich habe die Ob-ich-glücklich-bin-Frage   beantwortet.
   I   have the whether-I-happy-am-question answered
   'I have answered the question of whether I am happy.'

The indexical in the non-head in (34b) is interpreted in the same way as the indexical being the subject of the sentence: they both refer to the speaker of the sentence. The fact that the indexical in the non-head refers to the speaker of the sentence becomes even more evident when we modify the subject of the sentence: sentence (35) has the meaning that everyone answered the question of whether the speaker of (35) is happy, not the question of whether he himself is happy.

(35)   German (personal knowledge)
       Jeder hat die Ob-ich-glücklich-bin-Frage beantwortet.

       'Everyone has answered the question of whether I am happy.'

The relations change when we modify the compound into a quotative one. In this case, the indexicals are no longer interpreted with respect to the utterance situation of the sentence – note that (36a) and (36b) have the same meaning and cannot have the same meaning as (35):

(36)   German (personal knowledge)

       a. Jeder hat die 'Bin ich glücklich?'-Frage beantwortet.
       b. Jeder hat die 'Bist du glücklich?'-Frage beantwortet.

       'Everyone has answered the question of whether he himself is happy.'

Thus, we can use the interpretation of indexicals as a criterion to distinguish compounds of **Type I** and **Type II**. With this in mind, we find quite the same distinction in Turkish: Göksel (2015) distinguishes »quotational phrasal compounds« from »citational phrasal compounds«, and Trips & Kornfilt (2015: 305) distinguish between the »quotational« and the »nominalized« type of phrasal compounds. It seems that compounds of this type are ›genuine‹ phrasal compounds, i.e., compounds with a true phrasal non-head: syntax, semantics, and prosody point to this direction. Thus, they pose a challenge to the question of how to fit a phrase into a word.[4] We will approach this question by having a look at how quotative phrases are fitted into a word.

---

[4] Note that it is feasible to analyze the Dutch and German compounds in (i) and (ii) as non-heads corresponding to a plural noun phrase containing a noun only (cf. Booij 2002: 147).

(i) *Dächermeer* (German), *dakenzee* (Dutch) 'sea of roofs'
(ii) *Häuserreihe* (German), *hiuzenrij* (Dutch) 'row of houses'

3 Quotation and conversion

In an article from 1984, Jackendoff came to the conclusion that »the phrase structure rule responsible for introducing [quotes] violates the normal theory of syntactic categories by permitting a totally free expression« (Jackendoff 1984: 26).
This consequence, however, is not mandatory. I know of two options dealing
formally with pure quotes, both of which rely on conversion.

In their book *Beyond Morphology*, Ackema and Neeleman take quoting to be
zero-affixation: »[T]he operation involves a change in syntactic status, both with
respect to category and level of projection. Its input may be a syntactic phrase
of any category, but its output consistently shows the distribution of a nominal
head. [...] The formation of autoreferential expressions must hence be a case of
zero affixation« (Ackema & Neeleman 2004: 153-154).

Ackema and Neeleman further argue for an architecture where morphology
and syntax are distinct submodules of an encompassing module, generating distinct structures. Nevertheless, they tune their system in such a way that, under
certain circumstances, merging of a syntactic phrase inside morphology is allowed. Zero-affixation is a case in point.

Zero-affixation to a syntactic phrase, however, is not sufficient to deal with autoreferential expressions. Firstly, the phrases can be fully ungrammatical, purely
non-sensical, or they can mix different languages. Secondly, not only phrases and
words can be quoted, but also morphemes, phonemes, graphemes. Pure quotes
can thus not be built in Ackema/Neeleman's morphosyntactic module.

The alternative to zero-affixation is conversion by an input-output rule which
operates on expressions.[5] An expression can have several kinds of properties:
phonological, morphological, syntactic, semantic, and pragmatic ones. The rule
takes an expression as input and gives another expression as output whose properties partially depend on the properties of the input expression. In the case of
quoting a syntactic phrase, the rule takes an arbitrary expression (which is syntactically a phrase) as input and gives an expression as output which (i) surrounds
the input expression's phoneme, or, better grapheme, sequence with quotation
marks and which (ii) is morphologically a noun-stem. A decisive point of this
input-output rule is that we can convert an expression with syntactic properties
into an expression with morphological properties instead. This rule can be generalized as in (37) so that arbitrary linguistic elements can be converted into an
expression which is morphologically a noun-stem (for details see Pafel 2015).[6]

---

[5] Note that I am not interested in the general controversy of whether or not conversion can be
reasonably captured by zero-affixation.

[6] The pure-quotation rule can easily take the form of an input-output rule which is formally of
the same type as ›constructions‹ in the sense of Sag et al. (2012), ›unary phrase structure rules‹

(37) Pure-quotation rule (simplified)

$$\begin{bmatrix} \text{PHON} & phon \\ \dots & \end{bmatrix} \Rightarrow \begin{bmatrix} \text{PHON} & \text{`}phon\text{'} \\ \text{MORPH} & \text{stem[N]} \\ \text{SEM} & \text{being of shape } phon \end{bmatrix}$$

Phrasal compounds of **Type I** have a pure quote as their non-head. That this quote is an N is the result of the application of the pure-quotation rule. Thus, constructing a phrasal compound of **Type I** is the concatenation of two nouns. The phrase-to-word conversion occurs ›previously‹ and is not part of the process of compounding. See for illustration the output of rule (37) for the quote in (13) *His speech abounded in many I think so's*:

(38) Description of the pure quote 'I think so'

$$\begin{bmatrix} \text{PHON} & <\text{'}><\text{I think so}><\text{'}> \\ \text{MORPH} & \text{stem[N]} \\ \text{SEM} & \text{being of shape } <\text{I think so}> \end{bmatrix}$$

As for the morphology-syntax relation, pure quotations show that words can be built in tandem with syntactic phrases, i.e., that phrases can be built on the basis of words *and* words on the basis of phrases (phrase-to-word-conversion rules like the pure-quotation rule is the decisive element which makes it possible to build words on the basis of phrases). Nevertheless, we do not have to integrate morphology into syntax to get this result. We can keep the morphological and the syntactic level apart from one another, as two separate dimensions of linguistic expressions.

4 Three options of dealing with phrasal compounds

There are, in principle, as I mentioned in the introduction, three options of generating phrasal compounds if the task is to solve the problem of how a phrase can be a base for a word. The options are Merge, Insertion, and Conversion: we can form a phrasal compound either by merging an XP with an N (the head of the compound), or by inserting an XP to the non-head position of the compound, or by converting an XP into an N which functions as the non-head of a compound. These options come with different accounts of the morphology-syntax relation.

---

in Kay (2014), and ›lexical rules‹ in Müller & Wechsler (2014), which are all more or less on a par.

Jürgen Pafel

We know now that the different types of phrasal compounds require different analyses. Thus, it will not come as a surprise that these three options cannot account for all types of phrasal compounds. They are, first and foremost, options for dealing with genuine phrasal compounds (**Type II**), as we will see in a moment. Therefore, the question arises of how much these options differ from an adequate account of the other types. An option is preferred to the degree that it is related to the other accounts, i.e., an analysis of genuine phrasal compounds should not differ radically from the analysis of the other types.

The first option of dealing with genuine phrasal compounds is Merge. Lieber & Scalise (2006) favor this option. They assume that there is a limited access of morphology to syntax. Syntax and morphology have different principles in constructing phrases and complex words, respectively, and they »are normally blind to each other«. But for a limited domain, morphology can build complex words by merging syntactic phrases. The limited domain is determined in such a way that words with the structure $[[XP] Y]_Y$ become possible (cf. the very similar approach in Lawrenz (2006: §II.5) and the construction-grammar variant in Hein (2015: 42, 115)).

Merge seems adequate for genuine phrasal compounds (**Type II**), as their non-head constituent looks like a well-formed syntactic phrase (but note that we have a semantic interpretation which is typical for NN compounds (Lawrenz 2006: 141), Lieber & Scalise (2006) are silent on the semantic interpretation of Merge). This approach, however, is inadequate with respect to quotative phrasal compounds (**Type I, IV**) because they are NN compounds, as we have seen. Thus, a quite different approach would be necessary to cope with them, i.e., some kind of conversion. Merge is, also, inadequate for pseudo-phrasal compounds (**Type III**) whose non-head constituent is not a well-formed syntactic phrase. Summing up, the Merge approach plus an additional mechanism is best suited to account for morphology having access to syntax, but it does not cover all types of phrasal compound and leads to a view of phrasal compounds where they appear to be a very heterogeneous set of phenomena.

Ackema & Neeleman (2004) have proposed to deal with phrasal compounds by a certain way of looking at the nature of insertion: insertion in their sense is just a way of feature matching. Morphology and syntax differ substantially, but they are part of an encompassing module, and insertion allows for a limited interaction between them. A syntactic phrase (NP, for instance) can be inserted in an N slot of a NN compound as N and NP have matching features. In contrast to the Merge approach, Insertion takes phrasal compounds to be something which is made possible by the general way insertion works.

250

However, categorial feature matching seems inadequate, as the »inserted« XP can have various categorial features (nominal, verbal, prepositional, sentential etc.), which would predict that either the phrasal compound can be of a type which is ruled out in some languages (for instance, P(reposition)N(oun) compounds) or that is of a dubious type (non-head corresponding to a sentence should be a word of which category?), cf. Lieber & Scalise (2006).[7] Further, the following points speak against insertion. First, Insertion does not cope with quotative phrasal compounds. We have already seen that conversion is necessary to generate quotative phrasal compounds. Ackema & Neeleman would have to rely on zero-affixation to cope with them. Thus, quotative phrasal compounds would differ in structure from genuine phrasal compounds: no XP is inserted. Second, as for pseudo-phrasal compounds, the structure is inadequate as the non-head constituent is not a syntactic phrase. Ackema & Neeleman's defending claim that the non-head constituent be a well-formed syntactic phrase in telegraphic speech is unconvincing. Take the phrasal compound (39) as an example. We could have (40a) as a headline, but not the unacceptable (40b).

(39) Vor-Nobelpreis-Ära
      'before-Nobel prize era'

(40) a. Alles   besser damals
          everything better then
          'Everything was better in former times.'
      b. * Alles besser vor Nobelpreis
          'Everything was better in the times before Nobel prizes were awarded.'

Insertion doesn't have to treat phrasal compounds as a peculiar phenomenon because the general process of insertion builds them under the assumption that there is limited interaction between morphology and syntax. This predicts that we could find it in every language. But like Merge, it does not cover all types of phrasal compounds and leads to a view of phrasal compounds where they appear to be a quite heterogeneous set of phenomena. (For a similar approach with similar problems in a different framework see Sato 2010.)

The Conversion approach proposes to deal with genuine phrasal compounds by special phrase-to-word-conversion rules. According to Harley (2009), a phrase

---

[7] Should it be the case that Ackema & Neeleman take phrasal compounds to be always NN compounds, feature matching would become hollow (cf. Meibauer 2007: 243; Sato 2010: 392).

undergoes zero-derivation to a nominal category, i.e., the complex phrase is affixed by a zero n head (n^0):

(41) $[[XP] n^0]_{nP}$ (where 'nP' stands for 'noun')

Harley endorses Distributed Morphology, but has to make quite »speculative« assumptions to integrate her analysis into this framework (note that even in a framework which treats word-formation purely syntactically, it is by no means easy to cope with phrasal compounds). As for semantics, the derivation »will denote a concept evoked by the phrasal syntax, though not compositionally determined by it« (Harley 2009: 143); she further assumes that »quotative phrasal compounds evoke a particular attitude that might be attributed to a putative utterer of the phrase in question. Intuitively, the phrase has been fully interpreted, and an associated concept extracted from it — an attitude, in the case of quotatives, or an abstraction from an existing conceptual category, in the case of complex nP phrases as in *stuff-blowing-up effects* or *bikini-girls-in-trouble genre*« (Harley 2009: 142). Apparently, Harley wants to account for quotative and genuine phrasal compounds syntactically and semantically in the same way, which neglects, however, the differences between these two types which we have presented.

According to Pafel (2015), a special input-output rule copes for genuine phrasal compounds. The rule in (42) takes a phrase (XP) as input and gives a noun as output. The phrase and the noun have exactly the same phonology and semantics, and the noun is a bound morpheme, as it does not occur outside of a nominal compound.

(42) XP-to-N-conversion rule

$$
\begin{bmatrix}
\text{PHON} & phon \\
\text{SYN} & \text{XP} \\
\text{SEM} & \text{predicate(x)} \\
& mean
\end{bmatrix}
\Rightarrow
\begin{bmatrix}
\text{PHON} & phon \\
\text{MORPH} & \text{category: N} \\
& \text{valency: to-its-right-right(N)} \\
\text{SEM} & \text{predicate(x)} \\
& mean
\end{bmatrix}
$$

Given an XP with an arbitrary phonological form (*phon*) and the semantics of a one-place predicate with an arbitrary meaning (*mean*), the rule accounts for a word which has the same phonology as the phrase, as well as being of the morphological category N, selecting a noun to its right in morphology, and having the same semantics as the phrase. Note that SEM is a separate level for semantic structure, a level distinguished from syntactic structure (for arguments that it is, in coping with quantifier scope, necessary to distinguish syntactic and semantic level, see Pafel 2005). As SEM but not SYN is relevant for semantic interpretation, the missing SYN feature in the output does not jeopardize semantic interpretation.

This operation can be seen as a kind of nominalization. Thus, we finally would get a canonical NN-compound structure for genuine phrasal compounds. Compare the nominalized gerund-like clauses as non-heads in Turkish genuine phrasal compounds as discussed by Trips & Kornfilt (2015) and Göksel (2015).

(43) Turkish (Trips & Kornfilt 2015: 308)
[ic   camasir-in-i   göster-me]   oyun-u
internal laundry-3sg-acc show-nfnom game-cm
'showing-your-underwear-game'

Rule (42) is intended to capture genuine phrasal compounds only. Thus, there seems no progress with respect to Merge and Insertion. However, this time genuine and quotative phrasal compounds are captured by two variants of the same operation, i.e., phrase-to-word conversion. This captures the relation between the two phenomena. Additionally, there are two related morphological phenomena, namely phrasal derivation and phrasal conversion, which ask for similar conversion analyses. In (44) a VP or NP is the base for the German nominalizing suffixes *-er*, *-ung* or *-artig*, in (45) a sentence is converted into a noun, a kind of exocentric word formation, and in (46) it depends on the details of analysis of whether this is a case of derivation or conversion:

(44) German (Lawrenz 2006: 8-9)

   a. Licht-in-Strom-Umwandl-er
      light-in-current-convert-er
      'light-in-current converter'

   b. Kinder-über-Mittag-Betreu-ung
      children-on-noontime-caretake-ing
      'children caretaking at noontime'

   c. Ruhe-vor-dem-Sturm-artig
      quiet-before-the-storm-like
      'like the quiet before the storm'

(45) German (Lawrenz 2006: 9-10)

    a. (das) Wir-sind-wieder-Wer
       the we-are-again-someone

       '(the general) attitude expressed by the slogan 'We are somebody again''

    b. (das) Das-haben-wir-immer-schon-so-gemacht
       the this-have-we-always-already-so-done

       '(the) attitude express by the saying 'We have done this ever since''

(46) German (Lawrenz 2006: 8)
    (das) Arm-um-die-Schulter-Legen
    the arm-on-the-shoulder-put

    '(the) resting of one's hand on someone's shoulder'

As for the analysis of pseudo-phrasal compounds, we don't have to assume conversion, thus they differ from quotative and genuine phrasal compounds in this respect. They do, however, have the same structure insofar as they are XN compounds. Thus, there is only a minor difference to the structure of quotative and genuine phrasal compounds.

In summary, much speaks in favour of the conversion approach: it seems to deal with phrasal compounds in a satisfying manner, and it especially accounts for the relatedness of the four types of phrasal compounds without neglecting their differences.

5 Conclusions

Phrasal compounds are a challenge to the morphology-syntax relation. The conversion approach makes clear that we should distinguish between two aspects of this relation: the relation of morphological to syntactic structures, on the one hand, and the relation between word and phrase formation, on the other. As for the first aspect, the conversion approach presented presupposes a parallel architecture where morphology and syntax (and semantics) are separate structures (cf. Bresnan 2001, Spencer 2010, Trips 2016). It is not necessary to modify the standard parallel relation between morphological and syntactic structure in order to cope with phrasal compounds. Lexical Integrity in the sense that (morphological) words do not contain phrases is fully respected (cf. Pafel 2015). To the extent that the conversion approach is successful, it contributes to the plausibility of a parallel architecture framework. As for the second aspect, phrasal compounds point to a symmetrical relation between word and phrase formation: phrases can be built on the basis of words *and* words on the basis of phrases. This speaks against lexicalist approaches which claim that word formation strictly precedes the construction of syntactic phrases. Phrase-to-word-conversion rules (like 37 and 42) is the decisive element which makes it possible to build words on the basis of phrases.

So we can conclude that phrasal compounds are only a phenomenon at first glance which suggests the intrusion of syntax into morphology. A thorough analysis suggests just the opposite: morphology and syntax are separate levels with fully separate structures with distinct properties.

This, then, means that, in morphology, we are dealing with (morphological) words, stems, affixes, etc., and in syntax, we are dealing with (syntactic) words and phrases instead. The structures in morphology and syntax are of quite different character. There is, however, some overlap with respect to the features assumed in morphology and in syntax. Take the categorial and the gender feature as examples. In the default case, the morphological feature and its counterpart in syntax are identical (a morphological noun, for instance, is a syntactic noun). An appropriate general interface relation copes for this identity. But there are interesting asymmetries, i.e., exceptions to this general interface relation. In German, there is a class of words which, as far as syntax is concerned, are undoubtedly nouns. But nevertheless they inflect like adjectives, exhibiting the strong/weak contrast and this is something that nouns normally never do. See the contrast in (47).

(47) German

a. ein fleißig-er   Beamt-er
   a   busy-NOM.M.SG.STR official-NOM.M.SG.STR
   , 'a busy official'

b. der fleißig-e   Beamt-e
   the busy-NOM.M.SG.WEA offical-NOM.M.SG.WEA
   'the busy official'

We can account for this phenomenon if we distinguish morphological and syntactic categorial features. Spencer (2010) has proposed analyzing these words syntactically as nouns and morphologically as adjectives.

Concerning gender, we also find an asymmetry. Take a look at the Latin example *agricola* 'farmer'. It is syntactically masculine (as agreement suggests), but it is morphologically feminine (as inflection suggests).

(48) Latin

 a. sedul-us   agricol-a
    busy-NOM.M.SG farmer-NOM.F.SG
    'busy farmer'

 b. sedul-i   agricol-ae
    busy-NOM.M.PL farmer-NOM.F.PL
    'busy farmers'

In the default case, morphological and syntactic gender are identical, of course. So like phrasal compounds, these asymmetries get a straightforward analysis if morphology and syntax are taken to be separate levels related by interface relations.

Acknowledgements

I am grateful for the stimulating discussions at the workshop im Mannheim in June 2015, as well as for Carola Trips' and an anonymous reviewer's comments on the manuscript.

Abbreviations

AOR	aorist		PTCP	participle
CM	compound marker		STR	strong declension
COND	conditional		WEA	weak declension
NFNOM	non-factive nominalizer			
OPT	optative			

References

Ackema, Peter & Ad Neeleman. 2004. *Beyond morphology.* Oxford: Oxford University Press.

Bisetto, Antonietta. 2015. Do Romance languages have phrasal compounds? A look at Italian. *STUF–Language Typology and Universals* 68. 395–419.

Booij, Geert E. 2002. *The morphology of Dutch.* Oxford: Oxford University Press.

Botha, Rudolf P. 2015. Do Romance languages have phrasal compounds? A look at Italian. *STUF–Language Typology and Universals* 68. 395–419.

Bresnan, Joan. 2001. *Lexical-functional grammar.* Oxford: Oxford University Press.

Brogyanyi, Bela. 1979. Bemerkungen zu den Phrasenkomposita. In Bela Brogyanyi (ed.), *Studies in diachronic, synchronic, and typological linguistics: Festschrift for Oswald Szemerényi on the occasion of his 65th birthday,* 159–165. Amsterdam: Benjamins.

Fleischer, Wolfgang & Irmhild Barz. 1995. *Wortbildung der deutschen Gegenwartssprache.* Tübingen: Niemeyer.

Göksel, Aslı. 2015. Phrasal compounds in Turkish: Distinguishing citations from quotations. *STUF–Language Typology and Universals* 68. 359–394.

Harley, Heidi. 2009. Compounding in distributed morphology. In Rochelle Lieber & Pavol Štekauer (eds.), *The Oxford handbook of compounding,* 129–144. Oxford: OUP.

Hein, Katrin. 2015. *Phrasenkomposita im Deutschen. Empirische Untersuchung und konstruktionsgrammatische Modellierung* (Studien zur Deutschen Sprache 67). Tübingen: Narr.

Jackendoff, Ray. 1984. On the phrase: The phrase 'the phrase'. *Natural Language and Linguistic Theory* 2. 25–37.

Jespersen, Otto. 1924. *Philosophy of grammar.* London: Allen & Unwin.

Kay, Paul. 2014. Unary phrase structure rules and the cognitive linguistics lexical linking theory. *Theoretical Linguistics* 40. 149–16.

Klockow, Reinhard. 1980. *Linguistik der Gänsefüßchen. Untersuchungen zum Gebrauch der Anführungszeichen im gegenwärtigen Deutsch.* Frankfurt/M.: Haag und Herchen.

Lawrenz, Birgit. 2006. *Moderne deutsche Wortbildung. Phrasale Wortbildung im Deutschen: Linguistische Untersuchung und sprachdidaktische Behandlung* (Philologia 91). Hamburg: Dr. Kovač.

Lieber, Rochelle. 1992. *Deconstructing morphology. Word formation in syntactic theory.* Chicago: University of Chicago Press.

Lieber, Rochelle & Sergio Scalise. 2006. The Lexical Integrity Hypothesis in a new theoretical universe. *Lingue e Linguaggio* 5. 7–32.

Meibauer, Jörg. 2003. Phrasenkomposita zwischen Wortsyntax und Lexikon. *Zeitschrift für Sprachwissenschaft* 22. 153–188.

Meibauer, Jörg. 2007. How marginal are phrasal compounds? Generalized insertion, expressivity, and I/Q-interaction. *Morphology* 17. 233–259.

Meibauer, Jörg. 2015. On "R" in phrasal compounds – a contextualist approach. *Language Typology and Universals* 68(3). 241–261.

Müller, Stefan & Stephen Mark Wechsler. 2014. Lexical approaches to argument structure. *Theoretical Linguistics* 40. 1–76.

Ortner, Lorelies, Elgin Müller-Bollhagen, Hanspeter Ortner, Hans Wellmann, Maria Piimpel-Mader & Hildegard Gartner. 1991. *Deutsche Wortbildung. Typen und Tendenzen in der deutschen Gegenwartssprache. Vierter Hauptteil: Substantivkomposita.* Berlin: de Gruyter.

Pafel, Jürgen. 2005. *Quantifier scope in German.* Amsterdam: Benjamins.

Pafel, Jürgen. 2007. Ein Essay mit dem Titel 'On pure quotation'. In Elke Brendel, Jörg Meibauer & Markus Steinbach (eds.), *Zitat und Bedeutung*, 201–214. Hamburg: Buske.

Pafel, Jürgen. 2011. Two dogmas on quotation. In Elke Brendel, Jörg Meibauer & Markus Steinbach (eds.), *Understanding quotation*, 249–267. Berlin: de Gruyter.

Pafel, Jürgen. 2015. Phrasal compounds are compatible with Lexical Integrity. *Language Typology and Universals* 68. 263–280.

Sag, Ivan A., Hans C. Boas & Paul Kay. 2012. Introducing sign-based construction grammar. In Hans C. Boas & Ivan Sag (eds.), *Sign-Based construction grammar*, 1–29. Stanford, CA: CSLI Publications.

Sato, Yosuke. 2010. Complex phrase structures within morphological words: Evidence from English and Indonesian. *Lingua* 120. 379–407.

Savini, Marina. 1984. Phrasal compounds in Afrikaans: A generative analysis. *Stellenbosch Papers in Linguistics* 12. 34–114.

Schmidt, Hartmut. 2000. Hochkomplexe Lexeme: Wortbildung und Traditionen des Formulierens. In Mechthild Habermann, Peter O. Müller & Bernd Naumann (eds.), *Wortschatz und Orthographie in Geschichte und Gegenwart. Festschrift für Horst Haider Munske zum 65. Geburtstag*, 135–158. Tübingen: Niemeyer.

Spencer, Andrew. 2010. Lexical relatedness and the lexical entry – a formal unification. In Stefan Müller (ed.), *Proceedings of the 17th International Conference on Head-Driven Phrase Structure Grammar*, 322–340. Stanford: CSLI.

Trips, Carola. 2012. Empirical and theoretical aspects of phrasal compounds: Against the 'syntax explains it all' attitude. In Angela Ralli, Geert Booij, Sergio Scalise & Athanasios Karasimos (eds.), *Online Proceedings of the eighth Mediterranean Morphology Meeting*, 322–346. Patras: University of Patras.

Trips, Carola. 2016. An analysis of phrasal compounds in the model of parallel architecture. In Pius ten Hacken (ed.), *The semantics of compounding*, 153–177. Cambridge: Cambridge University Press.

Trips, Carola & Jaklin Kornfilt. 2015. Typological aspects of phrasal compounds in English, German, Turkish and Turkic. *Language Typology and Universals* 68. 281–322.

Vries, Mark de. 2008. The representation of language within language: A syntactico-pragmatic typology of direct speech. *Studia Linguistica* 62. 39–77.

Wiese, Richard. 1996. Phrasal compounds and the theory of word syntax. *Linguistic Inquiry* 27. 183–193.

Name index

Language index

Subject index

www.ingramcontent.com/pod-product-compliance
Lightning Source LLC
Chambersburg PA
CBHW080916100426
42812CB00007B/2290